W9-CAE-277

What people are saying about …

NUDGE

"This extraordinary book from an extraordinary author deserves an extraordinary recommendation. So here it is. Len Sweet calls us to pay attention, and you'd better pay attention while reading this book. It's wrong about a few things, most of them small but some of them big. It sometimes, and maddeningly, oversimplifies and underexplains. But it often startled me with insight and made me think harder about vital issues of evangelism than any other recent book I've read. It's meant to revolutionize our view of evangelism—and I think it just might."

John G. Stackhouse Jr., Sangwoo Youtong Chee professor of theology and culture at Regent College, and author of *Humble Apologetics: Defending the Faith Today*

"After decades of the church teaching that the key to converting culture is to criticize and boycott, *Nudge* is the corrective that will transform the way we look at evangelism. Leonard Sweet reminds us that to engage culture is a two-way conversation, and it starts with the words of Jesus: 'Pay attention.' Trust me, I did. Leonard Sweet has captured the secret of engaging twenty-first-century culture, and *Nudge* needs to be on every pastor's desk."

Phil Cooke, filmmaker and author of *Branding Faith*

"Three of Len Sweet's most obvious gifts are (1) he is the master of metaphor, (2) he is alive to culture, (3) he is not as bound by *what is* as the way it is *to be*. What I appreciate is that he uses all of these gifts to address one of the most crucial issues facing the church today: evangelism—what it is and how we practice it. I can't imagine that anyone interested in evangelism (and all of us should be) will not find help in this book. Thanks, friend."

Dr. Maxie Dunnam, author, evangelist, and
chancellor of Asbury Theological Seminary

"In this wake-up call, Len Sweet reminds us that literally everything we are and do as Christians is a living and active witness and, in fact, an invitation and 'nudge' to others to meet God and embrace God's reign. That sobering reality requires a watchfulness and attentiveness that are a far cry from older models of evangelism, which attempt to manage and manipulate our neighbors' responses to the good news. This book helps us understand the many ways that we communicate through pattern recognition, and in so doing it helps readers become more competent and joyful *nudgers.*"

Bryan Stone, E. Stanley Jones professor of evangelism
at Boston University School of Theology

"There is no other book like this on evangelism that I've ever read. I couldn't put it down. Sweet once again takes us back to the heart of the matter. In an era when everyone wants to redefine church, become missional, and even define the 'process' for making disciples, few are talking about where it all begins and where it all ends. What does that look like in the lives of the people who want to be witnesses to see God at work in people around them and then share in natural ways? What does it mean for evangelism to be more than a presentation—but a life? These are the issues that Sweet helps us wrestle with. What he writes about is real and alive, and it works. Evangelism is God's activity—not ours. We are merely to recognize him at work and join him."

Bob Roberts, senior pastor of NorthWood Church,
global engager, and author of *Real-Time Connections*

"Len did it again! He shifted the Rubik's Cube of my faith to show me a different aspect of God. This is the best book I have read on evangelism and sharing my faith in years. Reading it was a nudge of grace in my life. Thanks, Len."

Dr. David A. Anderson, radio host, author, and senior pastor of Bridgeway Community Church

"Much of what is being done today in the name of evangelism hardly resembles how the early apostles announced Jesus as the true Savior and Lord of the world. Len Sweet invites us to rethink our motives and methods and helps us recognize the risen Christ at work in the world today. Though it may startle some and seem too revolutionary to be true, Sweet is drawing on the long-held conviction that God loves his good world, fallen though it is, and has always worked from within it to call attention to himself."

Glenn Packiam, associate pastor at New Life Church and author of *Secondhand Jesus*

"This is one of the best books I've read in ten years. In *Nudge*, Len Sweet takes you on a journey of deep spirituality that lingers long after the book is closed. Every page is filled with wonder about how God is working inside of me and in the world. This is a life-changer!"

Tom Davis, author of *Red Letters: Living a Faith That Bleeds* and *Priceless: A Novel on the Edge of the World*

What people are saying about …

SO BEAUTIFUL

"Perhaps this says more about my own madness, but I think that this is Len Sweet's best book so far. Not only are the content critical and the literary style artful, but it delivers spiritual depth along with unusual insight into the nature and mission of the church. Missional, relational, incarnational—spot-on, Len!"

Alan Hirsch, author of *The Forgotten Ways*,
international director of Forge Mission Training
Network, and a founder of shapevine.com

"*So Beautiful* may be Leonard Sweet's magnum opus. It will explode your mind, open your heart, and guide your hand. The book flows from a beautiful life shaped by fierce followship of Jesus. It will inspire you to become so beautiful as well, so that the world is never the same."

Reggie McNeal, author of *The Present*
Future and *Missional Renaissance*

"In an age of privatized, commercialized, and culturalized Christianity, Leonard Sweet heralds a much-needed call to rediscover the biblical life, power, and purpose of the church. Contesting the 'if you build it, they will come' model so prevalent in the church today, Sweet demonstrates that the future of the American church does not rest on understanding and appropriating the latest trends, techniques, or methodologies but on the recovery of this biblical truth: The church is a community whose faith and witness is authenticated and formed in relationships that incarnate the life and love of Jesus Christ, and whose activity is missional—purposed and ordered by God's redemptive mission in the world. In what may be a pivotal moment in the history of the church, this book serves as a potential tipping point in her much-needed reformation and renewal."

S. Michael Craven, president of the Center for Christ & Culture and author of *Uncompromised Faith: Overcoming Our Culturalized Christianity*

"The landscape of today's Christianity is littered with 'church' movements: missional church, house church, megachurch, emerging church, the convergence movement, etc. In *So Beautiful*, Leonard Sweet explores three aspects of the church's inherent character—missional, relational, and incarnational, or MRI as he calls it. Sweet reminds us that these three aspects are not simply passing movements, but they are built into the church's very DNA. Moreover, they are attributes of divine life. While so much of modern Christianity restrictively thinks in terms of either/or, Sweet exhorts us to lay hold of the both/and of divine truth. Stimulating and creative, every serious follower of Jesus should own a copy of this helpful work."

Frank Viola, author of *From Eternity to Here* and *Reimagining Church*

What people are saying about …

AQUACHURCH 2.0

"*AquaChurch* remains the best introduction to the art of postmodern leadership on the market. Through a skillful weaving of metaphor, narrative, practice, and current church examples, the book draws us into the engagement of Scripture and our culture. Recognizing that the medium is the message, the book reflects something of what it teaches. It is a must-read for those wrestling with how to live out the gospel in the twenty-first century."

Dr. Donald Goertz, director, MDiv in ministry,
assistant professor of church history at Tyndale
University College & Seminary, Toronto

"*AquaChurch* is worth taking the time to read. Len Sweet is someone I greatly respect and appreciate. You will agree when you have navigated through this book. Thanks, Len."

Dr. Walt Kallestad, senior pastor of
Community Church of Joy

"Len Sweet is a master of the apt metaphor. He discerns today's invisible forces that make leadership more like a voyage than a march. His navigational aids help keep us on course."

Marshall Shelley, editor of *Leadership*

"Len Sweet is an ancient-future leader who navigates by God's North Star. This book is a must-read for Jesus leaders who risk navigating uncharted, postmodern seas."

Mike Slaughter, pastor at Ginghamsburg Church

"Len Sweet offers us a 'learning' manual on self-navigating the 'watery' world of postmodernism. Instead of describing a one-size-fits-all type of instruction manual on leadership, he shares with us the 'leadership arts' that can help guide us through the turbulent currents of today."

Bill Easum, senior managing partner
of Easum, Bandy and Associates

NUDGE

AWAKENING EACH OTHER TO THE GOD WHO'S ALREADY THERE

LEONARD SWEET

David C Cook®

transforming lives together

NUDGE
Published by David C. Cook
4050 Lee Vance View
Colorado Springs, CO 80918 U.S.A.

David C. Cook Distribution Canada
55 Woodslee Avenue, Paris, Ontario, Canada N3L 3E5

David C. Cook U.K., Kingsway Communications
Eastbourne, East Sussex BN23 6NT, England

David C. Cook and the graphic circle C logo
are registered trademarks of Cook Communications Ministries.

The Web site addresses recommended throughout this book are offered as a
resource to you. These Web sites are not intended in any way to be or imply an
endorsement on the part of David C. Cook, nor do we vouch for their content.

See Bible-resource credits at the back of this book. The author
has added italics to Scripture quotations for emphasis.

LCCN 2010927433
ISBN 978-1-4347-6474-4
eISBN 978-0-7814-0493-8

© 2010 Leonard Sweet
Published in association with the literary agency of
Mark Sweeney & Associates, Bonita Springs, Florida 34135

The Team: John Blase, Amy Kiechlin, Sarah Schultz, Jack Campbell, and Karen Athen
Cover Design: JWH Graphic Arts, James Hall

Printed in the United States of America
First Edition 2010

3 4 5 6 7 8 9 10

092010

For Leonard Humbert

Thanks for your attention.

CONTENTS

Discover More Online

CHECK OUT INTERACTIVES FOR YOUR PERSONAL OR SMALL-GROUP USE
AND MUCH MORE ON THE NUDGE WEB SITE:

WWW.NUDGETHEBOOK.COM

ACKNOWLEDGMENTS

This is a book about recognition, which places me under special obligation to make the right recognitions and acknowledgments.

So let me begin with a passage that I first memorized as a child in Vacation Bible School (King James Version, of course), a text that strangely testified about a prevenient God and a text that haunted this book out of me decades later: "The LORD, he it is that doth go before thee."[1]

Unlike one book I read recently, I can't recognize seventeen of my colleagues and friends who read and critiqued the book before showing up in my publisher's computer. But I can thank some of my doctoral students for reading and commenting with each other on the galleys: from Drew University, Jonathan Bower, Michael Cox, Troy Ehlke, Jacqueline King, John Landis, Paul Moon, David Noble, Patricia Rizor, and Mary Trank; from George Fox University, Doug Balzer, David Banks, Doug Bryan, Kristin Bullock, Matthew Deames, Kenneth Dove, Dottie Escobedo-Frank, Bill Gibson, Tom Ingram, David Parker, Jody Ray, Drew Sams, Alice Sawyer-Hainsworth, and Bill Watson. I only let two people see this offspring in its diaper stages: my research assistant, Betty O'Brien, who just may be the snappiest nappies changer in the publishing world; and Lori Wagner, who is now helping me write my first novel (*The Seraph Seal*). Lori's whole-earth perspective on living inspires a whole-gospel perspective on evangelism.

If Kafka was right that a book should be an axe for the frozen sea within us, then Michael Polanyi has so honed his axe on me that the shards of the axe-head (aka, *Personal Knowledge*, 1958) are scattered on almost every page of *Nudge*. So are flints and splinters from the writings of E. Stanley Jones, Lesslie Newbigin, David Bosch, and Andrew Walls.

My call requires me to do more than teach and write on evangelism. I must do evangelism. The directive of 2 Timothy 4:5—"Do the work of an evangelist"—has never been dodgeable. Certain people in my life enable me to be a participant-observer, to bring together the conceptual and the concrete, to cultivate both academic credentials and street cred: Lynn Caterson and Melissa Wilson, who run my New Jersey office; Michael Oliver, Jacob Lange, and Chris Eriksen, my TAs at Drew Theological School in 2009 and 2010; Kathi Ambler, who unsunk and unstuck my learning island (Mag Mell) in Second Life and made teaching from this platform possible once again; Thomas Ingram, my doctoral TA at George Fox University; and Loren Kerns, whose keen eye for the *Deus absconditus* constantly proved the wisdom of C. S. Lewis's motto "Jove is often Jehovah incognito." I am invariably led by my nose. My agent, Mark Sweeney, makes sure there are more senses engaged than that before I move forward. I can't thank him enough for being my guide and guard.

The whole field of semiotics was introduced to me willy-nilly by my holiness upbringing. I am a fruit of the holiness tree. My two brothers and I were taught from an early age to watch for signs of the Spirit, but to be equally watchful for signs of the world, the flesh, and the devil. As children, we couldn't bring a comic book into our house (among other things like cards, dice, novels, etc.). Our parents had been persuaded by Dr. Fredric Wertham that, as he put it, "Hitler was a beginner compared to the comic book industry."[2] I survived this crash course in semiotics because my two brothers, John and Phil, took the course with me.

My friend Chuck Conniry is a master of God-soundings and Jesus-sightings. Episcopal rector Michael Blewett is my virtual pastor. His sermons each week force me to search the same searing question, "Walk by a burning bush lately?" A burning bush was used by God to get Moses' attention, but a grain of wood is all it takes to get Michael's attention. A rooster is what got Jon Ludovina's attention, and when Jon attends to something, I listen and look. My wife, Elizabeth, and two kids still at home, Soren (age fourteen) and Egil (age twelve), keep forcing on me the question, "How nudgeable am I?" They never fail to teach me how to pay attention to ordinary things.

Colleague Dwight Friesen can spot shoots of hope in the most barren landscape of our culture and my mind. Brent Templet sent me an illustration that promises to secure firm footing for the hoped-for DVD version of this book. If there were an Oscar for nudging, Vern Hyndman would get one. I call Vern a soul otolaryngologist: an ear, eye, nose, and throat specialist whose office is always open to help me and others develop senses finely tuned to the presence of God.

Scholar Judith Maizel-Long has studied the Methodism hymnbook to chronicle the decrease of evangelism during the twentieth century. Where Wesley's 1780 hymnbook was organized around "evangelism as the organizing principle," by 1904 the rationale of Methodist hymnody was no longer mission but "handbooks for Christian life within the church."[3] My colleagues in the E. Stanley Jones Chair of Evangelism across the world of Methodism are doing their best to change this and to increase the number of those "whose hearts have been warmed at these altar fires," as that old Wesleyan phrase from "The Aldersgate Prayer" puts it. Stephen Gunter (Duke), Achim Hartner (Reutlingen), Scott Kisker (Wesley), John Wesley Kurewa (Africa University), Arthur McPhee (Asbury), Sergei Nikolaev (Russia UM Theological Seminary), Tumani Nyajeka (Gammon), Joon-Sik Park (Methesco), Douglas Powe (St. Paul), Bryan Stone (Boston), Mark Teasdale (Garrett-Evangelical), Robert Tuttle (Asbury–Florida), Laceye Warner (Duke), Elaine Heath (Perkins), and Wesley De Souza (Candler) never cease to inspire me for their vigilance at lighting the "altar fires" today. Thanks to Jack Ewing and the Foundation for Evangelism, the church's heart is warming to the mission of "strangely warmed hearts."

So far from a Christianity that sucks joy from the world, *Nudge* affirms the gospel's gravitational warping effects, the way we all feel dearer, deeper, more luscious in the presence of a Jesus follower. One of the most memorable Jesus followers in my growing up was Leonard Humbert, a soft-spoken Free Methodist pastor whose entire life and ministry were one of quiet nudges. He never preached hellfire and brimstone, but he brimmed and beamed with the presence of Christ, brightened every corner God gave him, and honed his spirit on the Living Cornerstone. Reverend Humbert even accompanied his young parishioners on their paper routes to shine God's light in some place other than the church. When I deconverted from Christianity at age seventeen, Reverend Humbert didn't judge me but kept up his gentle nudges to see the God who is already there, wherever I might have been at the time. If Simone Weil is right that "to treat our neighbor who is in affliction with love is something like baptizing him,"[4] then it was Reverend Humbert who really baptized me.

Reverend Humbert is now seventy-four, facing major health issues, but still pastoring full-time. Because he was the pastor who nudged me when others shoved me; because he specialized in seed planting rather than headlocks; and because he showcased with his style of evangelism that a conversion is never a coercion, I dedicate this book to one of the kindest, gentlest Jesus presences in my life story: Leonard Humbert.

Thank you for your attention.

—Leonard Sweet
16 April 2010
Seoul, South Korea

Preface

THE SHINING

> The world is charged with the grandeur of God.
> It will flame out, like shining from shook foil.[1]
>
> —Jesuit poet Gerard Manley Hopkins

Every bush burns with revelations. Are you alert to the shining? Are you able to see the shining? Can you read the shining? Rest assured, the fire does not burn berserk.

Evangelism for too long has been disconnected from discipleship. In *Nudge*, evangelism *is* discipleship. What yokes evangelism to discipleship, I propose, is the art of attention, attending to life and attending to God.

The art of attention goes something like this: You have an appointment with God. The address of that appointment? The dress of the next person you meet, whatever it is. Their dress is God's address. Want to find God? Look in the face of the person next to you or the next person you meet.

You will not find in *Nudge* a gospel of religion; what you will find is a gospel of Christ. What's the difference? The currency of the gospel of religion is fear and imposition. The currency of the gospel of Christ is love and invitation.

Love engenders a spirit of wonder, where fear spawns anger and distrust. Fear seeks to quash wonder and to impose. Love frees to wonder and invite.

Nicolaus Copernicus first argued that the earth was not the center of the universe, that in fact the earth revolved around the sun. The publication

21

of *De revolutionibus orbium coelestium* (*On the Revolutions of the Heavenly Spheres* [1543]) caused a reaction of fear in the religious establishment, which denounced the work and for a time waylaid the truth through imperfect interpretations of Scripture. But the discoveries of Copernicus, and those of Galileo Galilei, would make nautical navigation by the stars possible. It was a sense of wonder, not a sense of fear, that made discovery and invention possible.

Love, and the wonder that results from it, create a posture of invitation—as simply as the love and wonder of a wedding, as deeply as the wonder of the Spirit that nudgers invite others into, also known as evangelism. Such love is an outpouring of a sense of love, of generosity in love because of a deep sense of *being* loved.

The fear that permeates religion demands that to spread, a larger fear must exist. Selling or marketing religion, as opposed to offering the wonder of love, requires a maneuver not unlike that of a pots and pans salesman (I know because I was one in college for a week), who is taught to introduce people to a problem they don't know they have then to sell them a solution he happens to be selling. Or more precisely, "Spread fear, sell hope."

Fear breeds in a cocoon of scarcity and insecurity. A natural human response is to bargain our way out of it, the net result being that folks who have come to religion by fear have really made a business deal with God. We are sons and daughters of the living God. We are not business partners who have made a bargain to avoid some unpleasant consequences.

So, long before we can talk about evangelism, the spreading of the gospel, we'd best agree on what the gospel is. *Gospel*, the very word, means "good news." When we offer our sense of wonder, when we can see ourselves as bruised and broken yet beloved, as a people in process, the gospel is the good news that Christ is alive and with us, within and without, and that health and healing is ours through his death and resurrection.

It is wonderful news, for the emotionally worn out and strung out, that counseling could help them limp better. It is wonderful news, for the infirm of mind and spirit, that with enough good therapy, we can learn to compensate and moderate. But it is *great* news that Christ has come to bind up the broken hearted and to set the captive free. It is *great* news that healing and restoration is available to those who trust and obey.

The gospel is the sensational news that we can be the sons and daughters of the Creator, and that the One who created us loved us before we were even born. The gospel is the sensational news that eternity has already started and that the laws of sin and death need not apply to us. The gospel is the sensational news that life, and life more abundant, is ours. The gospel of Christ is a no-fear gospel. There is no push point to create a pots-and-pans sales close.

Nudge evangelism is the planting of seeds. With a motivation of love, nudgers meet people in their context and nourish their souls in some way. As in Jesus' parable of the seeds, planting frees us to be extravagant in love, yet leaves the results for God to germinate and grow. Nudging is an open-ended enterprise God may undertake directly. God may use others, and time, and circumstance to grow. Or God may even employ a continuing involvement from us. The main thing is that nudgers are free to love without consequences. Nudgers are free to invest in the lives of others through the generosity of life as a conduit of love from God.

In short, the gospel is the good news that Jesus is the Way—in a world that has lost its way and when there seems to be no way; Jesus is the Truth—in a culture of lies where deceit is king; and Jesus is the Life—in a world full of evangelists of death. *Nudge* is a call to evangelize life and to face death so that others may live.

Part I

NUDGE "SHINING"

Chapter 1

PAY ATTENTION:
EVERY BUSH IS BURNING

Pay attention.[1]

—Jesus

Brace yourself. This book is set to revolutionize your understanding of evangelism. Revolution—from the Latin *revolvere*—means "a fundamental change." This revolution stands to shake the very roots of your faith, rattle the range of your mission, and roll the very limits of your freedom.

Wait a minute, you say! There's a lot about me in that paragraph; I thought evangelism is about reaching out to others.

Remember "a fundamental change." I think evangelism changes me as much as anybody.

A friar returned to his monastery after an Ignatian thirty-day retreat. Over granola the next morning, he was interrogated by a grumpy old member of the community who complained, "We've been working like slaves while you've been swanning around doing nothing! And look at you! You don't look any different."

"You're quite right, I probably don't," was the reply. "But you do."

Jesus' last words in the gospel of Luke are these: "Go out and proclaim repentance and the forgiveness of sins."[2] But a biblical understanding of repentance is not red-faced anger at other people's sins but red-faced embarrassment at my own brokenness and complicity in the evils and injustices of

27

the world. Proclaiming repentance is as much about reminding me of my waywardness as it is about setting other people straight.

When I am engaging with people of other religious faiths, I find myself unable to commit to their conclusions or agree with their assessments. Yet at the same time I come away encouraged by the spiritual truths found in their traditions, thrilled by new insights into my own faith, and more passionate than ever about being a disciple of Jesus. The truth is illuminated and elongated in my mind, and my presuppositions and myopic perspectives are challenged and corrected in the process. Anything less would not be a conversation and would imply that truth is a proposition and not Christ.

> To be a real agent of God, to connect with the neighbor … each
> of us needs to know the truth about himself or herself.[3]
> —Archbishop of Canterbury Rowan Williams

I believe the lifeblood of evangelism is not propositions, but prepositions. For God to do something *through* us, God must be doing something *in* us. If we are not always evangelizing ourselves, we have no business evangelizing others. In fact, it is usually as God's grace courses *through* us *to* someone else that we become aware of God's love *in* and *for* us. Evangelism is an invitation for broken people together to meet the Christ who loves broken people. We all are damaged but loved, crushed but cherished, with a divine embrace. When love is the motivation for evangelism, *nudging* is love in action. And the cracks in our broken vases are where Jesus leaks out first.

Evangelism Jesus-style

I define evangelism as "nudge" and evangelists as "nudgers." Evangelism is awakening each other to the God who is already there. Evangelism is nudging people to pay attention to the mission of God in their lives and to the necessity of responding to that initiative in ways that birth new realities and the new birth.

God only asks that we do what we do best, which is nudge; God takes it from there. The nudging act—the human contact, the meeting of eyes, the sharing of space, the entanglement of words, the sense of bodily interaction—is to the soul what blood is to the body. Without nudging, the body cannot reproduce.

Every person who crosses your threshold today is ripe for nudging. A nudge happens in proximity. Even the nudges across the Internet or by phone take place in a proximity of relationships. The integrity of a nudge requires that it be welcomed and that it be reciprocal. The purpose of a nudge is to manifest Christ in a moment of mutual knowing, which benefits both the person being nudged and the nudger. Nudging is not best driven by fear or by some need within the nudger. Nudges are not contrived but are the natural consequence of being with someone in a moment and wishing them to join you in recognizing a God-moment. The best nudges culminate in a grunt of mutual recognition. God nudges me because God likes me. I nudge others because I like them. There is an implied caring that comes with nudging.

So there you have it. Nudge—gently pushing people off their seats more than it is sitting people down or driving them to their knees. Nudging is more about sowing than reaping. To be clear, nudging encompasses the full range of gardening—from dropping a tiny seed into the ground, to loosening the dirt, watering, weeding, fertilizing, protecting from predators, picking the fruit, and even helping, in Jesus' words, "the birds of the air … nest under its shade."[4] But every encounter is aimed not to "bring in the sheaves." Nudging aims to bring people less to a decision than to an impression: not just to an hour of decision but a lifetime impression of God's presence and the nearness of God's kingdom. In fact, isn't this the essence of sanctified living: to make our whole life a *Un Oui Vivant*,[5] a "Living Yes" to the living Christ?

This is exactly the opposite of ignoring the need for a decision. Rather, it is respecting and reverencing the process, if one looks back on it, by which each of us came to that place of decision. When an impression leads to a decision, it's "Hallelujah!" (or in my preferred way of stating it, "Javalujah!") time. But the ultimate answer to that question "Who do you say that I am?" is best forthcoming from another question: "What's up?" Or when translated theologically, "What's the I AM up to in your life?" We find the living One in the midst of living.

Images exist not to be believed but to be interrogated.[6]
—Andy Grundberg

Don McCullin is a British photojournalist who specializes in capturing images of the downtrodden and forgotten and making these moments of forsakenness universal. McCullin is also one of the greatest war photographers of all time. He says this about the role of a professional photographer: "If you take one good picture a year for each year of your career, you are doing well."[7]

If, for every year of your life, *one* person honestly relates that God nudged them through you, and that your nudge had kingdom significance to them, you are a master evangelist; well done! Of course, we ought always to be hoping and praying for what I call these ushering nudges. Always be closing. Even with a gentle nudge, or a God-wink nudge, always be closing in prayer and desire. But remember that every Jesus nudge, whether it leads someone to an altaring moment or not, is part of an answer to a two-thousand-year-old prayer in Matthew 9:38: a prayer Jesus prayed and taught his disciples to pray, when he asked the "Lord of the Harvest" to send out workers for the harvest. Sometimes a nudge will lead to conversion, but most often it will lead to a conversation, a confession, a connection, maybe a germination, but always a blessing.

Businesspeople who become entrepreneurs often learn the hard way that constantly chasing home runs will exhaust and bankrupt them. Good business strategists live on base hits. They are ready for a homer should it present itself but are not drawn into the delusive and elusive hunt for the home run. Evangelism is like that; too much emphasis on an evangelistic home run from a nudge is not only unlikely, but also prone to being motivated by impure and selfish motives.

Evangelists always nudge. They travel the Emmaus and Jericho Roads as often as the Damascus and Roman Roads.[8] They end up praying, "God is great, God is good" as often as "The Sinner's Prayer."[9] Their words when spoken are not so much "You are lost in sin" as "You belong to God." Their attitude is less "Look at what you're doing! What are you thinking?" than "Look at what God is already doing in you!" Nudgers give attendance more than they take attendance or count attendance. They less tuck people *in* than rustle them *out* of their sleeping quarters to awaken to more interesting, more humorous, more unique ways of being. Nudgers leave more tracks than tracts.

> All your words were one word: Wakeup.[10]
> —Spanish poet Antonio Machado referencing Jesus

Nudging is more about dialogue than monologue, more Facebooking than blogging. Acts of evangelism intentionally scooch and shimmy people in the direction of truth without the need for knee-bending, beat-my-back altar calls.[11] Evangelists nudge the Jesus in people to sit up and take notice. Evangelists are nudgers, not shovers. Whereas evangelism has been known to violate others' dignity,[12] which I call the reproach approach,[13] nudgers are not smudgers of the divine in people.

For the past century, evangelism has been built on this one question:

> *"If you died today, do you know without any doubt that you would wake up in heaven?"*

This is supposedly an updating of the evangelism of the eighteenth-century Wesleyan revival, which was mistakenly seen to have been built around:

"Do you desire to escape from the wrath that is to come?"

For the twenty-first century, evangelism will be built on nudges that have more to do with life before death than death and the afterlife, that focus more on the love of Christ than the wrath of God, that worry less about dying than about never having lived.[14] Some parts of the church have been slow to speak against the turn-burn evangelism of WOGS (Wrath of God Syndrome), which my friend Vern Hyndman calls "the bad news about the good news." James chapter 3 is quite clear here: *This should not be so.* If truth be told, love has always been paramount. In the definitive Wesley hymnbook, of the 525 hymns, only 1 is about hell.[15]

If you came alive today, would you think you had died and gone to heaven?

If you were offered to live forever, would you want to?

If you really woke up today, could you catch up to what God was doing in your life?

Why the focus more on life than death? The basic biblical distinction is not between "mind" and "matter" or "soul" and "body" but between "spirit" and "flesh." In one of the most helpful insights into recovering the mind of the Bible I have ever read, Cambridge theologian Nicholas Lash reminds us that when the Bible talks about living systems, it distinguishes "between things coming alive, and things crumbling into dust; between not-life, or life-gone-wrong, and life: true life, real life, God's life and all creation's life in God." That's why the metaphor of wind, or the breath

of life, is so important. Only the breath of God can neutralize the closed
system of death, also known as the second law of thermodynamics, with the
open system of life and the theodynamics of grace.

> Whether sent forth from God, breathing all creatures into
> being, renewing the Earth and filling it with good things;
> whether whispering gently to Elijah, or making "the oaks to
> whirl, and [stripping] the forests bare"; or breathing peace
> on the disciples for the forgiveness of sins—it is one wind,
> one spirit, which "blows where it wills and we do not know
> where it comes from or where it goes." To confess God as
> Spirit is to tell the story of the world as something, from its
> beginning to ends end, given to come alive.[16]

Evangelists nudge people to life. Evangelists nudge people to take deep
breaths. Evangelists blow breath into people. I often wonder how the literary career of French philosopher and novelist Jean-Paul Sartre might have
been different if he had been nudged at a time when his faith was trying to
take root. But I will let him speak for himself:

> I have just related the story of a missed vocation. I needed
> God. He was given to me. I received Him without realizing
> that I was seeking Him. Failing to take root in my heart,
> He vegetated in me for a while then He died. Whenever
> anyone speaks to me about Him today, I say, with the
> amusement of an old beau who meets a former belle: "Fifty
> years ago, had it not been for that misunderstanding, that
> mistake, the accident that separated us, there might have
> been something between us."[17]

Life and death are sometimes in the power of the nudge.

"Nudge evangelism" is based on the following three revolutionary notions (okay, some not so much "revolutionary" as hibernating—but when these "notions" cease logging zzz's, they *will* have revolutionary consequences). We will explore these more in depth a little later. But let's lay them out in full now:

Jesus is alive and active in our world.

Followers of Jesus "know" Jesus well enough to recognize where he is alive and moving in our day.

Evangelists nudge the world to wake up to the alive and acting Jesus and nudge others in the ways God is alive and moving (I call these nudges "small saves").

I was late to nudging. MSN Messenger first introduced the nudge decades ago, but it was not until I entered the Twitterverse in late 2008 and Facebook in 2009, that I was introduced to the "nudge" and "poke." The nudge has now even achieved elevated status in the leadership literature with a book by a Harvard law professor and a University of Chicago economist who argue that nudges are a form of "libertarian paternalism" designed to alter "people's behavior in a predictable way without forbidding any options or significantly changing their economic incentives."[18] In their opinion a nudge is not coercive, but cajoling.[19]

Even though I hold the E. Stanley Jones Chair of Evangelism at Drew University, I waited to write up my perspectives on evangelism until I had finished two other projects on "default systems." It's amazing the unintended messages we send, and defaults are some of the biggest "unintended" nudges in existence. Humans tend to live on autopilot, both as persons and as communities, which is why worshippers tend to sit in the same pew, and students in the same seat.

I am reminded of the mightiness of that default setting every time I approach a toll plaza on the New Jersey turnpike. A lane's white lines are like the strings of a corset, keeping the car in that configuration even though it would be faster and easier to turn the wheel, cross the line, and get in another lane. There may be twenty cars ahead of you in your lane, but you will sit where you are, ignoring the toll booths with only two or three cars in waiting, because of that mighty default setting.

If we don't set the correct defaults to faith, our evangelism will be full of sound and fury, but futile. Hence my books on the default interface that connects with a Google world (the EPIC interface)[20] and the default operating system that God designed for life and the church (the MRI default).[21] We often forget that Satan is an evangelist too. The forces of darkness want nothing more than to recruit people to the ethics of evil and the aesthetics of hell. And the pandemics of terrorism, ritualized violence, environmental degradation, and genocide attest to the success the enemy has had in writing a powerful counternarrative. As Alfred the butler (Michael Caine) says to Batman in *The Dark Knight* (2008) as they struggle to understand the psychology of the Joker: "Some men just want to watch the world burn." And judging from the seventy million people killed in the twentieth century, the bloodiest century in history, Satan may have been the most successful evangelist of the twentieth century.

Nudges are inevitable. We nudge even when we don't know it. For example, whenever someone says "most people," they are nudging you in the direction of conformity. And they don't even know they are nudging you. Conformism is one of life's (and evil's) biggest nudges.

Evangelism as we know it hasn't worked. Either evangelism is so aggressive you want to get a restraining order, or else evangelism is so restrained you want to call it to order. Our strategies have been spectacularly useless at best, counterproductive at worst. We have lived through an exodus, but not of the biblical kind.

God-guarantees

It's time to fundamentally change this approach: nudge. Nudge is built on five God-guarantees:

Every person you notice, every person you brush up against, is a child
of God, a Jesus-in-you noticer.

Every brush is a bush.

Every best is a blest.

Every worst is a juncture for grace.

Every noticer needs a nudge.

What does this mean?

Human beings are created in the image of God.

God is already present in that person's life in the form of some burning bush.

The best things about that person are blessings from God.

The worst things about that person are arenas for God's redemption.

People are hungry for encouragement and love and need help noticing the presence of the divine in their lives.

Nudge Trudge

Faith coaches and spiritual directors are God's A Team nudgers. They make
a life's work of carefully and skillfully nudging those who trust them. And
these wise and loving mentors have a saying:

Tell them: and if they can't understand,

Show them: and if they can't see it,

Do it to them.

There are three forms of nudges that increasingly demand more creativity from the nudger. These forms become more intimate and loving to the
nudge as they progress.

The trudge formula for nudge evangelism is simple: Start small;
scale fast; and live, Jesus, live! Nudge is encapsulated in Jesus' first postresurrection directive: "Go quickly and tell …"[22] To "go" is to move
forward and do something, however modest: "Start small." To be "quick"

is to use momentum to "scale fast." To "tell" is to lift up the name of Jesus, tell the good news that everyone has the potential to become a different kind of person, and with our ancestors, "speak that we do know, and testify that we have seen."

A brick wall is ... essentially
an aggregation of small effects.[23]
—Alec Clifton-Taylor

1. Start Small

Nudging is made up of small things, but it is no small thing. Small inputs can have massive consequences. It is less that "everything matters" than that small things matter everywhere. No moment is too small, no person is too small, to gently steer and move people down life paths and away from death valleys. Nudgers encourage first steps, small steps, and are open to the surprise of giant leaps forward.

One of the most distinguishing features of Jesus' teaching was precisely in this notion that from tiny beginnings God's reign grows. The ancient Hebrews compared God's workings to the monstrous cedars of Lebanon and wings of eagles. Jesus loves looking at mustard seeds, grains of wheat, leftover crumbs, and barnyard hens. He invites us to look around at our fields, our gardens, our orchards, our vineyards, our backyards. Jesus is not against large but invites us to start small and do little large. "Little is much if God is in it."[24]

It would be hard to overestimate the tremendous power you have to influence the direction of people's lives, even when that person is a stranger. Anthropologist Margaret Mead famously pronounced that we should "never doubt that a small group of thoughtful, committed individuals can change the world, indeed, it's the only thing that ever has."[25] The world has been changed by one word here, one story there, metaphors above and over all. It is not just that "a word aptly spoken is like apples of gold in settings of silver."[26] A nudge here, a nudge there are like baskets of blessings that pop out just when you need them the most to give life a burst.

In the animal kingdom, the bigger the brain, the smaller the face. We big-brained people do not know our face, who we are, and how severely we have been defaced from our original divine design. In the words of William Golding, whose book *Lord of the Flies* (1954) was inspired by his wartime experiences, anyone who could not see that "man produces evil as a bee produces honey must have been blind or wrong in the head."[27] In small, everyday ways, evangelists nudge out of others their original human face and what God is doing to summon them to become new human beings called to renew human society. The more I discover what I am, the more miserable I get; the more I discover who God is and who God made me, the happier I become.

In the Jesus kingdom, the bigger the brain in your head, the bigger the love in your heart. And that one-pound heart, made large with love and connected to a two-pound brain, made small by humility, can challenge the world to give peace and love a fighting chance.

To be sure, there is no path through life without detours. But detours, roundabouts, and imperfections, as the incarnation's setting straight of our sidetracked humanity makes clear, are the paths used by the Spirit to take us home.

2. Scale Fast

Once you have learned the nudge on a small scale, you can leverage and reuse attentional strategies to expand evangelism across every aspect of your life and across your connections.

You know a nudge is providential when the person being nudged already knows they need that very nudge. A nudge is only of value if there is an "aha" moment that accompanies it. Jesus never did anything the Father had not already been doing, and the very instinct to nudge is predicated by a knowledge that God had somehow prepared this very event. The most powerful nudges are those that coax someone in directions they already know they should be going. When a nudger pours fuel at the right moment to a low-grade fire already burning in the heart and mind, the combustion is explosive and the conflagration is breathtaking.

> In God nothing is empty of sense … so the conviction of a
> transcendental meaning in all things seeks to formulate itself.[28]
> —Dutch historian Johan Huizinga

To the ears of faith, we are never out of the range of God's voice: every distress a call, every surprise a service, every relationship a blessing, every phone call a connection, every hesitation or doubt a direction. We respond to each of these, trusting that our small saves will make a saving difference even if we never know how it all plays out or how it all works in God's scheme of things. Most often we never know "the rest of the story."

But we don't need to. What counts in evangelism is not cognition, but recognition. Can we identify the face of Christ when he shows it to us? What is our receptiveness to the Spirit, who appears in others and in one another? Are we able to decipher the playings of the Spirit in others' lives? That's enough. Jesus "appeared" to the Twelve, to Cephas, and to the five hundred; and Paul says, "He appeared to me." Has he "appeared" to you? If he "appeared" to you, would you know it? Can you apprehend his appearing?

3. Live, Jesus, Live!

Do we have any faith "to speak of"?

There comes a time when nudging means a no-beating-about-the-bush stepping forward to meet the other and tell it like it is, or in other words, to tell who Jesus is.

I call dropping the name of Jesus the "Nudge Bomb." Yet even when we throw the bomb, the nudger seldom throws his or her voice. While slow to speak,[29] we are always to be ready to give the "reason" for our high-hope living.[30] Jeremiah's confession about the futility of holding his breath is ours: "If I say, 'I will not mention him or speak any more in his name,' his word is in my heart like a fire, a fire shut up in my bones, and I am weary of holding it in; indeed, and I cannot."[31] Our nudges toward lives of freedom and communion and hope will require speaking the name of Jesus and inviting others to accept the liberation that comes with surrender, the communion that comes from submission.

One day a nudger asked a question of John Wesley: "Do you know Jesus Christ?" Even though Wesley was an Oxford don, a theologian, hymn writer, Christian author, and missionary to America, he realized that he really didn't "know" Jesus Christ in all of these activities like he was being called to know him. What Wesley had been living out of was a Christian faith based more on rational defenses of the cold logic and coherence of the Apostles' Creed or the Thirty-nine Articles rather than a personal experience of and a heart strangely warmed by the fires at the altar of Jesus the Christ.

Intimate spouses of fifty years *know* the nuances of their love, the snorts and grunts in sleep, what is normal and what is not. It's what poet Galway Kinnell calls the "familiar touch of the long married."[32] Do we, after years of walking with Christ, *know* him and his familiar touch?

In all of our nudges, in all of our helping people see the God who is already at play in their lives, we must never forget that we ultimately do not offer others our skills, our wisdom, or our expertise. We offer others Christ and the Holy Spirit, the only powers that can create the new humanity. Or as the apostle Paul put it, "To me, to live is Christ."[33] Not acknowledging Christ when he appears is dereliction of discipleship.

As you walk down the stairs toward baggage claim at the Memphis Airport, there is a sign that greets you when you land on the ground floor. It is the motto of Graceland. The sign reads: "Discover Your Inner Elvis." Nudgers help people discover their inner Jesus. Nudgers do that by lifting up Christ, not themselves, and trust Jesus to stir others to new life and new relationships.

Will someone mistake you for Jesus today?

Semiotics 101

For nudge evangelism to work, we must bring together two things seldom seen together: evangelism and semiotics. Since you now have some notion of what I mean by "evangelism," let me say a word about the more unfamiliar term *semiotics*.

A teacher walks up to a chalkboard and writes "H_2O." H_2O is an abstraction of water. You can't drink it, be quenched by it, swim in it, or float on it. It's a useful abstraction. Semiotics is an attempt to get our eyes off the chalkboard and into the real world. It is the art of making connections, linking disparate dots, seeing the relationships between apparently trifling matters, and turning them into metonymic moments.

Most important, *semiotics* is a Jesus word. In fact, Jesus instructed us to learn semiotics. It's a direct order.

One of Jesus' favorite sayings went something like "Red sky in morning, sailors take warning; red sky at night, sailors delight." He then went on: "You know how to read the signs of the sky. You must also learn how to read the signs of the times."[34] The Greek word for *signs* is *semeia* (from which we get the word *semiotics*). We are directed by Jesus to learn how to read signs, to read "the handwriting on the wall." God's hand is still writing on walls today. Evangelists are people with red-sky-at-morning sensitivities. Hence the yoking of evangelism and semiotics.

The world is ruled by signs, with money the most mastered semiotic system out there. We all do semiotics, whether we know it or not. Waiting on tables is a semiotic system, with every interaction an exchange of visual and verbal markers. At Le Peep restaurant in Peoria, Illinois, my waitress turned to her trainee and said, "See the crumpled-up napkin on his plate? That's the universal sign of 'I'm done.' Take his plate away."

Some things look easy until you try them (like juggling and jigsaws). Other things look hard until you try them (like semiotics).

Here's an example. You've just purchased a new car. You drive your new car out of the dealership, and as soon as you hit the highway, something happens. The moment your rubber hits the road, something starts to happen. What is it?

You say, "Depreciation." How true. You've just lost three thousand dollars, at minimum. I call the smell of a new car the most expensive cologne in the universe. Lasts about a month. You do the math: three thousand dollars divided by thirty days.... By the way, scientists now tell us that the smell of a new car is toxic.

But something else happens as well. You begin to see that car you just purchased everywhere. Am I right or what?

I don't think people are now buying that car to copy you. Nothing has changed except one thing: Because of your investment in that car, you are now in a state of "semiotic awareness."

And when people observe you and your car, they are also in a state of semiotic awareness whether they know it or not. In the land of semiotics, cars are driven less to get you somewhere and more to be seen and to be read. Cars are identity signals. They are signs of who we are or want to be.

We see what we choose to see, as artists have been telling us for centuries. Michelangelo is said to have remarked that he released David from the marble block he found him in. "The painting has a life of its own. I try to let it come through," confessed Jackson Pollock.[35] Artists are simply people with high levels of semiotic awareness.

Most disciples of Jesus are not in a state of semiotic awareness. The church especially is not good at reading signs. Those who are preoccupied with reading signs are looking for one thing only: not signs of our times, but end-times signs, signs of the return of Christ ... signs of the latter days and the end of days.

By reading the signs of the times, I am referring to the signs of the

Spirit's activity in the world. Jesus wept over Jerusalem because it could not read the signs: "You did not recognize the time of your visitation."[36] Nudgers are connectors of signs and channelers of their significance. Are you ready for signs? Are you able to read signs?

Nudge is an invitation to move beyond church-centric Christianity to a holistic, omnipresent theology of the signified reign of God. God is, Paul told the Athenians, "not far from any one of us."[37] If God can speak through a burning bush, through plagues of locust, through Balaam's ass, through Babylon, through blood on doorposts, through Peter, through Judas, through Pilate's jesting sign hung over the head of our Lord, and through the cross itself, then God can and will speak through art deco architecture, abstract expressionism, classic literature like Virgil's *Aeneid*, mass media, disease, Disney, hunger, Twitter, etc. The question is never, "Is God using this?" Rather the question is, "What is my/our invitation upon hearing?"

God meets us everywhere, in a bewildering variety of forms and fashions. Eighteenth-century hymn writer Isaac Watts called John's book of Revelation "the opera of the apocalypse."[38] We grow giddy over mystic numbers, signs and seals, heraldic beasts and composite beings, but what about the opera of the everyday? The ordinary and mundane? John Updike believed his only duty as a writer was "to describe reality as it had come ... to give the mundane its beautiful due."[39] Updike was a brilliant semiotician.

Nudge argues for the triangulation of all three: Scripture, Culture, Spirit. But we walk a tonal tightrope: *in touch* with the world but *in tune* with the Spirit through highly pitched souls, with heightened sensitivities that connect to the Scriptures and then to the Spirit and then to the culture.

As we watch for the signs of your kingdom on earth,
we echo the song of the angels in heaven.[40]

—Eucharistic Prayer F, *Common Worship*

Why are we fascinated with the CBS network's CSI franchise? We are transfixed by how investigators can "read" a crime scene. We read anthropologists' works because they can "read" a culture. We read Dan Brown novels in record-bursting numbers (*The Da Vinci Code*, *Angels and Demons*, *The Lost Symbol*) because of the power and mystique of symbology (the Hollywood name for semiotics) and our interest in the hidden forces at work in people's lives and in our world.

The ultimate in social as well as spiritual illiteracy is the inability to read the handwriting on the wall. There are many forms of biblical, cultural, and spiritual illiteracy that go beyond not knowing the difference between Melchizedek and Methuselah, or between Dorothy Day and Dorothy Sayers ... and Doris Day, for that matter. How many people have been waiting their entire lives for a message from God when they have been staring it in the face all along? How many people are deaf to the dog-whistle voice of the divine that only they are vibed to hear?[41]

Life without Landlines

To get into "Len's Lair" (aka, my study), I bend down and step up at the same time, and then pass through a small corridor to enter a totally silent room. I switch on some lights, burn some candles, and wake my computer.

Suddenly, there it is: the world. I'm connected to the far reaches of the planet. On our little island I've picked up signals that were there all the time. I have the world at my fingertips. All I need is the right apparatus, the right wireless card (or radio or TV or whatever) that can "connect" me with what was always there but was invisible and unavailable until the receiver was activated.

Think of semiotics as a receiver. We live in an ocean of waves—radio, cell phone, wi-fi, infrared, cosmic. These waves not only surround us; they pass through us and can even penetrate walls. These waves will continue to remain invisible unless there is a receiver that can channel them into forms we can hear and see. That "make me a channel of blessing" stuff? Semiotic awareness at its best.

This book is your wireless card to pick up the signals of transcendence, the immanent transcendent, that are out there but not being downloaded. Semiotics is the art of finding channels and making connections. Evangelism as semiotics is the art of tuning our receivers to the "I AM" channel and setting the controls to receive and transmit transdimensional frequencies. This book is your compass in a world where the magnetic lines of the earth are invisible. These magnetic lines have always been there and are not dependent on our compass. But the compass becomes our means of making visible and interpreting what we cannot see.

Marius von Senden, reviewing every published case of blind people receiving sight over a three-hundred-year period in his classic book *Space and Sight* (1932), concluded that every newly sighted adult sooner or later comes to a motivation crisis—and that not every patient gets through it.[42] There are plenty of people out there who are "seeing but not seeing." Or to put it another way, too many Christians are walking blind through life when they don't have to.

> Our survival, individual and cultural, depends on our ability
> to read and interpret ecologically what our man-made
> environments are saying to us and doing to us.[43]
> —Eric McLuhan

Throughout Scripture God uses sign language to communicate relationship: Noah and the rainbow,[44] Abraham and circumcision,[45] Moses and the Passover blood posts,[46] Moses and the exodus cloud/fire pillars,[47] Samson and his golden locks,[48] shepherds and the manger,[49] Jesus and the cross, and even Pilate's jesting billboard hung over the head of Christ on the cross was a sign.[50] The same sign can be different things to different people. The Passover was freedom to the Israelites and death to the Egyptians. The sign Pilate hung over Christ's head was irony to Pilate, blasphemous to the Jewish religious leaders, and truth to all followers of Christ. The same sign, different meanings. In fact, when Jesus turned water into wine, or fed the five thousand, or raised Lazarus from the dead, Jesus didn't think of what he was doing as a "miracle." He thought of what he was doing as a sign.

God is still signing us. God's finger is still writing. We may not be able to read the divine finger because we've got our fingers in our ears or are so fixated at the finger pointing to the moon that we can't see beyond the fingertips. But God's finger is busy writing in strange and sundry signs, designs, cosigns, and signals.

> Everything that surrounds you can give you something.[51]
> —Hungarian photographer André Kertész

I begin every day with what I call my "Bugs Bunny" ritual. Where Bugs Bunny chews his carrot and asks "What's up, Doc?" I drink my coffee and ask, "What's up, God?"

In fact, some sign readers are arguing that our very survival as a species depends on our ability to "read the signs." Jared Diamond, in his book *Collapse: How Societies Choose to Fail or Succeed* (2004), argues that the only common denominator behind all cases of collapse is not the destruction of the environment, as serious as that is. It is not economic collapse, as universal as that is. The one elementary but elemental factor in all civilizations that collapsed into extinction is the failure to read the handwriting on the wall, the failure to respond to warning signs. Every extinct culture hurled signs high into the heavens for all to see. But every collapsing culture failed to read and heed these flares.[52]

The Problem Is Not with Life

Sometimes my kids come to me and complain: "Daddy, I'm bored." I tell them, "Sorry. You aren't bored. You're having a semiotic breakdown."

They then run to their mother, who rolls her eyes and comforts them with "Don't worry. Your father is just having one of his semiotic spells. He'll get over it."

But I'm right.[53] And I'm not going to get over it. When my kids are bored, the problem is not with life. Life is full of wonderful, exciting, and adventurous things. My kids don't have life fatigue. The problem is not with life. The problem is with them. In a state of semiotic awareness, all of life is bathed in beauty and sacredness. When they get bored, they have entered a state of semiotic breakdown. The fact that many people live boring lives, the fact that many people make so little of their lives is not life's fault. People are in a state of semiotic breakdown.

Semiotic breakdown is the disconnect from all that is and can be from perceived possibility. Semiotic breakdown has degrees. The lightest of these is simply missing the message and doing nothing in most cases. The most serious is seeing the signs, believing they mean something, but having the wrong interpretation and setting off in a destructive path. The advice of park rangers applies here: If you're lost, stop. Call for help. Reorient yourself. Find true north. Suicide is the ultimate state of semiotic breakdown.

> The world is so full of a number of things
> I am sure we should all be as happy as kings.[54]
> —Robert Louis Stevenson

Much of the problem with the church is precisely this. The "ole ship," as Methodist cofounder Charles Wesley liked to call it, is in a state of semiotic breakdown. The church sees mysterious hieroglyphics all around, but because it cannot read the sign language, it fails to see that these are really hieroglyphics of holiness.

Without doing our semiotic homework, Christians can only follow trends. We can't create them. Faith widens the imagination and lengthens the horizons. So why is church so narrow in its imagination, so short in its scope of thinking? Why is the body of Christ not bursting with creativity, but a bastion of boredom?

It is in a state of semiotic breakdown. We are as clueless as to what the Spirit is up to as the critic who dismissed the Beatles when he first heard them as "strictly routine rhythm-and-blues."[55] One of the greatest examples of semiotics in the Scriptures is the story of the wise men, who were probably *not* "wise men" but Eastern magicians, sorcerers, or diviners (*magoi*).[56] In the Greek New Testament *magos* means most often "interpreters of dreams" or "experts in astrology." In other words, sign readers. These "magi" had the imagination to read the signals, register the early intelligence, and risk a long journey so that they got there first. Pagan semioticians got to Jesus before the holy and righteous.

If the inability to read signs is a surefire recipe for failure and extinction, the ability to read signs is now being defined as the key ingredient to success and leadership. Harvard Business School's Leadership Initiative has spent years developing a "Great American Business Leaders" database. The project identified and analyzed the accomplishments of some 860 top executives in the twentieth century, and the results are being made known through the writings of two leadership professors: Anthony J. Mayo, the director of the Initiative, and Nitin Nohria, the new dean of Harvard Business School. In the work titled *In Their Time: The Greatest Business Leaders of the 20th Century* (2005),[57] the coauthors distilled tons of data into three leadership archetypes: Mold-Makers, Mold-Breakers, and Mold-Takers (i.e., the entrepreneur, the charismatic, the manager). Whatever their style or "type," however, there was one ingredient that all shared in common: an outsized "ability to read the forces that shaped the times in which they lived ... and to seize on the resulting opportunities."[58]

The coauthors call this key leadership trait "contextual intelligence." In words that appear lifted from the biblical description of the tribe of Issachar (Israel's resident semioticians, who "knew the times" and "knew what best to do"),[59] Mayo and Nohria portray the century's best leaders as people who understood the forces that defined their eras, and as people who "adapted their enterprises to best respond to those forces." Both "knowing the times" and "knowing what to do" are what made them leaders: "Contextual intelligence is an underappreciated but all-encompassing differentiator between success and failure."[60]

The inability to read signs helps explain a great deal about the past, the present, and the future. For example, take the rise of Nazism. How did one of the most cultured and Christianized countries in the West succumb to the appeal of Hitler? How did the very culture that brought Christian arts and philosophy to their highest and most luminous levels become responsible for some of the most heinous atrocities in history? Its lack of attentiveness.

A few read the signs: Dietrich Bonhoeffer, Alfred Delp, Martin Niemöller, Joseph Ratzinger Sr., the policeman father of Pope Benedict XVI. But by and large the Christian church in Germany was as sign blind as the cousin of Winston Churchill, Charles Stewart Henry Vane-Tempest-Stewart, 7th Marquess of Londonderry (1878–1949), who after he met Hitler called him "a kindly man with a receding chin and an impressive face."[61]

Or to take one more example: The problem with the Iraq war was not so much bad military intelligence, but deficient cultural intelligence. There was very little contextual intelligence of the political, religious, and social culture of Iraq and its diverse peoples (Kurds, Sunnis). A decades-old reliance on relational intelligence was abandoned for satellites that could read license plates from space. Unfortunately, they failed to read the nuances of the population. There is also very little contextual intelligence of the mediated world in which we live. War has a very healthy future, but the future of war is inescapably global and fought not in physical space but in informational space. This is what Osama bin Laden and al Qaeda, and even the middle-class Iraqi citizen Salam Pax and his "Baghdad Blog,"[62] seemed to understand better than the United States.

Whether we know it or not, we all read signs. God is also a sign reader: The bow in the clouds is God's sign, not to us but to God to remind God that there is a promise in place never again to destroy the earth with a flood.

You do semiotics all the time. In fact, every one of you is a master semiotician. You may not know it, but you are. And I'll prove it to you one more time.

You can't get a driver's license until you learn your semiotics: You learn to read the signs of the road. In fact, you are given a test on your semiotic skills at reading road signs.

You can't balance a checkbook until you learn your semiotics: You learn to read the signs of mathematics. You learn the sign language of math.

You can't get a job until you learn your semiotics: You learn to read the signs of a language. You learn English or Spanish or Mandarin or Japanese. You can't read anything until you learn your semiotics.

Semiotics is the art and science of paying attention. Since evangelism is also the art and science of paying attention, I will argue that evangelism is semiotics. There is another book to be written on the prophetic role of reading the signs or semiotics.[63] *Nudge* argues that a semiotics evangelism is more pay attention than attract attention. The best evangelists are not the attention getters, but attention givers. Yet the most attentive semiotician is hopeless if the sign is read yet misinterpreted. Our quest is to be so filled with the Spirit of God, and to be wearing interpretive Jesus goggles, that we not only notice, but are able to interpret and respond.

Paying Attention

One of the earliest admonitions in life is this: "Pay attention." One of the hardest things in the world to do is this: "Pay attention." Nobody attends to attention. People teach us how to think, but not how to pay attention. But paying attention changes your brain, your being, your future. According to some scholars, the root *lig* in the word *religion* means "to pay attention."

If so, from its very definition, religion helps us learn to pay attention to people and to life.

Our poets and our artists have understood this better than our theologians. Poet John Ciardi defined human identity in precisely these terms: "We are what we do with our attention."[64] I call Mary Oliver the twentieth-century Thoreau. Oliver says, "This is the first, wildest, and wisest thing I know, that the soul exists, and that it is built entirely out of attentiveness."[65] In a poem Oliver says, "I don't know exactly what a prayer is. / I do know how to pay attention."[66] When poet Annie Dillard was asked by *Life* magazine "What is the meaning of life?" her response was very simple: "Pay attention so that creation need not play to an empty house."[67] "[God] asks nothing but attention," wrote poet William Butler Yeats.[68] Mexican novelist Carlos Fuentes calls "extreme attention" the number-one "creative faculty."[69] In fact, Fuentes defines love as "attention. Paying attention to the other person. Opening oneself to attention."[70] "To understand something," Indian philosopher J. Krishnamurti has written, "you have to pay attention, you have to love, and when you love something, the very nature of love is discipline."[71]

> Prayer is properly not petition,
> but simply an attention to God which is a form of love.[72]
> —Iris Murdoch

Prayer is where the Christian tradition attends most often to paying attention. Sixteenth-century Spanish mystic/poet St. John of the Cross said that the heart of prayer is giving "loving attention to God" so that even "when the spiritual person cannot meditate, let him learn to be still in God, fixing his loving attention upon Him."[73] Iris Murdoch, an Irish novelist and philosopher, argued in a quote so rich it needs to be cited twice, "Prayer is properly not petition, but simply an attention to God which is a form of love."[74] In her argument that prayer needs to become less a matter of what we say and more a matter of what we hear, the French mystic and philosopher Simone Weil liked to say that "prayer is paying attention."[75] Prayer is not getting God to pay attention, but learning to pay attention ourselves to what God is doing. Semiotic praying is listening, listening to God speaking to us now.

I would want to argue with Murdoch and Weil somewhat and say that prayer is what happens when you pay attention fully, when you are at full attention, and your attention always gets God's attention. Paying attention is a form of surrender. We are always surrendered and surrendering to *something,* but most of us live in the delusion we are in control. Surrender is a willingness to be open to possibilities we cannot imagine. Control suggests that if we can't imagine it, it cannot be, and we set about to ensure it.

British novelist and Christian essayist Dorothy L. Sayers in a letter written during World War II expressed her conviction that "we have rather lost sight of the idea that Christianity is supposed to be an interpretation of the universe."[76] The church has done itself a disservice, she argued, by presenting Christianity not as a way of seeing all things but as one competing ideology among many. "Instead of leading us to see God in new and surprising places, it too often has led us to confine God inside *our* place."[77]

There are a few in the theological world who have understood the importance of paying attention. "If I gave my attention to your handiwork, I should become your handiwork," wrote the English theologian and biblical scholar Austin Farrer, echoing the prophetic vision of William Blake, who believed you become what you behold.[78] Of anyone alive, however, British sociologist and theologian David Martin has cried the loudest and made the strongest case for the spiritual life being one of sign language. In words that led directly to the writing of this book, "I suggest we look at Christian faith as a code book for picking up signals of transcendence, and the question is how we are to pick up those signals and interpret the code?"[79]

But examples like these from the Christian world are exceptions that prove the rule. By and large, the Christian community has taken little notice of what it means to "take notice" and "pay heed."

Not so for the advertising world, which has made paying attention a science. What is public relations but the business of getting noticed. Umberto Eco defines semiotics in this way: "Semiotics is in principle the discipline studying everything that can be used in order to lie."[80]

Tell someone that they can read the signs of the stock market and in that way become rich, and people will do it in a New York minute. Tell someone that they can read the signs of the Spirit and become spiritually rich, and they yawn and walk away. We are more prone to read signs of someone's economic and social status than to read signs of the divine at play in people's lives. We have become experts at reading surface appearances and wonder why the number of what appear to be divine disappearances increases. You cannot serve two *Semeia*.

> But now ask the beasts, and let them teach you;
> And the birds of the heavens, and let them tell you.
> Or speak to the earth, and let it teach you;
> And let the fish of the sea declare to you.
> Who among all these does not know
> That the hand of the Lord has done this,
> In whose hand is the life of every living thing,
> And the breath of all mankind?
> —Job 12:7–10 NASB

We live in an attention-deficit culture more adept at gaining attention than at paying attention, furiously beating bushes that advance our interests while not paying attention to burning bushes that showcase God's activities.

Joseph Nye Jr. of Harvard's Kennedy School of Government names the "paradox of plenty" as one of the characteristic features of postmodern culture. In his words, "A plenitude of information leads to a poverty of attention.... Those who can distinguish valuable signals from white noise gain power. Editors, filters, and cue givers become more in demand, and this is a source of power for those who can tell us where to focus our attention."[81] If the future lies with those who can help people "focus attention" and "decode secrets,"[82] then the greatest days for evangelism lie in the future. In a world where everyone suffers from attention-deficit disorder, evangelists are people with "Attention Surplus Disorder."[83]

Whether attention is the highest goal of education, as some have argued,[84] is another conversation. But paying attention is the highest form of opening to life and to God. Unarguably the greatest gift you can give another is your attention, partly because it gets us away from our attention-getting "myness"[85] and places us in a larger attention-giving "youness" and "thereness." To pay attention means you are no longer the center of attention. Attention givers treat signs as subjects of multisensory study. Attention getters objectify themselves as the ultimate sign.

The greatest gift we can give God is our passionate attention, which as we have seen, is but another name for prayer. God pervades the world through the Spirit, but for most of us we live in a world without regard. The writer of Hebrews even goes so far as to suggest that the key to staying faithful and on track with the Spirit is our attentiveness. "Pay more careful attention ... to what we have heard, so that we do not drift away."[86] "Drift away" is a nautical phrase that beautifully conveys how easy it is for us to stray and go adrift without the focusing of attentiveness.

Our inattentiveness to the world contrasts so sharply to Jesus' attentiveness to all of creation. Jesus was a "dawn collector"[87] who found God's Spirit in all things, in all aspects of the natural world, both animate (birds, animals, flowers, seeds) and inanimate (pots, coins), yet showed how we can experience God's Spirit in ways that are beyond and "beneath language."[88]

> The moment one gives close attention to anything, even
> a blade of grass, it becomes a mysterious, awesome,
> indescribably magnificent world in itself.[89]
>
> —Henry Miller

Psalm 19 may very well be the greatest song in the Psalter and one of the most magnificent poems in all of literature. We have no evidence of Jesus ever citing it, but both the apostle Paul and John use it to reference Jesus and his mission.[90] We shall return to this profound passage and its early elaboration of the connection between voice and vision, or what I call a "sound theology." But for now let's pay attention to its declaration of God's universal disclosure:

> The heavens declare the glory of God;
>   the skies proclaim the work of his hands.
>
> Day to day they pour forth speech;
>   night after night they display knowledge.
>
> There is no speech or language
>   where their voice is not heard.
>
> Their voice goes out into all the earth,
>   their words to the ends of the world.[91]

The world is not God, of course, but the incarnation goes all the way down, and the Spirit indwells all that exists. Nothing is without a witness to the divine; everything that exists praises the Creator. If Christians are not the best at giving voice through art, poetry, and music to these unspoken voices, then something is wrong. We are living ADD lives.

Poet/critic Paul Mariani says it is our lack of imagination that has closed us to an awareness of God in the world.

> If the incarnation has indeed occurred, as I believe it has, then the evidence of that central act in human history—when the creator took on our limitations with our bones and flesh—should have consequences that are reverberating down to our own moment—evidence of God's immanent presence ought to be capable of breaking in on us each day the way air and light and sound do if only we know of what to look and listen for.[92]

This is part of our humanness: Homo sapiens are literally human knowers. And what are we to "know"? Know God, know each other, and know life. Since the days of cave dwellers, people have buried their dead with what they would need in the afterlife. We have always known instinctively that there is *more*. Enter into a relationship with a poem, a painting, a musical composition, a sunrise, a snowflake, a flower—know skunk cabbages in January, crocuses in February, cymbidiums in March, harebells in April, poppies in May, irises in June, cowslips in July, pansies in August, marigolds in September, toadlilies in October, mums in November, dahlias in December. God's creation is a revelation of divine presence. This is the genius of Christian theology: It radically reconfigures the human conception of the sacred. Nothing is inherently "profane." It may be profaned by sin; but it is inherently an arena of divine activity and spiritual insight. The locus and focus of biblical theology is the world, *not* the heavens.

What is the grass?
I guess it is the handkerchief of the Lord,
A scented gift and remembrance designedly dropt,

Bearing the owner's name someway in the corners,
that we may see and remark, and say Whose?[93]
—Walt Whitman (1855)

Jesus expressed an earthy, semiotic theology by materializing his message through various media, including images, stories, actions (stilled storms, healed limbs), and objects like spit, fig trees, bursting baskets, etc. He was a master semiotician. You might even say that Jesus' ministry was more a semiotics ministry than a preaching, teaching, or healing ministry. Instead of taking stands, Jesus took hikes during which he performed signs: like the coin with Caesar's image stamped on it, or the overturned money changers' tables, or the water-into-wine at small-town Cana of Galilee. Significantly, Jesus' "first sign" interceded not to sober up the party, but to make it more festive with 600 to 900 bonus bottles of vintage wine. Jesus' public entry into Jerusalem was a masterful use of signs: a donkey, not a dressed-up horse, as you would expect of a king. The ultimate sign that reveals Jesus as the life-giving Sign? The raising of Lazarus.[94]

Jesus' first postresurrection sermon is a sign. Jews raised their right hand to greet one another. The left hand was the dirty hand, the right the clean hand. When raised as a gesture of greeting, it showed that one was not carrying a weapon. Jesus greets his disciples with his right hand. To be sure, he has to walk through walls to get to them. But when he does, he raises his hands and reveals his real weapons: his wounds.

Jesus warns not to become dependent on these signs and rebukes those who get addicted to the signs.[95] If you followed Jesus because of the signs he performed, that wasn't all bad. But you had to move to something deeper. The ultimate sign was not a performing Messiah, but a participating people in the Messiah's death and resurrection.[96] The only sign that matters is a participation in the cross and resurrection. And those who follow Jesus without signs are more "blessed" than those who need the signs.[97] Fix our eyes on God, the starter and finisher of our faith.[98]

"What do you mean?" they asked composer Robert Schumann. "I mean this," he answered and played the piece again. "What do you mean?" they asked Jesus. "I mean this," he replied; and he took the bread, gave thanks, broke it into fragments, and shared those broken pieces with his disciples. And that piece, and those broken pieces, have been shared in every conceivable setting and played in every known language ever since.

Faith is the gift of reading the signs of the presence of God. The point of reading signs is not the signs themselves, but the Signifier, Jesus the Christ. Jesus is not some floating signifier at the whim of our advertising campaigns or some magnetic personality. Jesus is the ultimate Sign (*Semeion*—note the singular)[99] of God. The church is a sign of the revelation that Christ is and was. Or as Karl Barth puts it, "The church exists ... to set up in the world a new sign which is radically dissimilar to the world's own manner and which contradicts it in a way that is full of promise."[100] That is why the church will always be a sign that will be opposed.[101] But as with all good signs, the church points away from itself and toward the triune God. Its message is not "Come to church" but "Come to Christ."[102]

Nudge evangelism, or spreading the *evangelion* ("good news"), is announcing the good sign. I like how Bill Hull puts it: "If I am driving from Seattle to Los Angeles and see a sign that reads, 'Los Angeles, 400 miles,' I don't pull over and sit under the sign. The sign points me to my goal. Signs of God's manifest presence point me to Christ."[103]

Walk with thy fellow-creatures: note the hush
And whispers amongst them. There's not a spring,
Or leafe but hath his morning hymn. Each bush
And oak knows I am. Canst thou not sing?

. . .

Birds, beasts, all things
Adore him in their kinds.
Thus all is hurl'd

In sacred hymnes and order, the great chime
And symphony of nature.[104]
—Henry Vaughan

R-E-S-P-E-C-T

God posts all sorts of billboards and signposts on life's highway. Human circumstances have divine meaning. This book is designed to help you pay attention to the variety of signs and signals God gives us about what God's up to and what's up ahead.

The concept of paying attention is related to the ancient notion of respect, which comes from the Latin *respicere,* meaning "take account" or "pay attention." Key to this understanding of respect, however, is a form of observing that implies honoring. In the Latin meaning of respect, by paying attention, you value and honor what you are observing. When we don't pay attention to what God is doing, we dishonor and devalue him. In everything we do, whether it be reading the Word, hiking in the woods, watching a movie, viewing a painting, we respect God when we ask ourselves this question: "What is God's invitation here?" By not paying attention to life, we pay God no respect.

When we see all things in God, and refer all things to Him, we
read in common matters superior expressions of meaning.[105]
—Philosopher William James

That makes Christian semiotics more than awareness or attentiveness, however. That's Zen semiotics. Christian semiotics enters into the connections between signs and people and God. In other words, Christian semiotics is attention that leads to intention, attention that leads to transformation and remembrance. An attention that leads to remembrance is called a sacrament. The most sacred signs are called sacraments, and sacraments work through what they say; they impact what they symbolize. Sacraments are celebrations of our attentiveness and sign reading.[106] The more attentive you are, the more you will recover as well as discover. The more attentive you are, the more you see Christ in every person and the sacramental nature of all of life.

The practice of evangelism is, in many ways, life itself—being a true human being. It is to pay attention to life and to God. Evangelism is sensational: helping people hear, see, taste, smell, and touch the creativity of God in their lives and the necessity of their response to God's initiatives. Nudge evangelism is the decipherment of the workings of the Spirit in people's lives and nudging them in those directions. Evangelism is bringing people into contact with Jesus, who is already there.

> In Grandfather's mind, there could be no separation between
> awareness and tracking for they were one in the same thing.[107]
> —Tom Brown Jr., *Grandfather* (1993)

One of the best-loved stories about Emily Dickinson, perhaps everyone's favorite nineteenth-century poet, is the time her father rushed to ring the fire bell during dinnertime. The people of the village came running out of their homes, hugging napkins and silverware. "Where's the fire?" everyone wanted to know.

Emily Dickinson's father announced there was no fire. Just a beautiful sunset he didn't want anyone to miss. Hence he rang the bell before it was too late and the sun went down.

The villagers returned to their dining tables, shaking their heads at "that crazy Dickinson man."[108] But should we all not be ringing bells at the beauty of creation? When's the last time you rang the bell for burning bushes?

The church used to ring bells to call the community together and to announce the beauty of worship about to take place. Now we're in the bells and whistles business. I shall never forget the first time I attended a Roman Catholic Mass and heard the sanctus bell ring during the "Holy, Holy, Holy" and the sacring bell rung three times at the elevation of the host. I came home and asked my mother what all that bell ringing was about.

She said, "It's to tell you 'Christ is alive,' alive in the bread and wine."

"But why a bell?" I persisted. Her reason for the bell scared me at the same time it sparked my imagination. As a liturgical explanation it turned out not to be accurate, but it turned me into a lifelong bell ringer. In olden times, she explained, they used to bury people with strings attached to bells above ground, so that if perchance they buried you alive, you could ring the bell when you woke up. When people above ground heard the bell ringing, they would know "He's alive!" and immediately dig you out. My mother claimed that her grandmother knew someone who had been "saved by the bell."

Evangelists are bell ringers. We spend our lives digging people out of self-dug graves and ringing bells that say, "Christ is alive; Jesus is real; God's Spirit is active in your life." To people buried alive, trapped in tombs and wrapped in grave cloths, we speak Jesus' words to Lazarus: "Come out." Even those who are walking zombies can learn to pay attention to God's presence and movement. An old Methodist hymn says, "I can hear my Savior calling," and our response is, "Where He leads me I will follow, I'll go with Him, with Him all the way."

> I have freed a thousand slaves, but I could have freed a
> thousand more if they knew they were slaves.[109]
> —Underground railroader Harriet Tubman

At our home on Orcas Island, we like to feed the birds and hummers. This also attracts other less desirable wildlife like squirrels, ferrets, otters, and mice. But you can't have one without the other. We also like to leave our doors to the deck open, which means that more than a couple of times a summer a bird or hummer will get trapped inside the house.

When this happens, the whole family mobilizes into action, for we know that if we don't "help" it escape, it will die inside the house, and everyone knows this from personal discoveries of shriveled-up corpses found months later in the most unlikely of places. As soon as the bird or hummer sees one of us approach it, it will fly as fast as it can in the opposite direction, often smashing against a window or upending one of the colorful tumblers that attracted it inside in the first place. So another family member darts in that direction, nudging it from its place of hiding, only to have it fly even harder and faster to another part of the room, refusing to believe that it can't escape on its own. But wherever it flees, one of us will be there to nudge it toward the open door.

It is not usually until the poor little bird is so exhausted from trying to escape and its body is so crushed and beaten from its fear of our nudges that it can be guided to freedom or cupped in our hands and released. For some birds liberation takes only a few nudges. For other birds more self-reliant or stubborn, it may take an hour and dozens of nudges.

Never once has one of these freed creatures U-turned in flight and bounded back to say thanks. But the Sweet family always feels pride and joy when we work together to nudge a trapped and doomed bird finally toward life and food. Without our lifting that creature in our arms through prodding and nudging and poking and holding, it would have remained trapped and helpless, its fears sentencing itself to death.

Conclusion

Jesus said that our hearts follow whatever we "treasure" or pay attention to.[110] In fact, "Pay attention" may have been Jesus' signature phrase. Every speaker has pet phrases that they use over and over again. Sometimes these phrases are fillers, giving the speaker time to organize what comes next; sometimes these phrases are feeders, pumping new energy and punctuation into the speech; sometimes they become verbal tics … you know? … you know what I mean?

Paul's signature phrase was "Now!" Jesus' signature phrase was something that no one really knows how to translate. The King James Version renders it "Verily, verily, I say unto thee!" The NIV translates it "I tell you the truth." I really like that, because wherever Jesus went, there was truth. We cannot always give "the whole truth," and sometimes "nothing but the truth" is unkind, but we can always tell "the truth." Some contend that the most authentic twenty-first-century equivalent would be "Listen up!" I argue that today's version would be this: "Pay attention."

I have circled in my Bible every time Jesus says this phrase in the Gospels, and virtually every page is strewn with circles, sometimes five or six. It's almost as if Jesus couldn't tell a story or start a saying without reminding his hearers: "Pay attention."

You are what you pay attention to. No attention, no life. Everything comes to life when you pay attention to it. In a world of inattentiveness, a world that goes largely unregarded, it is the special mission given to humans to bring the world to life. How do we save the world? How do we keep the world alive? Through loving attention … by "tending and tilling," naming and cherishing the tiniest part of what God has created.

> I know that nothing has ever been real
> Without my beholding it.
> All becoming has needed me.
> My looking ripens things
> And they come toward me, to meet and be met.[111]
>
> —Rainer Rilke

 **Discover More Online**

CHECK OUT INTERACTIVES FOR YOUR PERSONAL OR SMALL-GROUP USE
AND MUCH MORE ON THE NUDGE WEB SITE:

WWW.NUDGETHEBOOK.COM

Chapter 2

WATCH AND WITNESS

The Two Phases of Paying Attention

My father-in-law, Gordon Rennie, whom the kids call "Par Par," has a hearing aid that occasionally emits a brief, high-pitched squeal that can be heard by anyone near him.

One day our daughter Soren was sitting next to him at the dining table when the device started to beep.

Surprised, Soren looked up at her grandfather. "Par Par," she said, "you've got mail."

Evangelism as semiotics is a fresh look at an evangelism that is based on three simple premises. These three were already introduced in chapter 1, but let me expand a bit more on each of them here.

Jesus is alive and active in our world.

Followers of Jesus "know" Jesus well enough to recognize where he is alive and moving in our day.

Evangelists nudge the world to wake up to the alive and acting Jesus and nudge others in the ways God is alive and moving. (I call these nudges "small saves.")

If any of these premises are wrong, you can stop right here and not bother with the rest of the book.

First, Jesus is alive and working in our world today.

I once heard Byron Klaus, president of Assemblies of God Theological Seminary (AGTS), challenge a gathering of clergy with, "I believe in the

present tense of Jesus." God once was human. And God still is human.
Many Christians are stuck in the Mary Magdalene phase of "They have
taken my Lord, and I do not know where they laid him."

> Let him easter in us,
> be a dayspring to the dimness in us,
> be a crimson-cresseted east.[1]
> —Gerard Manley Hopkins

Christ wants to become in your life and mine a verb, not a noun,
and in part it is nudging that turns the word *Christ* from noun to verb.
Christ is alive and at work in our world. In the words of one theologian,
"Theology, even at its most academic, is resurrection talk."[2] Or in the words
of one poet, "Christ plays in ten thousand places, lovely in limbs, lovely in
eyes not his."[3] How we discern the present tense of Jesus is the overarch-
ing theme of semiotic awareness. Every awakening of the Spirit in history
comes when the church no longer "remembers" Jesus as someone out of the
past, but "re-members" and reattaches itself to Christ as a living presence
and gets to know him afresh as a resurrection force.

The very word *Immanuel* is derived from the Latin word *manere*, which
means "to stay, to remain." "'The virgin will be with child and will give
birth to a son, and they will call him Immanuel'—which means 'God with
us.'"[4] But God with us, not for thirty-three years, but forever.

> The incarnation was not a thirty-three year experiment but
> the permanent mode of God's engagement to save.[5]
> —William Stacy Johnson

This is the key challenge facing semiotics, namely, our inability to take
seriously Christ in the present tense. Some theologians like to talk about
the role of the church as keeping alive the "dangerous memories" of the

classics.[6] If that's all there is to Christianity, keeping alive a dead person's memories, I've got better things to do with my life.

These classic texts are not there to report on what happened back then and long ago. The Scriptures offer signposts and specifications of a risen Lord who is accessible to the ongoing church.[7] Jesus, the church's being and body, the practices of the church, and the texts of the faith are one. So in the nudge sense, we are nudged to be aware of Christ through us when we read the narrative of the prodigal and recognize ourselves today as the elder brother. God speaks to us (convicts us?) about our 10:00 a.m. Tuesday attitude by resonating it with the timeless story.

I have a Jewish colleague who is more energized by a Messiah who has not yet appeared than many of my Christian colleagues are by a Messiah who is living in our midst. A Messiah who came two thousand years ago but does not come today is a what-difference-does-it-make? Messiah. The person and presence of Jesus are still available 24/7. "My Father is always at his work to this very day, and I, too, am working."[8] For this reason Augustine could say that God is *intimior intimo meo*, or "closer to me than I am to myself."

The fundamental fact of Christian faith is this: Christ is alive! "HE LIVES!"[9] "I know that my Redeemer lives."[10] "We Serve a RISEN Savior."[11] "Because He lives, I can face tomorrow."[12] The ideal of monastic holiness and in fact any tradition of holy living is precisely this: an awareness of the presence of Christ in all of life and in all things. When Benedict elaborated his rules in the sixth century, he understood prayer as a relationship with God that opens one to the awareness of God's presence permeating all of one's life. Back in 1998, George W. Stroup made this explicit: "Too often churches have understood themselves to be taking God to a godless world rather than following God into a world in which God is already redemptively present."[13] When we enter any context, we enter a world that is enveloped in divine nudges. Some folks wake to read their Bible and "find" Christ for the day (as if he wandered off over night), never realizing that their day was initiated by the nudge of Christ. Depending on the nudge we know and trust, nudge is a reliable way out of the obsessive-compulsive religious behavior that can usurp the motive behind the spiritual disciplines, rendering them less than moot. The spiritual disciplines are those practices that we engage in to become fully aware of the presence of Christ always in us.

Nudgers believe in the present tense of Jesus where Jesus is perceptible, able to be felt and sensed and experienced. "I will live with them and walk among them, and I will be their God, and they will be my people."[14] The great "I AM" is not the great "I was." Christians honor all the "omnis" (we especially celebrate omnipotence and omniscience) except one: omnipresence. I have a friend, Joe Myers, who observes that we believe more in the omnipresence of evil than in the omnipresence of God.

We can share time and space with Jesus even today in ways his disciples knew nothing about and would have envied. Nudge is more than connecting people to the Christ back then. Nudgers usher people into a relationship with the Christ who is alive and at work *today,* the Christ who is, who was, and who is to come. Nudgers are the living, breathing presence of Jesus Christ in the world because they take seriously the promise of Jesus himself to live among us and be present with us: "For where two or three come together in my name, there am I with them."[15]

> A person you don't recognize has taken his stand in your midst.
> —John 1:26 MSG

Second, nudge is recognition.

You may have heard the story of the research scientist hugging himself because he had just made a significant breakthrough: "I know something no one else knows, and they're not going to know it until I tell them."[16]

That's the evangelism of the past: "I know something no one else knows, and they're not going to know it until I tell them."

Evangelism of the future is "I know something everyone else knows, but they're not going to know they know it until I help them." Evangelism is less about trying to manage an outcome as it is sharing events and offering an advent alternative for what everyone clearly sees. Rather than wrestling the sinner's prayer out of a person who will say anything to get out of the headlock, it is a nudge toward the undeniable truth that is alive in all of us. Such a nudge is a shared moment over the crib of the firstborn of a friend counting toes and marveling at the entire miniature beauty, the acknowledgment of a miracle. What parent, in that moment, would contradict? There is little talk of primordial soup or big bangs in the hospital nursery.

It's worth repeating: What counts in evangelism is not cognition, but recognition. Can we identify the face of Christ when he shows it to us? What is our receptiveness to the Spirit, who appears in others and in each other? Are we able to decipher the workings of the Spirit in others' lives? The first step to Easter joy is recognition.

But recognition is easier said than done. One of my favorite Karl Barth stories is the one where he is riding a streetcar in his home city of Basel, Switzerland. He took a seat next to a tourist, and the two men started chatting with one another.

"Are you new to the city?" Barth inquired.

"Yes," said the tourist.

"Is there anything you would particularly like to see in the city?" asked Barth.

"Yes," said the tourist, "I would like to meet the famous Swiss theologian Karl Barth. Do you know him?"

Barth answered, "As a matter of fact, I do know him. I give him a shave every morning."

The tourist got off the streetcar at the next stop, quite delighted with himself. He went back to his hotel and told everyone, "I met Karl Barth's barber today."

We sit next to Christ all the time and yet fail to see that it is really Jesus himself.

Nudge is recognizing the "Jesus in you" so that we can help people experience what Jesus is already doing in their lives, encouraging and enabling them to say yes to God so that Christ can live his resurrection life in them and dwell in them.

Nudge is helping people connect the dots of what God is doing in their lives to the degree that their lives can be so "hidden with Christ in God"[17] that they walk so close to God as to cast only one shadow (and it's not theirs). Nudge is being reminded of "where we are weak, he is strong" and "a bruised reed he will not break." Nudge is to infuse some vexing failure with Christ so that it hardens like a shattered vessel so infused with epoxy resin that it is more durable than the unshattered original. Nudge is to amble right up next to the trigger that for so long has tripped the vexation, and to hear Christ saying "Watch this" as the Christ-infused "new being" watches the trigger activate, but for the first time is immune to the pull. Nudge is the shared Christ moment of celebration, the shared knowing it was the living Christ who transformed and infused. Nudge is the first reminder to lose the fear: *Why fear what is no longer true?* the nudge reminds us.

My favorite definition of church is this: "the community of competence to recognize Jesus as Risen Lord."[18] Can you come up with a better one? The ability to "recognize Jesus" Marianne Sawicki calls "ecclesial wisdom" and argues that real-time recognition of Jesus is as much "practical competence" as anything. The church is know-now as well as know-how, or better yet, the church is know-how know-now Jesus. The Gospels were written to help us recognize Jesus. To know. Now.

Nudge is poking the Jesus in you, inviting people to accept their great co-mission into what Jesus is already doing. Nudge is the Jesus in us poking the Jesus in them, but using the beings of two beloved children: us and them. In fact, nudge is not our working for God; nudge is God working in us and through us to bring to fruition what God is already doing. Scripture reminds us, like Neo in *The Matrix* (1999), that the spiritual world is more real than the physical. Nudge reminds us that what we see is not all that *is* and that the nudge we feel reminds us to remain firmly present in awareness of both. We achieve depth perception by seeing through a spiritual eye and a physical eye. The loss of either eye means a loss of depth or soul. Loss of soul drives us into the shallows spiritually; we become disconnected from what God is seeking to change in and through us. Depth perception is the cure for the dualism that plagues the church.[19]

People are already on spiritual journeys. Don't hinder the Holy Spirit's work in their charmed lives. *Do no harm!* It's the first rule of the Hippocratic oath. It's the prudential rule of nudge: Do no harm. Prudence nudges when it harmonizes, not harms. The word *prudent* is one of the most misunderstood words in the English language. It has come to mean cautious and timid, but it really means bold, daring, and magnanimous action that takes place after it is guided by the promptings of the Spirit. Prudent nudges are bold and daring nudges that are taken only after discernment of the divine will and proper probing of where the Spirit is moving.

In the Michael Jordan era of basketball, it was said that in the last seconds of the game, coach Phil Jackson would tell the team in the time-out huddle one thing: "Just give the ball to Michael and get out of the way." Our job is to give the ball to the Holy Spirit and get out of the way. It's not as if we have nothing to do. There are lots of people out there trying to keep the ball away from the Spirit of Truth. But once the ball is there, our job is to get out of the way and do nothing to handicap the Holy Spirit. After all, it is not by might (human resources); it is not by power (human resoluteness); but it is "'by my Spirit,' says the Lord."[20]

In short, nudge is saying to people, "Grandpa, you've got mail."

Third, evangelists nudge the world to wake up to the alive and acting Jesus.

Nudge is not bringing God to people or taking Jesus to the unsaved. Our "sentness" is not to stuff Jesus in our backpack and carry him out there into the world. Our job is not to initiate religious activity but to respond to God's directives and enlist in God's initiatives.

Nudge is not bringing people to Jesus or introducing someone they don't know but should. Nudge is introducing people to the "Jesus in them," to the God they already know but don't know it.

If you think about it, isn't it the height of theological arrogance the notion that you and I take Jesus to anyone? You mean Jesus never arrived on the scene until *you* got there? You mean Jesus wasn't present until *I* showed up? So, tell me again: God only lives where *you* are present? And were it true, what sort of Jesus container might work? You might as well try to save time in a bottle.

To make connections, you have to look behind, beneath, above, and within. But mostly you need to look ahead, which is difficult for a fore-sight-challenged church. Matthew's gospel says this about the risen Christ: "He has risen from the dead and is going ahead of you.... *There you will see him.*"[21] God is always in front of us, ahead of us. And God is always in front of our eyes, nose, ears, mouth, and hands. According to Augustine, Aquinas, Catherine of Siena, Luther, Calvin, Wesley, and every other major theologian in Christian history, God walks ahead of us and invites us to walk with him in such a way that our lives cast only one shadow. Think of Scripture as a window to be looked through and the resonance of our lives with the narrative in Scripture. This is their story, which appears similar to my story, and the resonance of the two eventually produces an expectancy. We have seen God move, and we depend on his movement, so we antici-pate the nudge.

You need to know what's in back of you to see and understand what's in front of you. But what's in back of us is not some "golden age" that we must return to. The "apostolic age" myth has been one of the greatest delusions of the Christian tradition. I call the notion that there was some "apostolic golden age" when everyone got everything right the ecclesiastical version of false memory syndrome. Church historian Robert Wilken counters our attempts to sanitize the past with these words: "The apostolic age is a creation of the Christian imagination. There never was a Golden Age when the Church was whole, perfect, pure-virginal. The faith was not purer, the Christians were not braver, the Church was not one and undivided."[22]

The "Eusebian view," as Wilken calls it, is the notion that the past defines an original gospel "somehow unsullied by the encroachments or even the context of the ambient culture." The "Gregory of Nyssa view" presents a more dynamic interplay of cultural engagement:

> It is the same with one who fixes his gaze on the infinite beauty of God. It is constantly being discovered anew, and it is always seen as something new and strange in comparison with what the mind has already understood. And as God continues to reveal himself, man continues to wonder and he never exhausts his desire to see more, since what he is waiting for is always more magnificent, more divine, than all that he has already seen.[23]

If God is always "being discovered anew," then the truth lies behind us; but the fullness of truth always lies ahead of us. The past is key in defining truth, but in conversation with present and future. What was and what truly *is* are harbingers of what will be. For a Christian, there are three (not two) sides to every story: past, present, future; absolute, relative, relational; timeless, timely, timeful.

For Jesus will not sit still … God is always on the move. God is always going ahead of us. We are always catching up to God. As with Peter joining Jesus in the water, can we go from thinking we need to come to Jesus ("Let me come to you, Lord")[24] to realizing that Jesus comes to us and reaches out his hand for us to grasp and not let go ("Truly, you are the Son of God")? Only by going ahead and getting to the future first do we get to "see God."

Evangelists give hindsight to the future. "You can see clearly something that is embedded in your culture only when it is in the act of receding into the historical distance."[25] That is why I personally don't conduct "retreats" ("He has sounded forth the trumpet that shall never call retreat"),[26] only "advances."

> The farsighted tend to get blindsided by the nearsighted.
> —Attributed to Barry Kolb

Top 10 Reasons for Missed Jesus-sightings

All the Gospels stress the difficulty experienced by the disciples in *recognizing* the risen Christ. In fact, sometimes the demons and evil spirits recognize Jesus before his followers do.[27] But if the disciples could learn to recognize Jesus, and they eventually developed the will and skill to do this, then I believe we can as well.

But what made it so hard for the disciples to recognize their friend, and what makes it so hard for us?

There is one major commonality to all the "christophanies," the resurrection appearances of Jesus. The gospel writers Luke and John make the biggest deal of the fact that the disciples have trouble recognizing the risen Christ. But all the Gospels make it clear that Jesus doesn't easily appear to his closest friends. Whether it's Jesus walking on water, or eating by the seashore, or walking on the highway,[28] or working in the garden,[29] or appearing behind closed doors where Thomas and the others were hiding,[30] the disciples have the same reaction: They *don't* immediately recognize him. Sometimes they take him for a ghost. Other times they are afraid to ask him, "Who are you?"[31] But in all cases, as Luke says bluntly, "Something prevented them from recognizing him."[32]

What was it?

You might call these the greatest semiotic "misses" of all time when they could have been the greatest semiotic "hits." What are some other great semiotic misses?

The birth of Jesus, as people were focused on the palace court and its golden cradles not the hillsides where shepherds herded sheep and stables housed mangers.

The greatest miss of semiotic awareness of all time: Pilate, staring at the face of Jesus, asking him the question, "What is truth?" and not recognizing that "I am the Truth."

One thief on the cross, who scored arguably the second greatest semiotic miss of all time.

> She turned around and saw Jesus standing there,
> but she did not realize that it was Jesus.
> —John 20:14

This is one of the most persistent themes of the Gospels: the inability of people to recognize Jesus, either before or after his resurrection. Either they totally missed him or insisted he prove his identity.

Why so much trouble recognizing him? Why did they then and do we today have such a hard time recognizing Jesus?

Here are my top 10 reasons:

1. Too Close

Who doesn't remember a parent sending us to find something, and after "looking everywhere," we return to proclaim its nonexistence? And who doesn't remember a parent's immediate retrieval of said object after a brief room scan, along with the inevitable reprimand: "If it had been any closer to you, it would have bitten you"? Jesus can be so close ("closer than a brother") to us it is like asking a bird to see air or a fish to see water. "What is water in the eyes of water?" asks poet Alice Oswald.[33] How does everything see itself in the world? Or in the words of Marshall McLuhan, "We don't know who discovered water, all we know is it wasn't a fish."[34]

Some things are so close that we are closed to them. And some things are so close—e.g., "Less of me, and more of him!"—okay, which one of us is which?

2. We Make a False Division between the Sacred and the Secular

We have trained ourselves to see God when we read the Bible. We hope to see God when we go to church. We count ourselves blessed when we see God through a friend or family member. And we're somewhat surprised to discover that God even shines the divine through nature. We choose to give God an ear in certain situations, selectively choosing when we open our ears so as to hear and when we open our eyes so as to see. Interestingly, the Bible is the inspired words of God, but the Bible itself says that God "spoke" creation into existence. *Both* the Bible and creation are the words of God. When we find that our interpretation of one doesn't jibe with the other, we can be certain that it is our incorrect interpretation of one or the other or both.

Unfortunately, the very privilege of choosing when to be open means we can miss God's presence in much of our experience. In limiting God's voice to certain "sanctified" media, we betray the dualistic tendencies we've inherited in our Western tradition. We wrongly assume that God speaks in church but not in the pub, that God speaks in Scripture but not in hip-hop. We live as though one is sacred while the other is secular; one earthly, one divine. Jesus says, "There's just one."

Life isn't sacred and secular. There is only life. Music isn't sacred and secular. There is only music. "Christianity is not about compartmentalization or withdrawal: it is radically and relentless life-encompassing."[35] A spiritual life is not isolated from the rest of life, but totally integrated into it.

Religion is not a separate subject or activity among others. You can't separate the secular and the sacred; you can't polarize the sacred and the profane. The doctrine of the incarnation, with its high view of the everyday and the ordinary, won't allow it.

3. We're Resurrection Phobic

We fear the living God,[36] or as theologian Marianne Sawicki puts it, "Our fear [is] that a living God is not a God we can live with."[37] God stuck between the pages of our Bible is a controllable God. We always have the option of snapping the book shut. It's the living, breathing Jesus who is dangerous.

Here are some manifestations of our fear of resurrection:

a) Worship of the Bible: I have been described as "one of the most Scripture-intensive people you will ever meet"—which may be a contemporary way of calling me a Bible thumper. But my mind is marinated in the Word of God, and everything that happens to me is put through the matrix of the Scriptures, so that my being can recognize the living Christ when he appears. For too many, "the Lord escapes the tomb only to be cloistered in the texts."[38] For some people Jesus went from one tomb to another: the garden tomb to the text tomb. We're afraid to let him out of either prison.

A young couple expecting their first baby were reading and studying everything about babies they could get their hands on. Not too long after the baby was born, they were frantically looking through their books to find any answer to their child's constant crying. In desperation, and hoping to get some sage advice, they called an older friend who had many children. Her suggestion: "Put down the book. Pick up the baby."[39]

Could it be that some of us should be putting the books down, lifting up our heads to see what is going on out there, and reaching out for those around us in distress? It is so much more difficult, but oh so beautiful when the Word becomes flesh.

b) Worship of worship and love of liturgy: We don't trust Jesus to "do it again" today, so we bring back the days when he did do it and try to replicate past victories. When we close the door to further appearances, we lock ourselves into packaged containers only opened by mandated "authorities" and transmitted by proper "authorizations." God's saving activity is thus safely located in the past and neatly wrapped in completion. Gerald May reminds us in his work interpreting St. John of the Cross and Teresa of Avila that the spiritual disciplines wonderfully provide an awareness of the Jesus *in* us, but at their end point, when they seem dry, it may well be because *everything* is dry relative to the felt presence of Christ in us.[40]

In the Iterative Semiotic and the College of the Retrospective, God has one-time-only signs, to be sure. But God speaks through signs often, and they're smaller and less obvious than many of us realize. Part of paying attention is to pay attention retrospectively. Was there a sign? Was I even looking for a sign? We can do postgame analysis and become more aware and more tuned in to what God is doing and the way God reveals himself in circumstances if we see backward. Most of us first see God after the fact. We live forward; we understand backward.[41]

Semiotics is often the art of reading where Jesus has just been, or seeing the movement of the air as he has just passed by, or discerning him imperfectly in the distance and trying to anticipate where we might intersect with where he has just left.[42] Jesus leaves behind signs like bread crumbs, which we must discern in order to follow and catch up to him on the road to mission. My Canadian friend Tom Bandy wants to refine this further:

> We assume that for Christ to be in the present tense, he
> must also be in spatial continuity with us. In other words,
> that Jesus can only be NOW in the sense that Jesus must
> be HERE. My challenge is that Jesus the Christ is not
> really "with us" but always down the road, a dust cloud
> on the horizon, a racing car just disappearing around

the corner of simultaneity. He is present tense ... he is
"eternally now" ... but not here in the present as we know
it.[43]

We wish signs would precede, but in biblical semiotics signs mostly
follow. You don't experience Jesus coming or going: only his "presence,"
his "prescience," or his "anamnesis." The twelfth-century French monk
Bernard of Clairvaux talked of God's presence during contemplation:

> I have felt that He was present; I remember afterwards
> that He was then with me; and sometimes I have sensed
> His coming in advance. But never have I been aware of
> the particular moment when He came or went.[44]

For the educational psychologist William James, this was the importance of both tutoring and tags, especially in the arts. First, our eyes must
be tutored to look for certain things and to dilate in advance or else we are
blinded by the magic of aesthetic moments.[45] Everyone knows this who
has ever viewed a painting or read a poem, and then had someone with a
practiced eye return you to that piece of art with new eyes. Second, we can
only preperceive what has been labeled and stamped into our minds. If we
"lost our stock of labels, we should be intellectually lost in the midst of the
world."[46]

4. Recognition Comes Out of Relationships

Beware of reasoning by rational associations rather than relational
associations. Lily Tomlin once noted that olive oil comes from squeezing olives, palm oil from compressing palm fruit, and peanut oil from
mashing peanuts. She then wondered about the source of baby oil.

For the gospel writers, recognition is possible only within a community that is being the body of Christ for the world, sensitive to the needs

of the whole body, especially the poor and dispossessed. That means it knows both how to be hungry and how to feed the hungry "in Jesus' name."[47]

Where is Jesus to be found? *In* the cry of the hungry.

The problem of recognition, according to Herbert McCabe, is asking the right pronoun: not What or Where or Which but Who.

> The question that mattered for those who met the risen Christ was not "What is it?", or even just "Which man is it?", but "Who is it?" There is a difference, a subtle difference between "which" and "who". And it isn't just that we keep "who" for human beings. "Who?" has a different kind of answer from "Which?" … When you ask *what* something is, you look for information about it, about its nature. When you ask "which?", you raise a different kind of question, though you are still looking for information of some kind … The who question is a "which man" or "which woman" question with a depth to it. To really know who someone is, is to know which person he or she is. But it is also to know him or her by a direct personal relationship … To know who she is in this sense is to know *her*, not just *about* her.… For Christ's identity is *recognized* by our faith; it is *established* by the *Father's* love. He is the one God loves.[48]

Sometimes it's less about our "witness" than our "withness." In fact, our best witness is our withness. Walking the boardwalk at Ocean City, New Jersey, I engaged a college student in conversation. He was part of some street evangelism team outfitted with a soapbox and microphone. When I walked away, it hit me that I had not been in conversation at all—the prefix *con* means "with." It was like I had been talked to by a computer program that just ran through its preprogrammed spiel as if that was what it was created to do. This college student was driving through life blind to the people waving at him from the sidewalks—his windows, tinted by an antiglare, sterilized, nonrelational faith.

To be a witness you have to have withness.

5. He Is Not Obvious and Appears Where You Don't Expect Him to Appear

Expect him where you least expect him—more in brokenness than in blessedness, more in the poor than the rich, more in the sick than the well. If it's really Jesus, he will not be immediately recognizable. He will appear unfamiliar, strange, estranged, and you will sometimes be frightened at first.

This means both that God is a God of surprises and that God is a God of suffering.

First, surprise. In the church, the unexpected is what we have come *not* to expect. It needs to be what we come *most* to expect.

The clearer the sense of vision a person/community has for the future, the less likely that vision is from God. That is not the way God generally appears. God leads us to the place where "we don't know" and "can't see." It is not God's way to give us specs or blueprints. God takes us to places where trust grows (or is more likely to grow) and often where we don't want to go. God leads us to faith, not certainty.

I collect stories from five-year-olds in the hopes of one day doing a book called *Kids Have All the Answers*. A kindergartner sat at her grandmother's feet to listen to the creation story from the book of Genesis. As the wondrous tale unfolded, the grandmother noticed that the child was unusually quiet. "Well, what do you think of it?" she asked the five-year-old.

"Oh, I love it!" the child answered. "You never know what God is going to do next."

Second, suffering. One of my favorite Latin expressions once learned, never leaves: *ubi dolor, ibi Christus*; "wherever there is suffering, there is

Christ." Or as C. S. Lewis is quoted in the movie *Shadowlands* (1993), "Pain is God's megaphone."[49]

> In God's kingdom, the basement is the penthouse.[50]
> —Neil Cole

The place to look for the *risen Lord* is not in the text. The text is his shroud, his covering, his compass that points to the North Star and Southern Cross. The place to look is where people are suffering from wounds of the flesh and spirit. In fact, if the disciples wanted to see their resurrected Lord, they had to look where he told them to look: "Whatever you did for one of the least of these brothers of mine, you did for me."[51] Our ability to see the Christ in others is how we will be judged. Much of the theology of the church rides on a concept of the judicial, and clearly there is an element of the judicial: God convicts and judges. But the bulk of the work of Christ, and therefore the bulk of the work of the church, is not done in a court context. It is done in a hospital context, which is all about health and healing. The quicker we can move those racked by their afflictions from the courtroom to the hospital, the quicker we're about the healing and restoring work of Christ and the church.

Every time the risen Christ appeared to his disciples, he appeared wounded and hungry.[52] We miss God-sightings by looking in the wrong places. The centers of power and wealth are a long way from the margins of our society, where the most creative stirrings of the Spirit are born and bring new life to the whole. It is hard to score semiotic hits from the centers of establishment power.

Rabbi Joshua ben Qarehah was once asked: "Why of all things did God choose the humble thornbush as the place from which to speak with Moses?" The rabbi replied, "If God had chosen a carob tree or a mulberry tree, you would have asked me the same question. Yet lest you go away empty-handed, here is why God chose the humble thornbush: to teach us that there is no place on earth bereft of the divine presence, not even a thornbush."[53] When there is a personal encounter with Jesus, the Bible says thornbushes burn: "The blind receive sight, the lame walk, those who have leprosy are cured, the deaf hear, the dead are raised, and the good news is preached to the poor."[54]

> Lord, when did we ever see you hungry and feed you?
> Or thirsty and give you something to drink?
> Or a stranger and show you hospitality?
> Or naked and give you clothing?
> When did we ever see you sick or in prison and visit you?
> —Matthew 25:37–39 NLT

How do we know "Is this the one?" Are the hallmarks of the kingdom present? Is there good news for the poor, the disabled, the disadvantaged? Where are the proud being humbled and the humbled things being treasured? The Beatitudes may be signs to watch for.

Where are people who realize their neediness?

Where are people mourning?

Where are people who are stung by injustice?

Where are the pure of heart, who are often taken advantage of?

Where are people losing themselves in the pursuit of peace?

By making being hungry the prime semiotics of the kingdom, Jesus inverted the customary meaning of hunger as divine displeasure, thereby threatening establishment positions on virtually everything.

6. Where the Spirit of Christ Is Joy …

Evagrius of Pontus, the fourth-century monk and desert father who conceived the "7 Deadly Sins" moniker, originally had eight, not seven, in his list. The one that got lopped off? The eighth deadly sin?

Gloom.

The spirit of joy was the dominant note of the NT church: overflowing joy, contagious joy, beautiful joy. Two things distinguished early Christianity from its pagan surroundings. Both of these two things are related: hope and joy (*chara*).[55] First-century paganism was steeped in despair, sadness, and pessimism. In fact, the Greek word for joy, *chara*, is mainly absent from the papyri of the ancient world outside of Christian sources.

The gospel begins and ends in "great joy." Here is its beginning: "I bring you good tidings of great joy." Here is its ending: "Then they worshiped him and returned to Jerusalem with great joy."[56] In Jesus' Farewell Discourse in John, he promises his disciples not just his "peace" but also his "full joy": "These things I have spoken to you so that My joy may be in you, and that your joy may be made full."[57]

When nudgers are looking for joy, we are looking less for an emotion that is based on an earthly, human foundation than a joy beyond the natural joys that come from friends and food, from beauty and beer, from dancing and drama. Beyond all these pleasures there is a joy free from the cages of circumstance, of mortality, of control, of individual fate. In his massive study of the history of joy, Adam Potkay says we live joyless lives because we seek pleasure, which is basically individual and solo, and not joy, which is by nature shared.[58]

In fact, joy is one of the chief attributes of God. God has joy at one sinner coming to faith. God lives in a state of perpetual joy. And the sign of God's presence is when mourning turns into joyful dancing.

> You turned my wailing into dancing;
> you removed my sackcloth and clothed me with joy.
> —Psalm 30:11

So look for jubilance! "Joy in the Lord" is the joy of the crib and cross, where we suffer with others, and where we see Christ in the joy of birth and death, beauty and ugliness, loss and gain, loyalty and betrayal. You might even call it "paschal joy."

One of the greatest indictments of the church is this: "Where's the joy?"

7. You Have to Want to See Him

You have to *want* to see Jesus to see him. God is already present everywhere and anywhere. But God doesn't enter where God isn't invited. Jesus does not force himself on us. Jesus is everywhere to be found knocking about and knocking. But he must be invited in. We must want the divine touch for God to touch us, and deep listening changes the desires of our hearts. As the poet of the Lord has written, "Delight yourself in the LORD and he will give you the desires of your heart."[59]

Jesus spoke in parables[60] so that not everyone would "get it." He unveiled the mystery only a tad, letting glimpses of truth escape. But only if you wanted to get it was Jesus willing to explain his parables and to reveal the "mysteries of the kingdom of heaven,"[61] and then he was quite eager to help. But he was not going to throw pearls before swine.

If you asked, you received. But you had to ask. We must ask. And to receive the hidden wisdom of the gospel, we have to become as children: "You have hidden these things from the wise and learned, and revealed them to little children."[62] Becoming aware of the kingdom has consequences. Once we have been exposed, we can't go back to not knowing. One of the worst aspects of drug addiction—crack, meth, heroin—is that once you've experienced it, you can't ever "unknow" it. The same principle applies to Christ's love and his kingdom. Once you are "experienced," as Jimi Hendrix reminded us in "Are You Experienced?" (1967), you are experienced.

> He comes to us hidden and salvation consists
> in our recognizing him.[63]
>
> —Simone Weil

8. I-Witness or God-Witness

Not an I-witness but a God-witness. I-witness evangelism features Christ "in me." God-witness evangelism features "me in" Christ. It is hard for anyone born after the mid-twentieth century to realize how recent this "I-witness" mentality is. You don't even have the concept or the word *self* as we know it today until the fifteenth century. And the concept of "self-fulfillment" did not appear until the nineteenth century. Descartes's "I think," Luther's "I stand," Schopenhauer's "I will," Kierkegaard's "I despair," and Sartre's "I act" underscore the modern world's preoccupations with the possibilities of selfhood. In 1968, Frank Sinatra's rendition of Paul Anka's "My Way" was for adults what Billie Piper's 1998 chart-topping hit "Because We Want To" was for kids: a mantra of me-ness.

The enthroning of the self is the author of countless sins, and is such a pervasive presence that it has infiltrated even some of our most hugged metaphors. "There is a God-shaped hole in the human heart that only God can fill" causes me to cringe every time I hear it, as if God exists to fill our holes, to fill our gaps, to be a pleasure plug. Every addiction is an honest attempt to fill the emptiness we feel when we deny Christ. Every addiction is self-medication. The "hole" is a metaphor for the sense of emptiness that consumes us when we seek independence. Desire is God ordained to encourage us to seek the divine and Christ's provisions, but a self-focused response is to stuff the desire with whatever will quell the discomfort.

From the time of the Protestant Reformation, the quest for self-fulfillment has made an evangelism that turns people toward God very problematic. Not too long ago it hit me that I had never preached on Jesus telling a ghost story about a haunted house.[64] Jesus told this story to warn his followers that we must be careful what we replace ghosts and addictions with, because more unholy ghosts than what were banished can refill the house to rule and reign. If we clean up our lives without replacing them with the true Spirit, the house is left empty and vulnerable for new evil spirits and worse dependencies to come back and take over. One of my Facebook friends, Isaac Arten, puts it like this: "I'm not interested in self-improvement but self-replacement." It is the difference between cleaning the house and turning the house over to Christ, letting him live there and leaving no room for malign spirits. As every science teacher can testify, young science students struggle when given the assignment to remove all the air from a beaker with self-created vacuums; each is destined to fail. It is the kid who completely fills his beaker with water that is first to get all the air out.

I-witness evangelism fills the world with more me-ness and the dramas of the self. God-witness evangelism fills the world with the dramas of the divine.

9. Confusion over "the Kingdom"

Another reason we miss the handoff is because we are confused about the language of "kingdom." The metaphor of kingdom has become for us a way of talking about a social and political agenda rather than a way of participating in God's activity in the world.[65] Wherever Jesus is found, the kingdom of God is a present reality. Jesus could not have been clearer when asked by the Pharisees about the coming kingdom of God: "The kingdom of God is not coming with things that can be observed; nor will they say, 'Look, here it is!' or 'There it is!' For, in fact, the kingdom of God is among you."[66]

Another way of asking "Would we recognize the living Christ if we saw him?" is this: "Would we recognize the kingdom of God on earth if we saw it?" Can we recognize only its absence and not its presence? We, too, can learn how to recognize Jesus and enter the kingdom. In fact, our task is to help others recognize the One who is already among them.

10. Missing Jesus through Resignation

Texan H. Ross Perot ran for president in 1992 with a running mate who was a war hero and vice admiral named James Stockdale. Jim Collins wrote a business book called *Good to Great* (2001) in which he relates a conversation he had with Stockdale regarding his coping strategies during his time in a Vietnamese POW camp. "I never lost faith in the end of the story," Stockdale said. "I never doubted not only that I would get out, but also that I would prevail in the end and turn the experience into the defining event of my life, which, in retrospect, I would not trade." Collins then asked about those who didn't survive. Stockdale replied, "Oh, that's easy, the optimists. They were the ones who said, 'We're going to be out by Christmas.' And Christmas would come, and Christmas would go. Then they'd say, 'We're going to be out by Easter.' And Easter would come, and Easter would go. And then Thanksgiving, and then it would be Christmas again. One by one, they died of a broken heart."[67]

Many folks lose heart because they start out with certain expectations of God. When their expectations are not met, they finally give up. They are seeking a nudge from a Jesus of their own making. Thomas Mulholland's *The Shack* introduced the concept of living expectantly, but without expectation.[68] When we have expectations of God, we're expecting God to come through *on our terms*; and if God doesn't come through on our terms, we deem God to have failed. When we live expectantly, we are living with the hope and the expectation that Christ will come through, but we've left the terms open. Living expectantly means always being aware of Christ in us, yet waiting for the how, when, where, and why to come from the nudge or a series of nudges.

Discover More Online

CHECK OUT INTERACTIVES FOR YOUR PERSONAL OR SMALL-GROUP USE
AND MUCH MORE ON THE NUDGE WEB SITE:

WWW.NUDGETHEBOOK.COM

Chapter 2 1/2

WATCH, WITNESS, AND BEAR WITNESS

In light of these three premises, let me propose two constituent parts to paying attention. Each one of these two components of attentiveness is a search tool better than Google. Except we're searching for the "Jesus in you."

> *Watch*
>
> *Witness and Bear Witness*

And they deserve a chapter all to themselves.

First, Watch: Show Up, Slow Down, Shut Up and Listen, and Wake Well

Show Up

Woody Allen's most famous line is "Eighty percent of success is *showing up*."[1] Nothing works without participation, whether or not you have a Woody Allen temperament. I teach in a state (New Jersey) that routinely turns out only 25 percent of its registered voters in elections. When only 15 percent of the potential voters participate in democracy,[2] democracy is in crisis.

Nudge is first and foremost showing up to life and to what God is doing in life in the universe. "My Father is always at his work to this very day, and

I, too, am working," Jesus said.[3] God created the world, and the Creator is not finished creating. But we who have been created in the Creator's image are invited to participate in God's ongoing creativity.

Did God make it all right the first time for all time? Or are we invited to attend God's artistry, to participate in creation, to anticipate God's creativity? I have a friend, Michael Blewett, who is a rector in Bowling Green, Kentucky. He informs his parish that they have three things to spend in life: time, money, and attention. And the greatest of these is attention.

We are so busy getting the world to pay attention to us that we don't pay attention to it and love the creative things God is doing in it. "Pay attention *to me*" is the drumroll mantra of a celebrity culture. The problem is, as Iris Murdoch points out, that loving the world and creating a work of art both require "morally disciplined attention"[4] to "something quite particular other than oneself."[5] If we can't stop being so self-centered, so preoccupied with our own "stuff," then we will never be able to pay attention. It is not by accident that Proverbs 8:34 links three things in this order: "listen," "watch," "wait."[6]

There is the silence that does without words. Then there is the silence that goes beyond words, beyond the reach of words, the word silencers. This is Gethsemane and Golgotha silence: "Abba, Father … everything is possible for you. Take this cup from me. Yet not what I will, but what you will."[7] Then comes the silence that you trust and obey, not debate or engage.

An ancient story is told of a rabbi who was brought into the presence of God in the high heavenly courts. When he arrived, he walked right up to the throne and called on God to justify God's silence in the face of so much human suffering. "Lord, we have prayed night and day, and yet your people have continued to suffer. You have heard our moans. You have seen our tears. Where have you been?"

God replied, "I am surprised that you did not recognize me. I was your tears. I was your moaning. I was your calling out to heaven." No matter how horrible the evil, God's Spirit is still working for the good. Like a compass, events help us see the invisible. The magnetic lines of force that envelop the earth are always there, but we become aware of how vast they truly are when we hold a compass and the needle aligns with them.

This is how Rabbi Jason Shulman begins his book *The Instruction Manual for Receiving God:*

> There are many books that tell us how to find God. But the truth is that God is not lost or hiding. In fact, it is the actual, continuous, omnipresence of God that is so hard for the human mind to fathom.[8]

When Christianity restricts God's presence to the sacred or denies God's presence outside the sacred, it mirrors an Enlightenment culture that crudely separated life into the secular and the religious, thereby making the omnipresence of God hard to experience. The apostle Paul called it "heart law."[9] John Calvin called it "common grace," and the Reformed tradition refers to the ubiquity of God's presence as the *sensus divinitatis,*[10] our innate tendency to apprehend God's hand in nature (in a sunset, on a starry night, under a waterfall, etc.). John Wesley called it "prevenient grace."

Whatever you call it, the Spirit of God is at work in all human beings, no matter what their religion, no matter what their morality or lack of it, no matter what they have done or haven't done. For many, the nudge is to repentance. For others, aware and committed to Christ, it is a nudge toward deeper relationships vertically and horizontally. Faith is more than learning to live in the reality of God's invisible presence. Rather, faith is living in the reality of God's *visible* presence.

If you don't find God in the very next person you meet
it is a waste of time looking for him further.[11]
—Gandhi

Many people are what Hebrew scholar Jack Deere calls a "Bible deist."[12] Like their eighteenth-century forebears who worshipped human reason as they worship the Bible, Bible deists believe in a Watchmaker God who wound things up and now watches as things run down. Worse than the eighteenth-century deists, who at least let God do the winding, for Bible deists it is the Bible, not God, who wound up the church like a big clock and keeps the clock ticking correctly.

God is no doubt watching what we are doing and weeping at how we are letting things run down. If you want to make God laugh, show him your plans. If you want to make God cry, show him your planet. But even more, we are called to watch what God is doing and wind up God's mission in the world.[13]

To be a Christian is to be a "watchman."

Ezekiel:

> Son of man, I have made you a watchman for the house of Israel.[14]

Habakkuk:

> I will stand at my watch and station myself on the ramparts; I will look to see what he will say to me, and what answer I am to give to this complaint.

> Then the LORD replied: *"Write down the revelation* and make it plain on tablets so that a herald may run with it."[15]

Often the prophet as watchman is not listened to.

Jeremiah:

> I set watchmen over you, saying, Hearken to the sound of the trumpet. But they said, We will not hearken.[16]

When no one hearkens, what to do?

Isaiah:

> "Watchman, what is left of the night?"

> The watchman replies, "Morning is coming, but also the night."[17]

Religious scholars talk about observant Jews, observant Muslims, but *not* observant Christians. Why? Because Christianity is about "observing" more than being "observant." Christianity is a religion that is less wrapped up in rituals and observances than it is in rapt attention to what God is doing in the world so that we can beat a path to where Jesus is living his resurrected presence.

To say that "Christ is alive" is to say more than we enjoy the possibility of transcending time. My relationship with my mother, Mabel Boggs Sweet, transcends time, even though she died in 1993. My relationship with my doctoral mentor, Winthrop Still Hudson, is such that he still lives for me even though he has been dead for some years. I commune with John Wesley daily in a discourse that crosses the boundaries of centuries.[18]

But with Jesus there is even greater possibility for relationship. Christ wants to live in each and every one of us. The unique claim of Christianity is that we can "know" Jesus now in the most intimate sense of "knowing," that we can know how to have a know-now know-Who relationship.

Once upon a time, in a small Russian village, there lived a rabbi who had a vision that the Messiah was passing through that part of the world. Fearful the Messiah might bypass such a small village, the people constructed a tall lookout tower on the main road. Then they hired a man to sit on the watch tower to look for the Messiah's arrival.

One day, a friend passed by the tower and called up to the watchman, "How do you like your job looking for the Messiah?"

The man in the tower yelled back, "The pay isn't much, but the work is steady!"

The work is steady because God is steady at work. "The Messiah is come." God is with us.

Slow Down

Why do we miss the signs? Simple. We travel too fast. We go so fast through life we can't see the signs.

In the high mountains, where the air is thin, people learn to do fast things slowly. The air is thin in the twenty-first-century-culture gospel of change. The pace of change requires a change of pace, which is birthing a batch of slow movements, from slow food[19] to slow sex[20] to slow parenting to slow travel to slow architecture to slow marketing[21] to slow brand to slow cities[22] to slow-down days at school, all of which are less about going back to "good old days" than learning how to shift gears and go into neutral. In baseball there is now even a "slow ball" strategy where the walk is as important as the hit. The aim is to win the game in small increments—stolen bases, sacrifice bunts, walk-in runs—as you capitalize on throwing errors and forced errors to put runs on the scoreboard.

The air is now so thin there is even a "slow philosophy" to go with our *Fast Company* magazines. In his introduction to a slow philosophy, Carl Honoré recommends that humans "seek to live at what musicians call the *tempo giusto*—the right speed."[23] A "right speed" does not evade fast lanes, fast foods, or the fast life. But the faster the world goes, and the more fast replaces vast, the more important it is to know how to slow down, freeze-frame the moment, and read the signs.

Farmer John lived on a quiet rural highway. But, as time went by, the traffic slowly built up at an alarming rate. The traffic was so heavy and so fast that his chickens were being run over at an average of three to six a day.

So one day Farmer John called the sheriff's office and said, "You've got to do something about all of these people driving so fast and killing all of my chickens." "What do you want me to do?" asked the sheriff. "I don't care, just do something about those crazy drivers!" So the next day he had the county workers go out and erect a sign that said:

SLOW: SCHOOL CROSSING

Three days later Farmer John called the sheriff and said, "You've got to do something about these drivers. The 'school crossing' sign seems to make them go even faster." So, again, the sheriff sent out the county workers, and they put up a new sign:

SLOW: CHILDREN AT PLAY

That really sped them up. So Farmer John called and called and called every day for three weeks. Finally, he asked the sheriff, "Your signs are doing no good. Can I put up my own sign?" The sheriff told him, "Sure thing, put up your own sign." He was going to let Farmer John do just about anything in order to get him to stop calling every day to complain. Finally the sheriff didn't receive any more calls from Farmer John. Three weeks later, curiosity got the best of the sheriff, and he decided to give Farmer John a call.

"How's the problem with those drivers? Did you put up your sign?"

"Oh, I sure did. And not one chicken has been killed since then. I've got to go. I'm very busy."

He hung up the phone. The sheriff was really curious now, and he thought to himself, *I'd better go out there and take a look at that sign … it might be something that we could use to slow down drivers.* So the sheriff drove out to Farmer John's house, and his jaw dropped the moment he saw the sign. It was spray-painted on a sheet of wood:

NUDIST COLONY: Go slow and watch out for the chicks!

There must be scores of decelerating rituals other than nudist signs that can be used to slow down in this fast-food, fast-cars, fast-talk, fast-service culture. Here are six of my most favorite decelerating rites: randomization, slow-boating, extra-ing the ordinary, focusing, fallowing, and silencing.

Learning to tell the truth takes time, attentiveness and patience.[24]

—Cambridge theologian Nicholas Lash

1. Randomizing Rituals. Call them "coincidences," "chance encounters," "God-incidences," or, my favorite, "godwinks,"[25] randomness is a reflection of the fact that spiritual forces move mysteriously and "blow where they will." But that very unpredictability is what brings life. Call godwinks "stealth nudges."

It is only when life slows and oxbows and loops that it can flood out to fertilize unfamiliar plains and terrains. A key way I keep creative is to engage in what I call "randomizing rituals" that rout routine in my life and slow me down enough to step outside the bounds of clique and convention. In fact, randomization may just be my number-one slow-down "secret" that opens life to "black swans"[26]—those unpredictable, hard-to-see, outlier phenomena—and forces me to stray from paddocks that quickly become padlocks.

One of the best compliments you can pay me is "That's so random!" In Gutenberg culture, a "random existence" was morally destitute, self-indulgent, and ruinously out of control. Puritans especially were fond of declaiming against the random existence of hedonists and other pagans. But randomizing rituals and practices help me escape aging's coffins of conformity. In fact, neuroanatomists who can read the colors of the "brainbow" are now telling us that dreaming requires randomization, since dreams are caused by random brain-stem brainstorms, stimulations of the cerebral cortex.

I am not the first to advocate randomizing rituals. Augustine liked to open Paul's epistles at random, and one day found a divine light flooding his heart when he did so. Leave it to Methodism's founder, John Wesley, to make a rule out of random, encouraging his itinerants sometimes to read the Bible using the "at random rule," stretching their hands randomly into the lucky dip, and then taking what their fingers plopped on as a providential passage. In *Either/Or* (1843), Søren Kierkegaard makes the case for crop rotation in life to curb boredom, keep the mental fields fertile and full of nutrients, and face the responsibilities of an ethical existence.[27]

> The surest way to stop thinking is to read books only in one
> field and talk only to people who work in one field.[28]
> —English philosopher John Locke

Here are some examples of randomizing rituals that slow me down as they open me up to new awareness:

a) Instead of picking out a movie to see, I "go to the movies" under the discipline of seeing the next movie that is showing when I arrive at the ticket counter. Yes, even if that movie is *27 Dresses* (2008).

b) Install the stumbleupon.com toolbar.

c) Pick with eyes closed from the racks of *Hudson News*, one periodical for every hour I'm in flight, with the discipline of reading every page (not necessarily every word) of the periodical in that one hour of flight. On a five-hour flight, I've been exposed to five periodicals that I never would pick up any other way.

d) Take make-it-up-as-you-go rides in the car, and stop at odd restaurants or coffee shops you never would pick out by natural inclination or interest.

e) Decline the passiveness of coincidence or chance. Admit no coincidences, only God-incidences, only connections. "As luck would have it, Providence was on my side," to quote the words of Samuel Butler's hero in *Erewhon*.[29]

f) Ask your waiter to pick out his/her favorite item on the menu, and on their recommendation order it. That one act will move you to a higher plane of relationship with that person and enhance your dining pleasure immeasurably.

g) Listen to the jarring juxtapositions of music that come from Jack radio format; or set your iPod to random shuffle. This will help combat the music snobbery called "playlistism" and reduce playlist anxiety and playlist pruning to suit the musical tastes of others. At your next party, invite your guests to bring their iPods so that the music of the evening can run off your guests' playlists, showcasing the digital diversity of your guests.

An organic as opposed to a mechanical approach to life is one where you grow in the direction of the light, and you make it up as you go along. Self-organizing systems are more symmetrical when their components are moving randomly than when they are marching lockstep in certain formations.[30] There can be a tendency to approach life one-dimensionally, with relationships frequently regarded as a means to an end or at least prescribed and programmed. Relational quality is enhanced by shared, random experiences and may actually be compromised by prescribed agenda.

Icons provide symbolic carriers for profound subjects like randomization, and my icon for these rituals is a book by Stanford computer scientist Donald E. Knuth, who is most known for his classic text *The Art of Computer Programming*. But Knuth has an iconic presence in my life because this lifelong Lutheran has memorialized in book form what he calls the most "scientific reading of the Bible." Using the random-sampling method of Bible reading, Knuth personally translated from the Hebrew and Greek all fifty-nine 3:16 texts, wrote a theological commentary on each, and commissioned fifty-nine of the world's greatest calligraphers to put these texts into visual form.[31] A signed copy of his book *3:16* and a poster with all fifty-nine calligraphers' art hanging in my Drew University office remind me of the change-my-mind creativity that is unleashed by randomizing rituals.

The killer app for Jesus as to whether or not his disciples were "born of the Spirit" was the first-century equivalent of "that's so random": "The wind blows wherever it pleases. You hear its sound, but you cannot tell where it comes from or where it is going. So it is with everyone born of the Spirit."[32] Are you predictable? Can people not always tell what you are going to do next? A windblown life is one going slow enough to be powered by the Spirit.

2. Slow-boating Your Journey. Ask someone, "How are you?" and they're likely to say, "Busy." Try saying, "Slow-boating it." Invite a little slowness into your high-speed life. Consumer culture wants us all to live as impersonations of the Energizer Bunny. After all, you can't pass in the slow lane. But the more we need to be "up to speed," the more we need to fast from fast.

> Praise without end for the go ahead zeal
> of whoever it was invented the wheel;
> But never a word for the poor soul's sake
> that thought ahead, and invented the brake.[33]
>
> —Onetime America's poet laureate Howard Nemerov

Instead of setting your GPS to "fastest route possible," set it to "no freeway." Take a seat-of-your-pants vacation where you take the blue highways and back roads, not the major thoroughfares. Instead of flying, take a train. Instead of driving, take a bus. Take every ferry you can find. Make "drive time" slow time, and stop to read every historical marker on the way.

Or here is a slow-boating exercise recommended by Metropolitan Anthony, the Russian Orthodox bishop in London. He suggests we sit down in a room somewhere, quietly, purposively for five minutes, and practice the Seinfeldian art of doing absolutely nothing. Relax intently and say this to ourselves:

> I am seated, I am doing nothing, I will be doing nothing
> for five minutes ... I am here in the presence of God, in

my own presence and in the presence of all the furniture
that is around me, just still, moving nowhere.[34]

One more quick tip in slow-boating (and hear the contradiction):
Declutter your life. Joyce Rupp uses the marvelous metaphor of "the cluttered cup" to explore the way our lives get cluttered. There are many kinds
of clutter, she says: anxiety, resentment, harsh judgments, self-pity, mistrust
… all take up a lot of inner space.[35] But even good things can become
clutter. Prayer can become clutter when it becomes a legalism. So start
decluttering: Drop membership in a club; resign from a position; cut back
on your commitments; take an extra year to get through college. One of
my sons gave me an orange T-shirt that testified: "U of T: The best 5 or 6
years of your life."

<blockquote>
In a world hard-wired for speed, the tortoise
still has a lot of persuading to do.[36]
—Carl Honoré (who got a speeding ticket going to a slow-food dinner)
</blockquote>

In Sweden not too long ago, a passenger on a train pulled an emergency cord. When it stopped, he distributed leaflets that read: "Speed is an
unnecessary evil that is destroying our lives and our planet."[37]

What cords are you pulling? In what areas of your life are you practicing less-hurried living? In Japanese fables, tortoises *do* win races.…

3. *Extra the Ordinary.* The holy haunts the everyday. "Heaven in ordinary" is how the seventeenth-century Welsh poet/Anglican priest George
Herbert put it.[38]

Where does God first address Moses? Not from the heavens or from
the heights, but from a lowly bush, from the midst of the commonplace,
the ordinary. Where does the risen Christ first encounter his apostles? Not
in Jerusalem but back in Galilee, where they were back to their businesses,
back fishing, in their old jobs, the memory of those three years spent with

Jesus wearing thin. The doctrine of the incarnation requires a high doctrine of the everyday, the ordinary.

In our daily lives we're in the thick of thickets all the time, and we can't hear the voice because we're listening and looking for the "high and lifted up" and forget the bushes and bulrushes. The holiest haunts are the common, everyday places.

Coming to appreciate life's common, everyday, ordinary miracles leads to some of the most surprising and theologically intriguing nudges.

> A leaf of grass is no less
> than the journeywork of the stars.[39]
> —Walt Whitman

Jesus is knocking at the door of the human heart, nudging us to come *out* and track the holy haunts. He comes in to get us to come out, and part of our "outing" is outdoors, into the world, to come out and play. How can you fail to see Jesus across the street? How can you fail to see the finger of God in nature: in a frog, in a fog, in a storm, in a thorn? Would you? Could you?

Nudgers are attendants in the house of God, which is the universe. What are we attending? The weft and weave of everyday life, without the expectation that the divine must manifest itself in riotous or raucous form. The ordinary is as emblematic of the movings of the Spirit as the spectacular or sprawling.

How many things do we attend without attention? Pay attention to ordinary things where realizing that there is no such thing as "ordinary." Nothing is ordinary. All things are out of the ordinary. Everything that exists is extraordinary and holds the secrets of the universe within itself. We need the eyes to see, the ears to hear, the nose to smell, the mouth to taste, and the hands to touch. Be transfixed by the ordinary so that you can see what you thought was ordinary is really a transfiguration.

The mundane can be sublime ... if we attend to it and peel away its inexhaustible mysteries like an infinite onion. The very word *mundane* reminds us to do this, since *mundane* comes from the Latin *mundus*, which means "world."

A retired songwriter in Nashville, remarking about country songwriter Tom T. Hall, points out what should be true of every preacher: "You know, some folks can go around the globe and never see a thing. Tom can go just down the road and see the whole darn world."[40]

Instead of looking for God in the heavens, why not look for God around us in everyday places. Or in the words of Cynthia Heimel,

> For God is always to be found at the back of the refrigerator behind the moldy tuna fish casserole, or sometimes He is found in the way the tailor at your corner lovingly stitches up the hem of your party dress, other times in the way a child sings along with a toothpaste commercial. Do not look for Him in the heavens; He only keeps a small locker there, only goes there to change.[41]

There are many definitions of *art*. My two favorites are by a poet and a factory worker. The poet, Denise Levertov, defined art as "the act of realizing inner experience in material substance."[42] The factory laborer-turned-philosopher Simone Weil put it like this: "Art is an attempt to transport into a limited quantity of matter, modeled by man, an image of the infinite beauty of the entire universe."[43] Both definitions understand art as a God-nudge, as the outer of an inner experience, which is as close to sacramental as you can get without being technical. I call art mystical materialism, and incorporate art into my everyday life in the same way our Orthodox ancestors would dip icons into beer to improve its taste. In fact, I can't get into my study (Len's Lair) without simultaneously stooping and stepping up as an expression of my daily need to bring together humility (stoop) and confidence (step up). When you nudge people to adopt material and concrete spiritual practices that connect with their everyday lives, you are nudging the Jesus in them. Any nudge that does not restore and renew our sense of the sheer mysteriousness of life isn't good, true, or beautiful.

> The sense of wonder
> that is the sixth sense.
> And it is the natural religious sense.[44]
> —D. H. Lawrence

4. Focusing Rituals and Attentional Strategies. Comedian Sam Levenson recounted the time his father was towing six or seven small Levensons, clasped hand to hand, through a museum. Suddenly, exasperated how slowly they were moving, the father snapped: "Look here, you kids. If you're gonna stop and look at everything, you ain't gonna see nothing."

In a world of overchoices and overdoses, a culture where overstimulation, information overload, hyperconnection, and Continuous Partial Attention (CPA)[45] are the states of normality, the more we fear we're going to miss something, the more we miss everything.

If I throw you one tennis ball, you can catch it easily. If I throw you six tennis balls, one after the other, you can catch them all. But if I throw you all the balls together, you will not catch any of them unless you focus on a single ball and let the other ones go.[46]

A life spent in soft focus needs focusing energy that will not drop balls. Without this laserlike focusing energy we suffer from what sociologists call "absent presence." Physically present we may be, but our attention drifts and pinballs, seldom in the here and now, "ever focused on the new rather than the now."[47] We enter every moment distracted and distant. This lack of attention and loss of intimacy lead to greater incidences of anxiety, depression, lack of fulfillment, poor school performance.

The need for focusing rituals that can keep our semiotic awareness on track is further evidenced by what is known as "emotion-induced blindness." Yale University researchers discovered this condition while exploring human reaction to violence and pornography. Images of sex and violence induce a period of blindness that lasts between two-tenths and eight-tenths of a second, long enough to cause a driver blinded by the billboard cleavage to veer off the highway. During this state of blindness, people simply cannot process what they are seeing.[48]

When important stimuli are presented, an information-processing bottleneck occurs in the brain. You can overcome the bottleneck with attentional strategies that refocus hard on the target images and resist the backslide from semiotics to hermeneutics, from experiential immersion in a sign to immediate interpretation of a sign.

5. *Fallowing Rituals.* When was the last time you gave yourself permission to "do nothing" without feeling guilty? Have you scheduled and protected on your calendar designated "do nothing" days? One of the worst mistakes you can make in life is to confuse fallow time with shallow time.

When you look at a field that is allowed to lie fallow for a season, it looks as if nothing is happening. But appearances are deceiving. In those fallow seasons, the soil is being replenished and restocked so it can continue producing a harvest. Seeds need rich soil for nature to work. When it looks on the surface like nothing is happening, down deep everything is happening.

When "nothing happens" is when life happens. "Do nothing" days get you daydreaming again. Recent scientific studies of the brain show that letting your mind wander, or daydreaming, is the seed corn of creativity and problem solving.[49] Let the soil of your soul lie fallow for a season, plowed but not planted. To rest from doing allows the soil to be enriched by God, making the soul more fertile for God's next planting.

That's why fallowing, and one of its expressions known as "vacationing," is part of the basic weather of living well. The value of vacations is that this is when we're most prone to vacate our minds, not to blank them out, but to fill them with restful and playful and mindful things. The change of venue enables us to rid our minds of the freight of the familiar. This defamiliarization imposes patience and lets things reveal themselves, lets something speak for itself without our thinking we know what it is or can speak for it. Some signs are more shy, even coy, than others. Travel writer Paul Theroux speaks from personal experience when he confesses that for him to really inhabit a culture he needs to empty both his mind and his space: "Luxury is the enemy of observation."[50]

This is where Christian mysticism is different from other forms of mysticism. The goal of fallowing is not to empty the mind or blank it. Mindfulness is not mindlessness. Rather, fallowing rituals help fill the mind with good things,[51] and whatever emptying (*kenosis*) takes place is for the purposes of filling (*plerosis*). "God's love has been poured into our hearts through the Holy Spirit that has been given to us"[52] Besides, try to rid your mind of negative or sinful thoughts, and guess all you will think of? Psychoneurolinguistic scientist George Lakoff got this right in his book *Don't Think of an Elephant* (2004). AA has a saying: "Thinking about not drinking is thinking about drinking." Our efforts at avoiding what we really choose to avoid often has the unintended consequence of keeping the issue forefront in our minds. Surrender is admitting that our efforts are not sufficient.

It's only the expulsive power of divine love that rids our hearts and souls of sin. This was John Wesley's most mature understanding of "Christian perfection," as outlined in "The Scripture Way of Salvation":

> Perfection … is love excluding sin; love … taking up the
> whole capacity of the soul…. For as long as love takes up
> the whole heart, what room is there for sin therein?[53]

A clothes closet is the best semiotic of sin I can think of. Every closet starts with a few pieces of clothes neatly hung and stacked. Within no time, every closet gets cluttered, messy, and scattered. Sanctification cleans closets by keeping them full of freshly laundered, dry-cleaned, and scented new clothes in which Christ can form and take shape in your life.

6. Silence Rituals. There is a joke circulating, partly inspired by television talk shows and news analysis, that goes like this: "Conversation: a vocal competition in which the one who is catching his breath is called the listener."

The more the discourses of society are designed to kill silence, the more garrulous the gospel in the church, the more disciplines of silence we need in our lives. The more people are discomfited by silence, as the rush of words washes over us in waves, the more we need to soak in silence.

Silence is God's First Language.[54]

—St. John of the Cross

True speech is a duet with silence.

The word *mystic* is related to the Greek word *mustes*, which means "close-mouth." *Mystic* and *mute* share the same roots and branches. The mystical nature of silence is key to the monastic life, as Philip Gröning's film *Into Great Silence* (2005) makes clear about the life of Carthusian monks. But it is not just monks who are sometimes called to live with background silence as opposed to background noise.

Much silence makes a mighty noise.

—African proverb

In the spiritual exercise of *hesychia*, which translates literally as the "silence of the heart," one tunes oneself to the rhythm of one's breathing through the use of what the early church called *monologion* or one-word prayers. First used by early Christian monks and continued in monasteries for centuries, these one-word prayers tuned the heart to the rhythms of the Spirit embedded in the self, community, and nature. Other religious traditions called *monologion* by another name: mantras.

There is no speed-reading in art. When it comes to appreciating any work of art, you need to slow down, stare it down, and silence your soul ... which is another way of saying that you need to look at God's participation in the universe, not yours. Only in this way can we reverse the bias of our blindness. Only in this way can we not "describe the world we see, but see the world we describe."[55]

I bring all of these together in certain personal rituals. Here are a couple of examples from my reading life. Every few months, instead of speed-reading, I try to read a book like I would want my books to be read: slowly, every word, almost devotionally. In the Great Books Seminars I conduct with the Indiana Conference of the United Methodist Church, we try not to consume a book. We try to receive it as a gift and let it call to us. Every book issues a call. Hearing the call is another way of talking about reading, and answering the call is how you allow the book to change you. And those books that have changed me the most, I reread every couple of years. Many books are readable; only a very few books are rereadable. C. S. Lewis said if you have read a great book only once, you haven't read it at all.

> What is divinity if it can come
> Only in silent shadows and in dreams.[56]
> —Poet Wallace Stevens

Shut Up and Listen!

Nudgers are listening posts.

Evangelism has been dominated by people who like to talk about talking. We think worship is about singing and speaking, not listening and praying. Nudgers are better listeners than talkers. You have two ears and one mouth. Seek that ratio as a starter.

In fact, the quieter we become, the chattier God gets. Just as when you keep silence, someone tends to talk more and reveal more, so when we keep silence before God, God tends to reveal more or we hear more. Do you want more of God? Then shut up and listen.

I call shut up and listen the "silent treatment." Gutenberg culture has programmed us to get our own views across, not to listen to other views and to coach others in listening to their lives. Therapy, known as "the talking cure," is based on "talking treatments" not "silent treatments," which have a negative connotation, not a positive one. But in this Google world, listening to the buyer has become so important ("the herd will be heard") that the economics of the future is being called "listenomics." The double-edged sword of this high degree of participation is that nothing belongs to the producer anymore. Who listens best and who best harnesses the wisdom of the crowd wins.

The essence of nudge: helping people to listen to their lives. The essence of faith coaching: showing people how to listen to their lives. By listening, I'm not talking about listening for flaws but listening for faith, listening for understanding, listening for the Jesus-in-you.

Flip and halve the word *listen* and what do you get? The word *silent*. The six letters that spell *listen* also spell *silent*. Silence is planted in, and the portal to, listening.[57]

It's not enough just to show up and slow down. You never resemble Jesus more than when you have your mouth shut. But I didn't say that. It was first said by Ignatius of Antioch.

Semiotic nudge is more about "Speak, Lord; your servant is listening" than it is "Listen, Lord; your servant is speaking."[58] This is what God said about Jesus, God's only begotten Son: "Listen to him." Listen to him. When you listen to him, you listen to each other.

We must watch carefully what God is doing. It is as important a part of nudge to learn when to keep our mouths shut as it is to learn when and how to speak. In the "Show Up" stage of nudge, the less said the better. We need to clamp our mouths shut and sit on our hands more so that we don't jam up or interfere with what God is already doing. Nudge is less "show and tell" than "shut up and listen."

> The beginning of wisdom is silence.
> The second stage is listening.[59]
>
> —Hebrew sage Solomon ibn Gabirol

Nudgers go beyond seeing and hearing to looking and listening. David Henderson proposes a 10 to 1 ratio between listening and speaking. "If you have ten minutes to share the gospel with someone, spend the first nine asking questions and listening. When we speak more than we listen, it is like flying a kite in the dark. Our words go out, but we have no idea if they ever get off the ground."[60] For the corporate world, MIT scientist Peter Senge says something similar: "Generative listening is the art of developing deeper silence in yourself so you can slow your mind's hearing to your ears' natural speed, and hear beneath the words to their meaning."[61]

But my favorite way of remembering Henderson's 10 to 1 ratio and the meaning of deep listening is through the glorious word HEART. Mark Brady, who teaches Deep Listening courses, invites us to circle the last three letters of the word HEART (the last will be first, after all). Now circle the first four letters of HEART. Now circle the middle letters of HEART. Now circle the whole word. What do you get?

ART of HEAR-ing is the EAR of the HEART[62]

The ear of the heart is often called the "third ear." Prayer is an invitation to "listen with the ear of your heart," the first words of the prologue that opens the whole Rule of St. Benedict, the most famous guide for living in community in Western Christianity.[63] The better you are at third-ear listening, at exercising your "listening ear" (Wordsworth) and "gazing heart" (Yeats), the better you are at talking and praying.

The first duty of love is to listen.[64]

—Paul Tillich

We pay for everything, and you have to pay to pay attention. There is a cost, there is payment due. All practices take practice, but listening practices may require more practice than others. Listening is exhausting, maybe more exhausting than speaking. It certainly makes more demands.[65]

The biggest demand is for us to get out of God's way. We use the third ear to get ourselves out of there, to take ourselves out of the picture. The foundation of nudge is not your story or my story, but God's story and another's story. To pay attention means you are no longer the center of attention. We are so busy, so self-centered, so preoccupied with our own "stuff" that we need deep listening to pay attention, to stop paying attention to ourselves and start attending to the divine presence that is everywhere.[66]

To pay attention also requires availability, or *disponibilite*. The French concept of *disponibilite* is almost untranslatable, but it is best defined as the capacity of being available, of being willing to interrupt your work and your agenda for generous acts and nudges. *Disponibilite* involves noticing and nudging people by giving them more than a name tag or even a name; more than making them stand up or making them a loaf of bread. Even more than the take-a-pagan-to-dinner approach to evangelism. *Disponibilite* is interrupting your personal agenda to enter into the reality of who they are ... and you've got about fifteen seconds to decide to do it and begin it. How do you know if you've succeeded? When you find a person "existing in excess of themselves."[67]

Ubique credimus divinam esse praesentiam.
We believe that the divine presence is everywhere.[68]
—Rule of St. Benedict, chapter 19

When we fail to shut up and listen, we fall out of step with the rhythm of God's presence.

The shut-up-and-listen mixture of silence, listening, and waiting, or the "silent treatment," can be compared to fermentation: a messy, tumultuous, yeasty process that eventually results in clarity. But the fermentation is laborious, and people often mistake fermentation for failed implementation. Teresa of Avila used to shake her hourglass to make the sand go more quickly during her silent treatment. The worse his day was going, the more Martin Luther used his third ear and gave God the silent treatment. John Wesley spent a minimum of an hour in silent treatment. If we spent half as much time preparing to listen as we do preparing to speak, there might be more around of what is called communion.

There might also be more around of what we call "victory." There are few more misquoted verses in Scripture as this one: "Be still, and know that I am God."[69] When placed in the context of the whole psalm, this is not a validation of ease and serenity. Rather, it is an invitation to preparedness for struggle and pilgrimage. When we say with the psalmist "Wait upon the Lord," we have almost lost the original meaning of that word *wait.* The Latin word for "to wait," *attendere,* means to stretch oneself forward. We are attentive, still, opening ourselves to what will come so that we might hear inside words, phrases, lyrics, and images "the history of its future echoes."[70] Waiting is not passive lounging. Waiting is active stretching into the future, to the God who is already ahead of us, to hear in the present the future of the past.[71] We aren't waiting for something to come; we are waiting for the future that is already here to appear. We are waiting for something to be revealed from a source beyond ourselves. From a biblical perspective, the present is not the past becoming future; the present is the future becoming the past.

Listening is a gift. In fact, the gift of listening, the gift of attention, what the Quakers call "devout listening" or what Kay Lindahl calls "the sacred art of listening,"[72] is the greatest gift you can give to someone. Next time you have coffee with someone, consciously say to yourself: "I am now gifting you with my listening. I give you my total attention as an expression of my love and respect for you." The gift of listening is a gift you choose to give or not to give. But when you choose to give it consciously, notice how your whole demeanor changes: Your voice softens, your body relaxes, you lean into the person, and you enter a whole new way of being in the world.[73] In fact, notice how you start communicating with the other person without words. We are nourished and flourish in the gift of another's attention.

What you need … is a good listening to! My Gramma Boggs had a saying that was a variation on the folksy scold "What you need is a good talking to!" (although she was known to say that, too). Her version was this: "Some people need a good listening to." Remember what it felt like when someone really "got" what you were saying? When you were at the receiving end of this holy practice of listening, it inspired you, and freed you, and healed you. The words "I hear you" have magical healing properties: "Listen, that you may live."[74] Listening heals the soul.

Some have suggested that being understood is at times even more of a fundamental human need and a more powerful healing force than being loved. In fact, David Augsburger contends that "being heard is so close to being loved that for the average person they are almost indistinguishable."[75]

Listening looks easy, but it's not simple.

Every head is a world.

—Old Cuban proverb

Wake Well

> Wake up, O sleeper,
> rise from the dead,
> and Christ will shine on you.
>
> —Ephesians 5:14

Once nudgers have showed up, slowed down, and shut up, it is important to wake well.

The wake metaphor was an important one to Jesus, who was constantly saying in one form or another: "Stay awake, be alert, watch." In fact, Jesus often put two words together: "*Watch* and *pray*."[76] To watch means to be awake, to be aware, to be mindful. In the book of Revelation there is the drumbeat refrain: "Be watchful," "Be attentive," "Keep watch." Isaiah beats the same drum, but with a bigger stick: *"Wake up!"*

The blowing of the ram's horn to begin the Jewish New Year, Rosh Hashanah, is not intended to usher the Hebrews musically into the future. In fact, the ram's horn is the furthest thing from a musical instrument. Its blasts are harsh, grating, groaning, even threatening. The six blows of the ram's horn—two broken blasts, two warning sounds, two shouts of victory—are the call to wake up from slumbers, to repent of lethargies, and to provoke new ways of seeing and being in the world.[77]

For Cistercians like Thomas Keating and Esther de Waal, the Cistercian rule of prayer is a shofar sounding. De Waal, an Anglican religious in a Cistercian order in England, explains the meaning of "Vigils."

> The daily framework of prayer starts in the dark in the
> hours before dawn. Its name, Vigils, is significant for it
> is the daily call and commitment to be vigilant, awake,
> aware, alert.[78]

In this sense of shofar soundings, nudgers are artists. Art critic and philosopher Clive Bell used to say that "the artist is not one who dreams more vividly, but who is a good deal wider awake than most people,"[79] which may be the source for composer John Cage's more well-known thesis that the function of art is to wake us to the life we are living. No wonder artists can seem so wailing and annoying.

> Now those persons who wait are awake and on the look-out for
> their Lord, whom they are expecting. And they are expectant
> whenever anything comes, however strange it may be, and look
> to see whether perchance it is He who comes. In the same way
> we should be on the look-out for our Lord in all things. This
> requires diligence and we must be prepared to give everything
> that one can contribute in mind and strength. It is well with
> those who so act; they will apprehend God in all things equally
> and they will find God in an equal extent in all things.[80]
> —Meister Eckhart

Nudgers do not necessarily dream bigger dreams than other people, but they are more wide awake than most. They unabashedly wake the slumbering to the present tense of Jesus. And all of us are sleepwalking in some areas of our lives. I guarantee you have become so habituated to the humming and thrumming of your refrigerator, or air conditioner, that you no longer notice it. I once saw a camper in the front yard of a home on Bridge Street in Lafayette, Oregon, who was literally becoming organic and returning to the earth. I guarantee you that the owner of that house drove in and out of his driveway every day without seeing that eyesore who flew in the face of every person who drove down that street.

Christian scholar Origen walked among his contemporaries in third-century Alexandria with the shofar cry: "Wake up to the love that sleeps within you."[81] Even when something has slumbered for weeks, months, years, decades, nudgers are the ones to give it a wake-up call. That's why nudgers will get pushback and blowback. My kids hate me when I wake them up. They call me names and gripe at me. Never once have I gotten hugs and kisses from a wake-up call. When we wake the church from its dogmatic slumbers, and point out that the old responses no longer get the needed reactions, we shouldn't expect flowers and hugs.

> While the mother sleeps, her toes are awake.[82]
> —Creole proverb in Guadeloupe, French Antilles

Semiotics is the doctrine of watchfulness, and nudgers are wakers. Ronald Reagan once fell asleep during an audience with the pope. Much of the church has fallen asleep during other audiences—with postmodernity, with post-Christendom, with a posthuman culture. But watchfulness entails more than not falling asleep or waking up. The Spanish greeting of a morning is "Did you wake well?"

Once you wake, you must wake well to the day. You can wake up and stay in bed. Or you can wake and stand and shake out those lower extremities. Are your clothes laid out, and are you ready for the excitements and challenges of the day? Or are you like that bumper sticker that reads: "New Day, Same Underwear."

For nudgers, every awakening is a meeting—a call to connection with some one, some event, some One. Every awakening is a special openness to the strangeness of the world. The world is a strange but splendid piece of music, sung by messengers, intermediaries from God. Part of waking well is hearing the world sing. Can you hear the strangeness in a person's song that makes it theirs? Can you hear God sing in the world, and the different notes and beats that go with different cultures? This is what semiotic nudges do ... help people, starting with ourselves, wake well and hear the music of the spheres.

> The sin of inadvertence, not being alert, not quite awake, is the sin
> of missing the moment of life; whereas the whole of the art of the
> nonaction that is action (wu-wei) is unremitting alertness.[83]
> —Joseph Campbell

John Gardner, founder of Common Cause and mentor to best-selling business guru Jim Collins, told him one day: "Jim, you spend too much time trying to be interesting. Why don't you invest more time being interested?" Collins commented:

> If you want to have an interesting dinner conversation, be interested. If you want to have interesting things to write, be interested. If you want to meet interesting people, be interested in the people you meet—their lives, their history, their story. Where are they from? How did they get here? What have they learned? By practicing the art of being interested, the majority of people become fascinating teachers; nearly everyone has an interesting story to tell.[84]

Waking well brings us to the second component of semiotic nudging: Witness and Bear Witness.

> Only that day dawns to which we are awake.[85]
> —Henry David Thoreau, *Walden* (1854)

Second, Witness and Bear Witness

Survivors of Auschwitz and Hitler's other death factories are called "witnesses." The early church called the first Christian martyrs "witnesses." What right do nudgers have to use this word?

The Bible has two Great Commissions. The more familiar one is from Matthew. But before you quote it to yourself, let me defamiliarize it a bit by the discipline of historical context: This ambitious strategic plan, the most lofty assignment in history, was spoken to a tiny, pathetic, and impoverished band of followers who had no idea what to do next:

Go into all the world and makes disciples of every culture.

But Luke gives us another rendition of the Great Commission in two other places: Luke 24:44–49 and Acts 1:8.

You will receive power when the Holy Spirit comes on you; and you will be my witnesses in Jerusalem, and in all Judea and Samaria, and to the ends of the earth. (Acts 1:8)

Matthew's Great Commission is "Go and make disciples!"

Luke's Great Commission is "Wait and be filled with power!"

We need both.[86] Even in our evangelism, we are primarily followers … God is faithful, Christ is present; will we participate in the presence? Will we be witnesses to Christ's presence and power? Can we shout out the Spirit's activity?

Whether or not your tribe recognizes every baptized Christian as an evangelist, there is no tradition that does not call every Christian to be a witness. We are called to be as much a witness to the resurrection as the first disciples were witnesses to the resurrection. The central statement of the church's earliest affirmation were these words of Acts 2:32: "God has raised this Jesus to life, and we are all witnesses of the fact."[87]

Storycatchers before Storytellers

Nudgers are first storycatchers and only then storytellers.

Nudging is recognizing the Jesus-in-you story and saying, "Look here!" Nudge is identifying what Jesus is up to in your story and saying, "Look out!" Once someone has listened up and looked here, it's time to look out.

As nudgers are catching a person's story, you are all the time trying to connect that story, not to your story, but to the gospel stories and to the Greatest Story Ever Told. In fact, nudgers are reluctant to tell their stories of what God is doing in their lives too soon in fear of overloading or overdetermining the action of the Spirit.

Parents tell children something that no child likes to hear: "Don't speak until you're spoken to." This is one of the earliest lessons in life we fail to learn at our peril. But whether we like to hear this truth or not is beside the point: It's precisely true. Nobody can every really speak until they're spoken to. Cambridge theologian Nicholas Lash puts it like this: "We cannot speak unless we are spoken to; all speech is, in the last resort, response."[88] St. Augustine put it like this fifteen hundred years earlier: "Each one of us learnt our native language by habitually hearing it spoken."[89]

There is no understanding without standing under. Nudge is not taking or talking God to people. Nudge is helping people speak for themselves after they realize they've been spoken to. Nelle K. Morton taught theology for many years at Drew. One of her most memorable mantras was the importance of people in their relationships to "hear into speech."

Nudgers "hear into speech" the hearts and minds of others yearning for connection to God in a world where we are easily disconnected from both reality and eternity. Nudgers help others to listen to their lives and to hear, see, taste, touch, and smell the sacredness of their own journeys.[90] Nudgers help others "hear into speech" so that they can "speak for themselves." Most importantly, nudgers never speak until they've been spoken to.

> Truth is tradition-dependent, and learning
> how to speak the truth takes time.[91]
>
> —Nicholas Lash

It requires an act of imagination to enter a frame of reference different from your own.

It requires an act of discipline not to default to generalizations and preconceived categories once we hear someone say something different from what we expect.

It requires robust concentration not to induce "functional deafness" into ourselves, which is what S. I. Hayakawa, the greatest semanticist of the twentieth century, called it when we hear things we have already worked through and have come to different conclusions.[92]

It requires deep compassion to care enough to bear another's burden.

It takes a bent ear to hear words as the speaker intends them, not as we use them or think they should be used.[93]

When we don't hear into speech and let our definitions of someone's words trigger deep revelations, a lot of these deep revelations will consist of reaffirming exactly what we had always thought.

It is one thing for someone to get you to tell your story. But it takes it to a whole new level when someone else gets your story so right that they can tell your story better than you do. How much does it mean to you when someone knows your story so well they tell it in front of you? Can you fail to be moved when that happens?

The best evangelists are those who can first define what people are already thinking and then say it for them as they would like best to say it. This is especially the case for the revoicing of marginalized and repressed voices.

The issue is not to avoid controversy or argument. The issue is for nudging to foster dialogue more than discussion. "Our duty is not to see through one another, but to see one another through."[94] How many of us, when we come away from a conversation (or a sermon), come away with agreement or disagreement, like or dislike? Or do we come away with new insights, fresh understandings, refreshed connections, and varied ways of looking at things, regardless of whether there is agreement or disagreement?

There is an important difference between dialogue and discussion. Dialogue comes from Greek *dia* (through) and *logos* (meaning). Dialogue is the use of words "through," which flow and flux "meanings" that issue in new perspectives of dissolution and metamorphosis that can only be gained from shared conversation.

Discussion comes from the Latin *dis* (apart) and *quatere* (to shake). As Kay Lindahl notes, "It has the same root word as percussion and concussion—to break things up." A dialogue aims to open things up. A discussion aims to break things up, to answer a question, or to win an argument. Too much evangelism has been discussions aimed to persuade and produce results and not dialogues aimed to explore and connect.[95] A dialogue aims for clarification and connection. A discussion aims for victory and conquest.

There is one nudge rule that keeps a dialogue from turning into a debate or a discussion. Hayakawa calls it the "one basic conversational traffic rule" that can prevent many "verbal traffic snarls." The traffic rule is this: "We refrain from agreement or disagreement with a speaker, to refrain from praise or censure of his views, until we are sure what those views are."[96] My way of putting it is this: I have no right to argue with you until I can state your case to your satisfaction. I have no right to tell your story until I can state your story to your satisfaction. This is a rule easier to embrace than employ.

Join Up, Get Behind

We witness and we bear witness. Witness is not enough. We must bear witness. God expects us to do more than worship and witness; we are to join God's activity in the world and participate in the signs of God's presence wherever they may be and pass that on to someone else. We are obligated to share in some way, partly because our own cup can't be filled up without it being emptied out.[97]

Nudgers refuse to settle for anyone or anything less than the best: Only Jesus will do.

It's a sin to speak if you're not moved to speak.
It's a sin not to speak if you're moved to speak.[98]
—Quaker principle

Penn Jillette of Penn and Teller is an atheist. But his response to being evangelized after a show is revealing. Penn was deeply moved by his encounter with this lover of Jesus who treated him with dignity and respect. Penn says:

> I don't respect people who don't proselytize. If you believe that there's a heaven and hell, and people could be going to hell, and you think, "Well, it's not really worth telling them this because it would make it socially awkward." ... How much do you have to hate somebody not to proselytize?[99]

Do we bear a message of universal importance, or don't we?

Do we bear a message of eternal import, or don't we?

If we do, can we afford not to bear witness? Can we afford to ignore the real needs of people? When we hear these words, "Tell me, please!" can we not just be a bramble bush that burns for God, but a conveyer of the promise that Christ is here waiting to be lived completely in you? Evangelism is more being the good news than telling the good news. But sometimes you tell.

In fact, the first postresurrection of Jesus contains the whole of nudge: "Go quickly and tell."[100] "Go" means to get off your seat, on your feet, and leave your secure world to venture forth into where God is up to something. Forget about hijacking people into holy places. Fish where the fish are. But go fishing.

"Quickly" means that time is precious and of the essence, and that in some ways we battle against time. There is an urgency and we're using up our allotted time, and the time is "ripe" and the fields are "white [and brown and yellow and red and black] for harvest."[101] There is a race going on, and that race we're running is a big one for each of us, and for all creation.

"Tell" means that while actions speak louder than words, words still speak, and people still need to sign an inner contract: "How, then, can they call on the one they have not believed in? And how can they believe in the one of whom they have not heard? And how can they hear without someone preaching to them?"[102]

One day Dwight L. Moody, the Rick Warren of his day, was walking down a Chicago street and ran into a complete stranger. Filled with faith's fervor and passion for Christ, he walked up to the stranger and said, "Excuse me, sir. Are you a Christian?" Offended, the man stepped back, stared Moody in the face and snarled, "Mind your business, sir."

Moody smiled at him and said, "Sir, you are my business."

Nudgers aren't starting up something. We are joining Christ's initiative and catalyzing what Jesus is already doing. The first recorded words of Jesus: "Did you not know that I must be about My Father's business?"[103] Nudgers are busy with God's business, not ours. Our nudging is not toward the end of what you can do for God; it's what God has done, is doing, and wants to keep doing for you and for the world. That's what keeps us taking the hate and heat.

Nudgers need to think of themselves as baton passers in a race that may run for decades and centuries, not just weeks and years.

It may even be that we're part of the nudge that exists beyond time. Nudge doesn't need to lead to closure, at least not the nudgers' closure. Our trust is in the promise that our nudges will start something through a word or witness that God will send someone else to take further. Maybe our role is simply to start the Spirit ball rolling in someone's life and never see it come home....

If you think about it, this is how it has always been. God uses more than one person to lead people to Christ. It may take ten, twenty, fifty, and we may be number twenty-three. George Hunter, professor of evangelism at Asbury, says that thirty years ago it probably took five significant encounters before a person would accept Christ. Today, he argues, it usually takes no less than twelve to twenty nudges. Only a few times are we privileged to be the closer.

Margery Wilkie was my closer. But I was brought to faith by dozens of nudgers, some present, some past. Reading Martin Luther changed my life, and in the roll call of nudgers for Len Sweet, Luther is high on my list, even higher than John Wesley. John Irving's *A Prayer for Owen Meany* has the best opening line of any book—the first sentence ends, "I am a Christian because of Owen Meany."[104] But "Owen Meany" is a semiotic symbol: a sign for all those nudgers who enabled Owen Meany to bear witness. I am a Christian because of Mabel Velma Boggs Sweet.

Discover More Online

CHECK OUT INTERACTIVES FOR YOUR PERSONAL OR SMALL-GROUP USE
AND MUCH MORE ON THE NUDGE WEB SITE:

WWW.NUDGETHEBOOK.COM

Chapter 3

SENSATIONAL CHRISTIANITY
AND
THE SEMIOTIC 5

Nudge best occurs in good company, and with good sense. I did a whole book about the meaning of good company (entitled *11*) and the role of the community in the nudge factor.[1] In the second half of this book, I want to look at the good sense(s) and to bring good company and good sense together.

But let me loop back a bit and revisit Jesus' image of evangelism as "fishing." I guarantee that when you hear Jesus say "Come, follow me! I will teach you how to catch people instead of fish,"[2] the image that comes to mind is of a lone individual fly-fishing. Actually, the fishing Jesus is alluding to here is net fishing where an entire village would fish together and often two boats would work in tandem drag-netting fish in between them. Jesus' image of fishing was not solitary but social.[3] In the Jesus story of the miraculous catch of precisely 153 fish,[4] the number 153 is the celestial calculus for completion. The ancient world believed there were exactly 153 different species of fish. A catch of 153 fish symbolized the church's need to reach in its communal netting every culture upon the earth.[5]

Perhaps if a more communal mentality of nudging were adopted by our churches, the fear of evangelism would diminish, and our nudge potency would increase. For our ancestors the essence of heresy was a preference for individual truth over communal truth. The concept of orthodoxy was slow in coming. In pre-Christian Greek, *heresy* (*hairesis*) meant nothing more than a school of thought. The negative sense of the word *heresy* came when Christians returned the word to its original etymological meaning: a belief adopted by personal choice rather than by communal consensus.

Unus christianus, mullus christianus
The single Christian is no Christian.
—Old Latin saying

We are more comfortable with church as masks of community rather than as manifestations of communion. A great example of communal nudging comes from John O'Keefe, a colleague and fellow collector of frequent-flier miles. He tells of attending a church that he had been going to on and off for a year when he was home. One Communion Sunday, after a long time on the road, a young usher came and sat down next to him and began to explain to the "visitor" what was happening in the liturgy. "I'm sure it looks strange to you what is happening, but when I motion, I'm inviting people to the Communion rail, which is right up front. See it there? When I come to your pew, just walk over to me and then I'll lead you up to the rail if you want to partake in Communion." The usher then went on to explain what Communion meant, that at this church Communion was open to all people, and that John was welcomed to partake if it seemed like something good for his soul. "In all my time in the church, and in all the churches I've been part of, this usher was the first person who took the time to explain what was happening in the liturgy."

A semiotician sat down by him—an usher who morphed into a nudger.

My favorite example of the communal nudge is my Facebook page, which I opened up only a year ago but which now has been rated by Twitter Grader as one of the top spiritual-oriented Facebook pages. I have sought to surround myself not just with Christian friends from the full spectrum of Christian faith but with people who have been burned by Christianity and now are dropout agnostics or drop-dead atheists. I also have many friends who are part of other religions. In making the plural de rigueur in building an online community, my Facebook world is filled with people from well over fifty countries representing a wide array of cultural and social perspectives.

This means the last things you will not find on my Facebook wall are straight-laced establishment blather or straight-faced PC cliches of any stripe. In fact, most often someone is stirring strange ingredients into the theological goulash or, in the words of William Blake about Christians of his day, "Both read the Bible day and night / But thou readst black where I read white."[6] In other words, my Facebook wall is usually crackling with dramatic energy.

When I have been away from my wall for a while and then check in, I often think of the early church (second thru seventh centuries), when theological debates raged so widely that one bishop complained that he couldn't buy a loaf of bread without the baker wanting to debate "whether there were one or two natures in Christ."[7] If you went to a shop in Constantinople to buy a loaf of bread, St. Gregory Nazianzen (died 389) sounded off, "The baker, instead of telling you the price, will argue that the Father is greater than the Son. The money-changer will talk of the Begotten and the Unbegotten instead of giving you your money, and if you want a bath, the bathkeeper assures you that the Son surely proceeds from nothing."[8]

Yet when someone posts something that misses the forest for the fruit trees, or swings into action as the Tarzan/Jane of the Ivy jungle, my Facebook community does not become the "I know better" brigade. Nor do they assign anyone to spend long stretches in the social-networking equivalent of the stocks. Rather, they respond organically as a communal nudge. In fact, I have learned to count on that word *angel* in *evangelism* because of my Facebook friends. Some "angel" will post a comment that explores another aspect of the question from a more historical perspective. Another angel will pour some oil on troubled waters. Another angel will bring some sacramental gratuity into a more and more utile debate.

A nudge faith eschews the following: a merely mental or intellectual matter, a solitary experience, or a spiritual sensation that disregards the material. A nudge faith is an embodied, lived, communal adventure played out in the context of ordinary life with all of its sensory experiences.

It is one thesis of this book that if we only knew how to sense God, to see, hear, smell, taste, touch the divine, we could nudge the world with the consciousness that "everything that lives is holy"[9] in some way.

The Puritans who settled New England are known for the wrong things and unknown for the things that really set them apart. The Puritan world was not one of sensory deprivation, nor was the world of the senses a foreign country where secrecy was the *lingua franca*. In fact, the Puritans were convinced that God gave us the senses to perceive the world in order that sensuous experiences might lead us to God.[10] When the Puritans looked at the sin in their lives, and what drove their unholy allegiances, they found passion lying at the root. But instead of rooting out passion as the enemy and killing it—and since passion is enflamed by the senses, making the senses the enemy too—the Puritans sought to align their passions to God's purposes, and to find freedom in sensual desires always being aligned to Christ.

When my friend John Dill was pastor of a church in Camden, Arkansas, a tornado hit the area and did serious damage to property throughout his parish. One church member in particular, a chicken farmer, found that part of his chicken farm was totally destroyed, while another part was virtually untouched. By the time he got around to surveying all the damage, over a week had passed. In one remote corner of his farm he found a chicken coop that the tornado had lifted up whole, roof and walls together, leaving the cement plank and chickens undisturbed. Almost all of the five hundred chickens in the coop had died. But they didn't die from the tornado. They died of starvation. They had been used to the industrial feeding of pellets that came to them if they stood in place. So they stayed on the cement plant, remained in the status quo, and waited, and waited, and died. Only five of the chickens decided that maybe they needed to use the senses they were born with. Only five ventured to step off the plank and eat some awful things that had never touched their mouths or been seen with their eyes: slimy, grubby worms; creepy, crawly bugs; yucky green grass; hard seeds; etc.

Once they started eating these foreign substances, however, they discovered what they had been born to taste, hear, see, smell, and touch: *real chicken food*. Only if we have the courage to get off our comfortable planks and into the sensational world out there will we discover that our food for the past five hundred years may actually have been unnatural, foreign food. Christianity's native food may be more what we today think is slimy and creepy ... the real, "pagan," sensate surroundings we find ourselves in.

Jesus comes to us through five primary regimes of presence:

> *Jesus comes to us ... through eyes.*
> *Jesus comes to us ... through ears.*
> *Jesus comes to us ... through smells.*
> *Jesus comes to us ... through touch.*
> *Jesus comes to us ... through food.*

Each one of the senses has its own energy, its own culture. Collectively, they come together to form the energy of the body, a culture of the body that William Blake defined in precisely these terms: "A body is that portion of Soul discerned by the five senses."[11] We receive Jesus with our ears, our mouths, our eyes, our hands, our noses so that we can hear reality with Christ's ears, and taste reality with Christ's mouth, and see reality with Christ's eyes, and touch reality with Christ's hands, and sniff out reality with Christ's nose. We receive Jesus into our hearts so that we can be Jesus in our world.

These are big dreams and bold metaphors: Paul says that Christ and we are all one body. Then he gets even bolder: We are all one Christ. Not because we are good people, or better than anyone else. But because Christ is at work and at play in us.

Become what you preach, and then preach Christ in you.[12]
—Presbyterian minister Joseph Ruggles Wilson (father of President Woodrow Wilson)

We are better at asking questions than inhabiting our regimes of presence, at hearing, seeing, tasting, touching, smelling answers. Nudge evangelism helps people to make sense of life, or as the Bible puts it, to "come to our senses"[13] in order to find God and to find life. Nudging is endowed with a biblical world of perception and presence—seeing, hearing, touching, tasting, smelling. It is so much less demanding to think than to be. Words vaporize quickly; hands, stomach, eyes, ears, nose remember.

The blessing of science and technology is that they can expand our ability to see, to hear, to taste, to touch, to smell—and in so doing increase our nudging capacities. The curse of science and technology is that they can also entrap our senses and awe us with the wonders of the technology itself rather than what they can enable us to experience. The rich foods we eat can so overstimulate our senses that we lose the ability to appreciate a cup of pure water.[14]

Throughout history, there has been a philosophical hierarchy that has placed sight and hearing above all other senses as "the higher senses," because they were associated with the mind. Taste, smell, and touch were deemed "the lower senses," because they were associated with the body. Aristotle made sight the primary sense, with the problem senses being taste (after all, the organ of taste was the troublemaking tongue) and touch (another mischief maker).

But this is not always the case. Some cultures order the world principally by sound (the Andean Incas), others by temperature (the Tzotzil of Mexico), others by smell (the Onge of the Andaman Islands), and even some by color (the Desana of Colombia) or more precisely "color energies," which is far afield from the Western stress on critical observation and surface showings.[15] In fact, the history of warfare has yet to be written from the standpoint of sensory warfare and sign manipulation. For example, Native Americans and Europeans lived in different sensory universes. Native Americans integrated the senses, while the English privileged the eyes. By changing the scenery, or sign manipulation, the British transformed the landscape (the English fort at Roanoke was famous among Native Americans for "hurting the eye"). Post fences rather than plant hedgerows, felled forests, cleared fields, wooden buildings, linear towns, and church bells disoriented Native American sensibilities and imposed the sensory regime of Europeans. Camp meetings and revivals were forms of spiritual warfare against "the world, the flesh, and the devil" based on sensory conflict through sound ("shouting Methodists," "hooping" preaching, dress parade), sight (gestures, night torches), smell (burning oil, the sawdust trail), touch (healing dramas, courting grounds), and taste (love feasts and delicious meals).

Nihil est in intellectu quod non sit prius in sensu.
Nothing is in the intellect that was not previously in the sense[s].[16]
—Arguably Thomas Aquinas's favorite quote of Aristotle

What did Jesus spend his ministry doing? He had three years in which to save the world, and how did he spend those three years? He spent his time creating a new sensory regime of the Spirit: telling stories (sound and sight), sharing meals (taste and smell), healing people (touch), and traveling the countryside and building his team while connecting and praying with people (all five senses) that they might have life more sensational in all its dimensions, in all its senses.

The Spirit of Christ is not vagrant or homeless, but incarnate and embodied in whatever gives life: a fish, some flesh, the aroma of bread and wine, an accent, or an appearance. How do the disciples recognize Jesus?

His wounds, which they touch.

His food, which they eat.

His presence, which they see.

His voice, which speaks their names.

His aroma, which they inhale.

We recognize Jesus the same way today. It is not we who pound down Jesus' door. Jesus is the real seeker. It is Jesus who is knocking at *our* door, saying, "Can't you hear me? Touch me? Smell me? Taste me? See me?" Are you finding Christ in the people you meet? Are you finding Christ in the things you handle? Are you finding Christ in the food you eat? Finding Christ in the voices you hear? Finding Christ in the smells you breathe?

Hearing, Tasting, Seeing, Touching, Smelling

The availability of Jesus requires a new kind of literacy, semiotics of skill and will. Since evangelism is a "community project,"[17] these skills and wills must be embedded in the lifeblood of the community itself.

> *Hearing is a skill:*
> *but first a will to Hear.*
> *Seeing is a skill:*
> *but first a will to See.*
> *Tasting is a skill:*
> *but first a will to Taste.*
> *Touching is a skill:*
> *but first a will to Touch.*
> *Smelling is a skill:*
> *but first a will to Smell.*

There must be will before the skill is developed. Jesus is signaling all the time and inviting us to more sensational ways of living. In fact, Jesus' knuckles are raw from knocking on the door of our hearts, begging us to come out, discover for ourselves his sensory truths, and "bless what there is for being."[18]

Jesus is saying, "Enjoy your senses, I gave them to you to enjoy. Come, let me guide you into finding life through your senses, because it is through your senses that I will reveal myself. Lose the fear, my child, and come out and experience *life*." Fear of the senses is the sharp point of the wedge that Gnosticism uses to separate the physical from the spiritual.

The phrase "bless what there is for being" is one of the most powerful and mysterious of all lines in the poetry of W. H. Auden. In a poem dedicated to his senses, "Precious Five," with a stanza of gratitude to God for each of the senses, Auden concludes by invoking:

> That singular command I do not understand, / *Bless what there is for being*, / Which has to be obeyed, for / What else am I made for, / Agreeing or disagreeing?[19]

Part of the secret to unlocking that magical phrase "bless what there is for being" is to understand that what matters in life is not being good but being God's. One of the most difficult tasks in life is to know the difference between "be good" and "be God's." It's a lot easier to "go and do likewise" than to "go and be likewise." But Jesus calls us to a doing based on being. Jesus is saying, "Don't *act* like me. *Be* me!"

Jesus gave us more than a command of likeness; he gave us a command of oneness. Nudgers need to worry less about doing evangelism, or getting evangelism done, than about being with Jesus. Jesus acts on us. You don't need to do anything. Just being around him acts on us. And sets us free, to be. It is and always was an issue of freedom—and God's teaching us to use our freedom well.

The twentieth-century poet Denise Levertov, a wizard with words too little known these days and in her own day, has a collection of poems called *Evening Train* in which she quotes an ex-slave:

I sits here, in my rocker, evenin's,
and just
    purely
       be's.

Toward the end of the poem, Levertov writes,

as the task before me, to be,
to arrive at being.[20]

The ultimate nudge in life is helping others "to be" and "to arrive at being." It's the ultimate art form: the artistry of being.

If God wanted you to sit and relax, how would God need to deliver the message? Usually, if God tells us to move a mountain, we break out the pickaxes and shovels. But if Jesus says, "Sit with me for a while," we act like we can't hear him. If Jesus says, "Let's take a walk. I want simply to enjoy your company for a while," we walk to church. We live in the falseness of believing that Christ really wants us for what we do rather than for who we are. I can sing "Jesus loves you" rather loudly. But to sing with any degree of deep feeling "Jesus loves me this I know" is a lot harder.

A Sensational Christian is one whose faith uses all five senses. A Sensational Christian has a mouth, hands, ears, eyes, and a nose connected to the soul as well as to the brain. But there is a holy hierarchy to the senses: If you don't hear it before you see it, you'll never ever taste it, much less smell it and touch it.

Nudge evangelism must pass Jesus' "The LEAST Test": "Whatever you did for one of the *least* of these brothers of mine, you did for me."[21]

L ... listen ... Do you have ears for the kingdom?
E ... eyeball ... Do you have eyes for the kingdom?
A ... aroma ... Do you have a nose for the kingdom?

S ... savor ... Do you have a taste for the kingdom?
T ... touch ... Do you have a touch for the kingdom?

The Celtic tradition is known for its fivefold symbols and motifs. In an attempt to integrate the "whole" and the "parts" where the whole is greater than the sum of its parts, the Celts pioneered the fifth element and five prime themes. For example, there are 4+1 directions: North, South, East, West, Center; there are 4+1 seasons: Spring, Summer, Fall, Winter, Transitioning.

One of the least known but most suggestive of the Celtic Fives is the Five-P Exercise of Spiritual Awareness. To be aware of God in any moment, you put yourself through the five Ps: Pause, Presence, Picture, Ponder, Promise.[22] I call these the Semiotic 5, because each of these is associated with a function of a primary sense organ:

Pause ... Hear

Presence ... Taste

Picture ... See

Ponder ... Touch

Promise ... Smell

In the second half of this book, we will explore nudge evangelism from the perspective of the Semiotic 5 and the multiple sensory nudge points. One of the central things every human knows: *There is always more and there is always meaning.* We cannot exhaust a sign. There is always more meaning than we can perceive. The assumption of the Semiotic 5 is that there is more to anyone and anything than we initially notice or receive, and there is always more meaning, both intended and unintended meaning, that can be discovered from the senses God has already given us.

When we assume to "know," we rule out the possibility of receiving more from God. Three of the most important words in the universe are these: "I don't know." The engineer's creed—"the more I learn, the less I know"—is based on these three words. Some forms of Christianity are built on a series of "untouchable signs" and thus miss God's living presence in their closed perspectives of those signs. For the Christ follower to be open to the reality of the living God in real time and real space, the person must leave "knowledge" open to God for shaping, reshaping, replacement, or removal. When you fail to do your Semiotic 5, when you "know" too much or autopilot too quick to "sense" the way things are and the way things are going, you easily lose your path in life.

But it is not just enough to study and read emerging patterns. We also are called to nudge those patterns into shape and give form to spirit. It's not so much about reading or recording signs as it is about transposing and transfiguring signs. Nudging is sign reading that rewrites the text of the sign within the text of our lives. Nudging is the reading of signs so that the signs of the Spirit can be rewritten within the sign of our life and the lives of those we nudge. This is what makes nudging so endlessly fascinating, difficult, and important.

Fully immersed in our sensory world, nudgers need sensory training, the iterative process of experiencing, sitting with God in the result, and engaging all over again. This Semiotic 5 is not meant to lock nudging into some sequential, linear grid. In some ways, I am mixing and matching the five Ps all the time, and also doing them all at once. Simultaneity is important, for the senses need to check one another and especially move us beyond the dominance of the traditional sensory channels of sight and sound. Sign reading is not easy, for signs are deceiving. In fact, the greatest smoke signals out there are often smoke screens.

Two examples must suffice. Italian paparazzi started noticing how often the new Pope Benedict XVI slips out of the Apostolic Palace and hangs out at his old flat just outside the Vatican's St. Anne's Gate. Italian newspapers used this sign to conclude that the new pope misses the academic life and anonymity of his prepapal life.

The truth of the matter? The pope loves cats, especially stray cats. One day he fell in love with a sick, stray tabby he named Scherzo and nursed her back to health in the Apostolic Palace. When the pope found Scherzo swinging from some brocade curtains and bounding from one priceless antique to another, he decided that he had to find a new home for her. So he hid her in an empty miter box and took her to his old apartment, where he visited her and played with her regularly.

This sounds like a great story of the difficulty of reading smoke signals. But wait: The newspaper issue where this story appeared was the first week of April 2009. And *scherzo* means "joke."[23]

Another example: Mildred was the "Tongue of the Church" and the self-appointed monitor of the church's morals. She could not stop sticking her nose into other people's business and gossiping what she sniffed out. Several members did not approve of her extracurricular activities, but feared her enough to maintain their silence.

Mildred made a mistake, however, when she accused Henry, a new member, of being an alcoholic after she saw his old pickup parked in front of the town's only bar one afternoon. She emphatically told Henry and several other members that everyone seeing it there would know what he was doing. Henry, a man of few words, stared at her for a moment and just turned and walked away. He didn't explain, defend, or deny. He said nothing.

Later that evening, Henry quietly parked his pickup in front of Mildred's house, walked home, and left it there all night. You gotta love Henry.

We borrow the ears of God, the eyes, the mouth, the nose, the hands of God, to hear and see, taste, touch, and smell as Jesus did from the cross. Not to condemn but to love. Here is where Christian semiotics diverges from prevailing semiotics: Disciples of Jesus are to "take up the cross daily." We are to see the world as Jesus sees the world, and Jesus sees the world *from the cross*. He looks *out* from the cross. We are to see others looking *out* from the cross. And we are to nudge others looking *out* from the cross.

This means nudgers live and love as Jesus lives and loves: with a blend of *fortiter in re, suaviter in modo*, or to translate this ancient theological phrase into English, "resolutely in action and gently in manner." Or as I shorten it: Our nudges should be strong and sweet.

To be a nudger is to recognize Jesus where he is appearing all the time—in situations, in people, in creation. To be a nudger is to watch Jesus express himself in others and *in me*. A nudger is a close relative to a nodder; and a nodder nods and says, "Yup, that was Jesus." Acknowledgment is the first step toward a nudge.

 **Discover More Online**

CHECK OUT INTERACTIVES FOR YOUR PERSONAL OR SMALL-GROUP USE AND MUCH MORE ON THE NUDGE WEB SITE:

WWW.NUDGETHEBOOK.COM

Part II

NUDGE "SENSING"

Chapter 4

PAUSE: USE YOUR EARS

Do You Give Ear to God?

Hearing Jesus

One of the most resonant words in the Greek language is *logos*. It has as many meanings as *heart* does in English but is best translated to mean story, speech, saying, sound, voice, or a combination of all. Perhaps the least satisfying translation of *logos* is "word."

"In the beginning was the Voice …"

The creativity of the Multivoiced One wells over and makes a world, a world made for relationship and designed to connect to the Multivoiced One through speech and song. The Voice that created the universe never stopped. It is still voicing, still creating, for ever and ever, for eternity. It can still be heard today, inviting all mortals to "join the mighty chorus / Which the morning stars began."[1] It is speaking in multivoiced accent all the time. But we must be ready to do the listening.

Music is everyone's first language.[2] That's why we remember more musical melodies than we do prose passages. The human brain is wired for sound. From twenty-eight weeks' gestation, the fetus can respond to auditory stimulation: The fetus experiences the mother's voice not just as sound but also as vibrations on the skin. Even infants don't like "devil's notes" like uncertain C and F sharp but smile at stable fourths and fifths like C and G or C and F.[3]

UCLA nanotechnologist Jim Gimzewski has discovered cytological music by listening to the "singing" of cells. He calls this new field of bio-physics "sonocytology," and scientists can now receive a PhD in cell sonics and explore the vibrational life of cells. For example, when you douse a cell with alcohol, the frequency of vibrations increases as if the cell were scream-ing; when you change the temperature of a cell, you speed up or slow down cellular harmonics; once a cell dies, its vibrations flatline.[4]

In other words, according to sonocytology, every person sings his or her life.

"Do You Hear What I Hear?"

A church secretary was accustomed to answering the telephone, saying, "Jesus loves you. This is Alice. How can I help you?" Once, the telephone rang while Alice was deeply engrossed in a conversation with an office col-league. Thus distracted, she picked up the phone and said, "Alice loves you. Jesus speaking. How can I help you?"

After a long pause, she heard the caller say reverently, "I thought your voice would sound different."

Nudging is most fundamentally sound awareness and potent sonic pokes. Except when it comes to ecclesiocracies, where much less is usually going on than meets the eye, the rule of thumb is this: Much more is always going on than meets the eye. But before it meets the eye, it meets the ear.

> The air of life is music, and I live.[5]
>
> —Poet Denise Levertov

Nudgers learn to use their ears to move people toward health and holi-ness. In John 20, Jesus is not seen, but he is recognized. How? Peter first *hears* that it is Jesus.

This chapter explores what it means to hear the voice of Jesus in others and to use our ears to nudge others with the voice of Christ. It presupposes a belief in the *viva vox*, the living voice of Christ, spoken through another human being, through the voice of tradition, through the voices of culture and nature, reason and experience, shouted out through the Scriptures. Usually it comes in the form of an interruption, often at a difficult time. Commonly it comes in the form of what Margaret Feinberg calls a "sacred echo."[6] Always it comes with the ring of resonance, often as a corrector, sometimes as a celebrator.

Christianity is not about "Do you believe?" but "Do you hear?"

Do you hear something different from what the world hears? Followers of Jesus hear something different…. "Do you hear what I hear?" rings the Christmas carol. Evangelism is not getting people to believe this or that and they will be saved. Evangelism is getting people to hear it for themselves.

Christianity is a nudge to the listener: "I'm hearing something amazing. Do you hear it? I hear a star … do you hear what I hear? I hear a song … do you hear what I hear? I hear a child … do you hear what I hear? I hear cries of goodness and light in midst of badness and gloom … do you hear what I hear? I hear a cross … do you hear what I hear?"

One of the greatest compliments a nudger can ever receive is this: "I can hear the song/star/child/cross in your voice."

Faith is song. Christians are constituted by faith through sound. When you nudge, you place a musical deposit in someone's life.

> Sense almost always follows sound,
> so I've found.[7]
> —Welsh/English poet Gwyneth Lewis

A Sound Theology

Tell me who can make as much noise as they want, and I'll tell you who has the power. We used to regulate our lives according to sacred sounds, especially the ringing of church bells. But a new soundscape emerged in the early twentieth century where the older sounds faded away, and new sounds were being born (siren, hum of electrical wires, phonograph).[8] With this increasing noise of modernity, where could one find silence? In the world of the Spirit.

Did you hear something?

The first evidence of the divine often comes as a wisp and a whisper. And if we don't pause, it will whisk on by us and we'll be left floundering in the backwash. I call this the warning of the wind.

The classic film portrayal of the warning of the wind was a scene in the first *Jurassic Park* movie. The power has gone out, and the park visitors are stuck in automated vehicles just outside the T-Rex pen. Thunderous vibrations cause ripples in a visitor's cup of water. T-Rex is approaching. Some of the visitors heed the warnings of the wind and of the paleontologists. Others, like the lawyer who ran frightened into an outhouse and left the two kids to fend for themselves, became dinosaur grub.

No parent needs the movies to teach them that you hear the future before you see it. You saw your kids before they were born. An ultrasound reveals the secrets, or the horrors, of the future. Sonograms are images we can see with our eyes that are first formed by vibrations and sound.

The most important guy in Homeland Security? Not the one who monitors the photographs. A picture tells you what already happened. If you want to know what's going to happen, plug into the communications network and listen.

Nudgers are sonographers of the Spirit. Aristotle said sight is the primary sense. But Thomas Aquinas thought different in *"Adoro Te Devote"*:

> *Visus, tactus gustus, in Te fallitur*
> *Sed auditu solo tuto creditur*[9]

> Sight, touch and taste in Thee are all
> deceived;
> The ear alone most safely is
> believed.[10]

"The vision thing" is so yesterday. The future is all about vibe and voice.

It has always been such. Mary is now officially called the "apostle to the apostles" because she was first to see Jesus and proclaim his resurrection. But when Mary saw Jesus with her eyes, "the vision thing" failed her. She thought he was a gardener. Her recognition awaited voice activation.[11] Jesus' first words to Mary were distancing: "Woman …" Then when he speaks her name, "Mary," she knows who he is.[12] Jesus shows us who he is by first showing us who we are. And we show others who Christ is by first calling each other by name.

Humans are constituted by sound. These days, if it doesn't get in the iPod, it doesn't get in the heart: To get in the surround-sound system is to get in the soul. In many ways we all go through life blind and find curbs along which we can tap our white canes. We hear our way forward. When Jesus is our leader, he asks us to stay close and trust him. He seldom gives us the vision of "This is exactly where I'm taking you" but takes us one step at a time, one day at a time, one call at a time, one curb at a time. You think Jesus was a visionary planner? Check out the strange, bizarre routes he took in the Gospels as he zigzagged and careened the countryside.[13] The pause of the ear is less "What is God's vision for my life?" and more "How can I hear and catch up to God's mission in the world?"

The Semiotic 5 begins with the pause of the ears.

> Sound is to the nervous system what food is to our physical bodies.
> Food provides nourishment at the cellular level of the organism, and
> sound feeds us the electrical impulses that charge the neocortex.[14]
>
> —Sound researcher/author Joshua Leeds

Give "Ear" to God

"Heard any good books lately?"[15]

With audiobooks becoming better sellers than print books, it's an apt and app question.

"Heard any good news lately?"

With the Scriptures linking hearing and seeing, it's an apt and app question.

The Bible, once called "The Talking Book," is an ear app: It pauses us to "see" what God "speaks," to "hear" what God is doing into "sight." You can trust what you see, only when you see what you hear.[16] The nudge challenge is to hear with our eyes, to see with our ears, to use our nose as our mouth, and our mouth as our nose.

> The ear is the only true writer and the only true reader.[17]
>
> —Poet Robert Frost

To read the Bible, the ears come before the eyes.[18] For Semitic peoples, the ears not the eyes were the most trustworthy organ for perceiving divine truth.[19] In the Torah, God is heard, never seen. The divine vision is heard. This is in stark contrast to Greek cultures, where divine apparitions are a literary commonplace. In Numbers, God speaks to Moses "mouth to mouth."[20] In Exodus, God speaks to Moses "face to face,"[21] which means much the same as "mouth to mouth."

A Facebook world needs more not less face time that is face-to-face, in-your-face, and especially in God's face. That kind of face time is less seeing "eye-to-eye" than "lending an ear" and becoming "all ears" to one another. Nudging is more about learning how to be an ear-witness than an eye-witness. Evangelism is nudging others to see the sacred harmonies. Evangelism is helping people to name what is resonating in them. Again, a good ear-mark to follow is the 10 to 1 rule: In ten minutes of nudging, nine minutes should go to listening and asking questions and one minute to speaking. But all ten minutes should be seen as a nudge.

> When we speak more than we listen, it is like flying
> a kite in the dark. Our words go out, but we have
> no idea if they ever get off the ground.[22]
> —David W. Henderson

The owl is the symbol of the sound nudge. The owl brings sound and sight together in its "ear-eyes." When we look at the heart-shaped face of an owl, we are looking at a creature whose eyes looks like satellite dishes because they are: Its eyes are also its ear. The proverbial wisdom of the owl comes from this extraordinary sophistication of overlapping sense organs.

As far as I know, only in Chinese is ear-eyes conveyed in one word. The Chinese word for hearing or listening is a combination of four characters: ear, eye, heart, and emperor. The heart of evangelism is the development of ear-eyes that more than anything want to follow and please the "emperor." And our emperor is Jesus.

> Wisdom is the reward you get for a lifetime of listening
> when you'd rather have been talking.[23]
> —Aristotle

Dietrich Bonhoeffer organized an underground seminary at Finkenwalde in the 1930s for theological students opposed to the Nazis. The students of necessity lived in a closed community where the relational health of the community was literally a matter of life and death. Out of the experience Bonhoeffer wrote a remarkable little book, *Life Together*. One of the sections is entitled "The Ministry of Listening." Let's listen to Bonhoeffer:

> The first service one owes to others in the community involves listening to them. Just as our love for God begins with listening to God's Word, the beginning of love for

other Christians is learning to listen to them. God's love
for us is shown by the fact that God not only gives us
God's Word, but also lends us God's ear.[24]

Bonhoeffer notes that "so often Christians, especially preachers, think
that their only service is always to have to 'offer' something when they
are together with other people. They forget that listening can be a greater
service than speaking."[25]

"To hear" in Hebrew is *šāma*, which means something richer than "to
listen to." *Šāma* means to listen with response, and not repose, to hear and
heed at the same time. Unlike every other sense but touch, sound is an
interactive and relational medium. Have you ever read an email and gotten
angry? The more times you eyeballed it, the angrier you got. But call that
person up, and you calm down. The more you hear what they're saying, the
more soothed and smoothed your response gets.

Since that little flap of skin on the side of your head was thought
to be a direct conduit to the heart, *šāma* also means to obey or become
obedient.[26] To "see" God was to hear and channel the commandments
of the righteous. Hence the centerpiece Hebrew prayer, the *shema:*
"Hear, O Israel: The LORD our God, the LORD is one."[27] That word *hear*
could equally be translated from the Hebrew as "discern," "discover,"
or "perceive." To "hear" God's Word for the Hebrews was to respond
in obedience, to make the journey from the head to the heart. It is two
different things to hear with the head and to hear with the heart, which
itself can be an organ of perception. In today's language, the *shema*
might begin: "Here's the Vibe, Israel." Put your ear up to God's Word,
so that you can put your ear up to life, to people and to projects, and
discern: Does it sound like God or not?

Where the eye divides, the ear connects.[28]
—Composer John Luther Adams

The same linkage of hearing and obedience is found in English and Latin. The English word *obedience* comes from the Latin word *oboedio* ("to obey"), which has as its first meaning "to hearken, give ear, listen" and only means "to yield obedience" as its second meaning. Further, the Latin *oboediere* is cognate to the word *obaudire* ("to listen carefully," thus *audire*, "to hear"), from which we get words like *audio, audition,* and *audience.*[29] Anyway you look at it, obedience means to listen deeply.

Obedience is listening. We all listen to something. The question is will we pause to listen to God? In the story of Samuel and Eli, it takes God four times to get through to Samuel to the point that he would listen. It's the same with most of us. We are what we hear and "re-sound," the technical meaning of "re-sonate." Deep listening leads to resonance, and resonance produces change that sets new things in motion. Jesus came to set humanity in motion.

For this reason the first word of St. Benedict's sixth-century "Rule of Life," the most famous of all the rules of life, is the hortatory "LISTEN!"[30]

> Listen, carefully, my son, to the master's instructions, and
> attend to them with the ear of your heart.

Toward what end? Listening is how you arm yourself with the "strong and noble weapons of obedience."[31] We lean our lives into hearing God with the heart that we might trust and obey.

Enough philology. Here's the theology: From a biblical perspective, you hear a vision more than you see it. Paul has a vision where he hears these words: "My grace is sufficient for you, for my power is made perfect in weakness."[32] Or go back further in time to a seldom-read passage from Habakkuk that states explicitly what is implicit throughout the Scriptures: "I will stand on my guard post and station myself on the rampart; and I will keep watch to *see what He will speak to me.*"[33]

Sound becomes sight. Vibes become vision. The first manifestation of the Spirit at Pentecost? Sound (communal wind) became sight (personal fire). The creation of the universe? Sound ("And God said/sang") became sight ("Let there be light"). Nudgers listen for that background hum of the Creator built into the universe.[34] Nudgers hear melodies of the Spirit long before they understand all that they might mean.

> Music may be the closest human analogue to the mystery
> of the direct and effective communication of grace.[35]
> —Scottish Jesuit John McDade

An old film about the physics of sound shows a handful of iron filings placed on a thin sheet of metal. A musical tone was played near the sheet. Suddenly the filings arranged themselves in the form of a snowflake. Sound became sight, as vibrating energy took physical shape. Another tone was sounded, and the treasures of the invisible world became manifest—this time into a star. Every note sounded transfigured filings into physical formation. Similar things have been done more recently with water.[36] The invisible became visible. Vibration became vision.

Communities of faith might better be called hearing rooms where God is given listening room. To hear the Gospels is to hear the voice of Christ,[37] and with that hearing comes obedience. In a Harry Potter world, a magical world exists just out of sight. In a Jesus Christ world, a magic heavenly kingdom exists just within earshot. Nudgers are always listening for vibrations of grace, evidences of Christ's visitations in people's lives.

God's words to us at the transfiguration were these: "Listen to him."[38]

Talk is cheap. The reason is simple: The supply exceeds the demand.

Listening is expensive. For the opposite reason: The demand exceeds the supply. Just ask any therapist, hairstylist, or pastor.

Where are your nudges heard most loudly? In your speaking? Or in your compassion and compunction?

Notice the order:

> That which was from the beginning, which we have heard, which we have seen with our eyes, which we have looked at and our hands have touched—this we proclaim concerning the Word of life.[39]

First comes the ears. Then the eyes. Then the handles of touch, taste, and smell.

Nudge begins with sound. Nudges are heard first, then seen; then handled through touch, taste, and smell. Disciples of Jesus nudge more by the ear than the eye. Since disciples are constituted by sound as "hearers of the word," nudge evangelism begins first in being tuned to the Voice ... the Voice that created us, and the Voice that one day will call us home.

In contrast to other deities that surrounded the Hebrews, Yahweh is Perfect Voice. The Hebrew word for *voice* (*kol*) is a key word that is used in many ways. Sometimes it conveys to those who know how to listen to voice the ability to fathom what is fantasy and what is truth. But almost always it is used to express or summon up the will of God. Voice is the pleasure and privilege of the bodyless God.[40]

Music is sonorous air.[41]
—Ferruccio Busoni

Symposium as Symphonium

As any video-game designer will tell you, our ears are the emotional real estate. Our eyes are the fiefdoms of our rational minds. That's why sound envelops the body, while sight traces lines and dissects, focusing the object in ever-sharper detail.

When you start talking to contemporary physicists about matter, what comes out of their mouths is not math and formulas but a Dantesque netherworld of words like *quarks* and *squarks, leptons, gluons* and *muons,* and *bosons.* Or when they're not sounding like scientists, words like *vibrations, resonances, strings, entrainment.* In other words, they start sounding like musicians. And Christians.

With Einstein's 1905 equation $E=mc^2$, we began the twentieth-century learning that matter and energy are essentially the same thing. By and large the church has yet to come to terms with an Einsteinian world where time is relative, mass and energy are interchangeable, and space can stretch and warp.

Wake up, church. Already we are post-Einstein. As we begin the twenty-first century, some are making the case for mind and matter being essentially the same thing—matter is just dense mind.[42] We now know that mind affects matter. We now know that mind affects matter at a distance. We now know our minds operate beyond space and time. A mind of unique power can collapse the quantum wave into a particle, in one famous instance (among many) turning water into wine.[43] We now know our severely limited special senses do not define what is real. All sound, taste, sight, touch, and smell do is help us negotiate our three-dimensional space-time world in an eleven-dimensional (at least) universe.

If you think the doctrine of the Trinity is hard to understand, you need to read a science text published in the past ten years. Actually, a good way to think of matter is less mind than music. If super-string physics is right (and the loop gravity school says it's not),[44] then the basic reality of the universe is vibration or sound.

This is what makes the sound nudge so important, and so dangerous. If you doubt the power of vibrations to tear down as well as build up, remember what brought down the Walls of Jericho, or the Tacoma Narrows Bridge, or look into what shut down the opening of London's Millennium Bridge, or is causing the marble to disintegrate in Michelangelo's statue of David.[45] Music can also cause altered states of consciousness or trigger seizures, the style of music that triggers the epilepsy depending on the patient.

> Now then, my children, listen to me; blessed are those who keep my ways. Listen to my instruction and be wise; do not disregard it. Blessed are those who listen to me, watching daily at my doors, waiting at my doorway. For those who find me find life.
> —Proverbs 8:32–35 TNIV

String theory (recently renamed M-theory, for reasons I don't quite understand) posits an original number of ten to eleven spatial dimensions—"or maybe twenty-six," which is a scientist's way of saying, "We really have no idea, but it's a lot more than the three we know anything about." No wonder the M in M-theory can stand for *mother, matrix, magic, mystery, membrane,* or even *murky.*[46] And I haven't even mentioned field theory (Einstein deemed this his greatest discovery),[47] morphogenesis, wave mechanics, the "tunneling" of electrons through neutrons, etc. As science turns toward the realm of the Spirit to understand the physical universe, Space, Matter, Time are more prone to induce reverence than arrogance among scientists, who are sounding more like Isaiah in the temple than Isaac Newton under the apple tree.

String theory defines matter as "vibrating strings of energy."[48] That's it. What makes a turnip a turnip, and a carrot a carrot? A change in vibrations. Vibrations are what turn one vegetable into another. Why? Because matter is but vibrations, notes on God's violin. Anything that vibrates does so at speeds called frequencies, and the frequencies of vibration create sound. When sounds are shaped together, that's called music. Words like *vibration, frequency, sound,* and *music* are in some ways interchangeable. Oh, I forgot one term that should be added to that list: *matter.*

We are all string instruments, and our thoughts and emotions are the notes struck by life's playing on the strings of our souls. Whether you can carry a tune or not is irrelevant. We are all made of rhythm; we have a beat, whether we can sing or not. It is less accurate to say that we live our lives than that we sing our lives.

> Trust thyself; every heart vibrates to that iron string. Accept
> the place the divine providence has found for you, the society
> of our contemporaries, the connection of events.[49]
> —Ralph Waldo Emerson

Unhappiness and depression begin the day the music stops or when we try to sing someone else's song. An "iron balloon" is a Jamaican expression for a singer who has not found his or her own voice. God wants each one of us to sound like no one but ourselves. The psalmist musician complained, "When I kept silent, my bones wasted away."[50] If you don't sing your song, or people can't hear your song, or the music of faith stops for you, your health deteriorates, and others discount you for not speaking from the soul. We listen for music from our politicians more than we look at their platforms, as King David proved.

When your song is right, your crowd is captive. But there are two kinds of captivity depending on the singer: those who sing a song that points to their voice and virtuoso, and those who get out of the way and let the music sing, who let the song flow and glow.

The greatest task of a human being, your greatest mission in life? To find and sing your own song … to the glory of God. In "sacred harp" music, the harp was the voice you were born with or your voice was the harp you were born with. Either way, your song was sacred.

Everything that exists has a sound, a unique vibration that some call a "home frequency." When someone walks into a room who shares those wavelengths, you start to sing along willy-nilly, and spontaneously vibrate. You become a "resonant system"[51] of eurythmy, of harmonious rhythm, or even holy harmony. Nudgers trust that humans are designed to sympathetically vibrate with Jesus when their souls are "struck" by his grace and truth.

A vibrant faith is a vibrating faith. Nudgers give off good vibes. It is not enough just to be present. You must be present with voice. Nudgers have a vocal presence. The best nudgers are those with a voice that's being authenticated by vocation and lifestyle.

I have not been able to shake the mantra of the film *Australia* (2008): "I will sing you to me." Nudgers sing you to you and to me. Nudgers sing others to healing and wholeness. Nudgers sing Jesus to one another. Most of all, nudgers help others hear God say to them, "I will sing you to me."

Poets have understood this better than philosophers: from John Donne, who insisted that creation was a sound event and that the "word" with which God created the universe was a song, to Welsh priest/poet R. S. Thomas, who called God "a poet who sang creation."[52] God is Pure Voice. In fact, scientists even contend that the background "noise" of creation ("The Big Bang"?) is still out there. An incarnational God means that God-stuff is found in the matter of the universe. Consider R. S. Thomas's "matter is the scaffolding of spirit."[53]

The Gospels record nine times Jesus saying, "He that hath ears to hear, let him hear." What did God tell John to tell the seven churches in Revelation? "He that hath ears to hear, let him hear."

What we see depends on how we look, and we need to look with our ears; the radar-dish ear is the best reader of sound.[54] Jesus is the Ear Restorer. He gives us back our ears. How sad that the church's street cred is more that of Peter than Jesus, more known for cutting off ears than putting ears back on.

Peter didn't get his name changed to "the Rock" until after he proved he could be an ear-witness and he had listened to what the people were saying. *Simon* is a form of *Simeon,* which in Hebrew means "hearing." In Hebrew custom this meant Simon was "one who hears God" or even "one whom God has heard." Because he listened to what the people were saying, while at the same time was the first to confess Jesus as "the Son of the living God," Simon the Ear became Peter the Rock.[55]

> While there's music, there's hope.[56]
>
> —Wilfrid Mellers

My next quote will be one of the most memorable metaphors for the ear nudge that you will ever hear. It comes from the Scottish poet Hugh MacDiarmid (1892–1978), who called music "the gate which separates the earthly from the eternal."[57] Pause to take this in: By using music as an ear nudge, you are a gatekeeper of the eternal. You swing the gate back and forth from the visible to the invisible.

British researcher Jill Purce took MacDiarmid's metaphor more literally in her argument that it was the unique mission of humans to use sound to mediate the translation of spirit into matter, and matter into spirit. "If spirit can become matter through sound, then matter can become spirit again through sound."[58] British literary critic and Columbia professor Sir Frank Kermode (he was knighted in 1991) contends that any interpretation that moves something from the physical to the spiritual is an "angel." When crusty English professors and philosophers start talking about angels, I sit up and take notice. Kermode is no less than making the case for music as an angelic force in our lives and those who wield its powers "angels."

> Oh, to be delivered from the rational
> into the realm of pure song.[59]
>
> —Theodore Roethke

Tech Support for Sound Architecture

1. Turn Off: It's a Pause

A pause means we turn off the noise. We live in sound. Sound lives in us. We must choose carefully the sounds that surround us. If we listen carefully to what our ears are picking up, a lot of what we're hearing is not signal or even sound but noise. But therein lies our problem: A lot of noise is pleasing to the ear. The word *noise* is derived from the Latin for *nausea,* which means to make physically sick. A pause can radically change the signal to noise ratio.

Is there anything that will bring you to full attention more than a phone ringing in the middle of the night? But God doesn't just call in the middle of the night with loud rings. More often God uses the "still small voice,"[60] or even silence, to bring us to attention. William Wordsworth talked of "a soft eye-music of slow-waving boughs."[61] Silence can be absence of sound; but it can also be, as many deaf people "see" silence, the absence of movement.

> Silence is now a commodity of the same sort as darkness;
> we buy polarized sunglasses, heavy curtains, and blindfolds
> to tone down the light as we buy noise cancellation or
> white noise devices, soundproofing panels, and ear plugs
> to keep ourselves, or others, safe from excess noise.[62]
> —Hillel Schwartz

Every culture is hearing impaired, but Google culture seems especially prone to the overamping of our bodies and souls. Surrounded by sound boxes, cell yells, and background buzz, how do we recognize God's voice calling us?

I am writing these words in the Paramount Hotel in Portland, Oregon, where I woke up this morning to the sound of hammers, jack-hammers, and cranes constructing a city park across the street. One of the biggest problems in hospitals? Noise. Hospital beds are noisy places. Hospital sounds can be as loud as jackhammers. With all the buzzers, alarms, carts, telephones, wheels, shouts, joking at the nurses' station, a morning shift change can generate sounds in the jackhammer range of loudness: 113 decibels.

You can listen to 100+ decibels once in a while. But if you're listening to 100+ decibels all day long, you're going to go deaf. And if not personally then culturally we're going deaf. In the second half of the twentieth century, the human ability to perceive sounds has plummeted. In the 1980s, the human ear could subtly distinguish 300,000 sounds. In the twenty-first century, we have the ability to distinguish just more than 180,000 sounds, a loss of almost 50 percent.[63]

> If Bach continues to play in this way,
> the organ will be ruined in two years or
> most of the congregation will be deaf.[64]
> —Members of the Arnstadt council, employers of J. S. Bach

The church handles silent pauses like our worship handles its favorite call to worship. No sooner are these words out of our mouths—"The LORD is in his holy temple, let all the earth be silent before him"[65]—than the first hymn fills the earth with sound.

Nudgers are like old-time stone masons/artisans, who would not work on a wall when heavy machinery was operating nearby. It seems they placed the stones by the sound they made as they set them in the wall. If they couldn't hear that proper sweet sound, the right *plunk,* they couldn't work.[66]

The test of whether it's a true pause or not? Does the pause refresh? Architect Frank Gehry, justifying some of the fun flourishes at the Walt Disney Symphony Hall, said, "If people feel good, they hear better."

And soon the night of weeping

shall be the morn of song.[67]

—"The Church's One Foundation"

2. Turn On and Tune In: Don't Tune Out

Once you've turned off the frequencies of the world, you turn on your being to the frequencies of God's Spirit and tune in to what medieval cosmologists called "the music of the spheres." These new stations specialize in love, not fear; grace, not guilt; promises and possibilities, not handicaps and limitations. It is these frequencies that produce in us a sound mind. Fear of the unknown causes some who tune in to quickly tune out, so a "No Fear" nudge is often needed.

My favorite way of understanding Jesus is in musical terms: In Jesus, God gave us a tuning fork to the eternal. Jesus is God's Perfect Pitch. His atonement is our attunement.

Sound (low frequencies) becomes sight (high frequencies). Light is just revved-up sound. Sound, which everyone can hear, became light in Jesus, who is "the true light that gives light to every man"[68] and enlightens everyone with evidences of God's power and love.

When I tune my vibrating strings of energy to his frequencies, as a sheer gift of grace, there will come a moment of resonance. You have seen what happens when resonance is reached in the old Ella Fitzgerald commercials, or in opera singer Caruso's ability to launch notes at will that could shatter glass.[69] When resonance is reached, there is a tremendous explosion of energy, and something has got to give; and it's not going to be Jesus. The weaker instrument is transformed into a new identity, and we become "new creatures in Christ," with resurrection wavelengths.

In this state of resonance, we truly become the Jesus Vibe and "all things are possible." In sync with the Spirit, we are one "in the Spirit."[70] In this stage, ear cliches sound like tinnitus, and bad theology like botched tunes. In a resonant state, your life is plugged into the soundtracks of the Spirit, which are the soundtracks of holiness, health, and healing.[71]

> Musical training is a more potent instrument than any other,
> because rhythm and harmony find their way into the inward
> places of the soul, on which they mightily fasten.[72]
>
> —Plato

3. Tune-ups and Fine-tuning

The problem is that every musical instrument quickly goes out of tune. Every concert, whether of grade schoolers in a gymnasium or professionals in a philharmonic hall, accommodates time-outs for the musicians to tune up. That's why one conversion is not good enough. We need a daily re-turning and re-tuning to the frequencies of the Spirit.

Our soul is an organism, and organisms possess internal, daily clocks, of which two things are constant: (1) It has twenty-four-hour periodicity; and (2) it needs to be reset daily by external stimuli, especially the light. Our internal clock gains or loses time if it isn't constantly being reset by the light. Wait, there's a third constant I almost forgot: Everyone is born with different biological rhythms. I am sensitive to this because I live with a rhythm disorder: My daily rhythm is disordered, arrhythmic, and more in need to attunement than others'.

There are a few people whose internal rhythms never seem to be "off." When I encounter someone with perfect pitch, I marvel and say: "What an ear!" In "Name That Tune" some people can hear one note and the song is revealed (I hate those people). Some people are born with an internal tuning fork that can tell them the pitch of a burp. These people are called saints and mystics.

The rest of us learn to develop better pitch and more calibrated internal tuning mechanisms. We do this through what the Christian tradition has historically called "practice." People today work on their bodily appearance and looks like our ancestors in the faith worked on their souls. If we worked as hard trying to stay in tune spiritually as we do staying in shape physically, our world would be a very different place.

There are two levels of truth: matter-of-factual truth and incandescent truth. The latter is accessible only through life practices and rhythms of discernment. The church is fundamentally a community of practice that teaches rituals that enable resonance with incandescent truth. These rituals (or "drills") brought a certain litany and rhythm to life, and out of that rhythm or "groove" came growth and confidence and courage.[73] In fact, ritual is embedded within the spiritual. You can't even spell the word *spiritual* without *ritual*, much less *doing* spiritual without doing ritual. Didn't Jesus invite a faith rooted in relationship and lived out in rituals of practice?

Some people call these "spiritual disciplines" rather than what I prefer to call them: "life practices" or "rhythm grooves." For me the problem with "spiritual disciplines" is that they can quickly become symbols of our piety rather than instruments of our human formation. Spiritual disciplines became open-sesames to our holy clubs rather than means of learning and life formation.

What are some of these "life practices," these tune-ups and fine-tunings that can keep us attuned to the Jesus wavelength? How is life tuning best done for you?

First and foremost is Scripture study. In order to listen and tune in, we first must learn the score and the language of the music. Do you know the language of the faith, the language of the Spirit? Or are you always looking up words in the dictionary? Try going to an emergency room and having the attendant say, "I'll look that wound up in the books and see what it is…. Get back with you when I find out."

Second, for the Wesley brothers singing hymns was a key communal practice. A hymn was what they called the common person's theology. By inviting direct, emotional participation, hymns fixed doctrine in the soul. *There's within my heart a melody....*

The sonic saturation of your life in the music of the faith, always allowing God to "put a new song in my mouth,"[74] is one of the most powerful fine-tunings you can undergo. To nudge a song in someone's life is to stimulate their soul to vibrate at a particular frequency that can strike a resonant note. These resonant notes are healing zones. Already hospitals are being designed around "harmonic zones" and "prescriptive sound," which empower the healing process for patients, staff, and visitors.[75] I met a bone surgeon on an airplane who encourages his patients to bring their own music into the operating room, so that as they go under anesthesia and under the knife, they are listening to their favorite music. The original sound therapy[76] can be found in the story of David. Whenever he was down and depressed and couldn't feel the goodness of the Lord, he would bring in the minstrels to minister to him with music. Only then could he feel the experience of God.

Third, we need to learn how to be better "receivers." My father was an army–air force shortwave radio operator in the Second World War. In the unit he set up at our home, he showed my brothers and me how to tune into the invisible and broadcast aspects of the universal.[77] What made all the difference in the world was the receiver. Fine-tuning makes us better receivers, better able to pick up the soundings of the Spirit. You are reading this book in a room. That room is full of signals. But unless you have the right receivers, you will never pick up the images (TV) or the music (radio). You can't receive them without a receiver.

There are some voices that are so resonant they can be heard all over the world, if only we had the receivers to hear them. The voice of a child starving to death. The voice of the homeless Vietnam vet in a snowstorm. The voice of a teenage sex-worker slave about to see her tenth client in ten hours. We can't hear these voices because of fingers in our ears, or because our receivers are dog-tracking the fingers that point to the moon and not the moon itself, or because we are in love with the sound of our own voices.

Our receivers may be off also because we are fooling with the speaker systems of the establishment, which override our internal receivers with the voice-overs of power and prestige.

Our receivers may also be wrongly mistaking an echo sounder for an echo chamber. In the Jewish tradition there is something called *bat kol*. Literally translated "daughter of a voice," *bat kol* means you don't hear the voice itself, or even where the voice comes from. You only hear the child of the voice, the echo. The "voice behind you," telling you go left or right[78] is heard mostly indirectly, as an echo, as a *bat kol*, the daughter of the voice, which Margaret Feinberg calls "the sacred echo."[79] The "sacred echo" may come as a sound or a note, but it may also come from one of the other senses. An angel spoke to Jacob directly. But Ezekiel felt a hand on his shoulder, while Isaiah felt a fire on his tongue. We need to learn how to receive the echo, to prepare ourselves for its soundings, and to expect periodic Doppler effects. When we are headed in the opposite direction of the echo, it can create a kind of Doppler effect that can be hard to figure out.

One of the dangers of fine-tuning in church circles is when we start twisting our tuning pegs to produce ever smaller intervals only the highly pitched can hear. This is why the fine-tuning cannot be toward doctrines or propositions but the frequencies of Jesus the Christ. Three-time Pulitzer Prize winner Carl Sandburg got his start as a sportswriter. One of his favorite stories was his interview with Babe Ruth for the *Chicago Daily News* in 1928. Sandburg asked the Babe: "People come and ask what's your system for hitting home runs—that so?"

"Yes," said the Babe. "And all I can tell them is I pick a good one and sock it. I get back to the dugout, and they ask me what it was I hit, and I tell 'em I don't know except it looked good."

The Babe had no complicated formula for hitting homers. He was in tune with the game, and the home runs came. It's the same for those who are in tune with God's Spirit. There is no complicated system that can bring you homers and bring you home—except tuning yourself to the Spirit of love, tuning yourself as a "hearer of the word" to the Voice.

> Since I am coming to that holy room
> Where with thy choir of saints forevermore
> I shall be made thy music; as I come
> I tune the instrument here at the door,
> And what I must do then, think here before.[80]
> —John Donne, "Hymn to God, My God, in My Sickness"

4. Entrainment

There is a difference between resonance and entrainment. Resonance is a participatory phenomenon between two items sharing the same frequency. Entrainment is the gravitational pull of resonance from a stronger frequency onto a weaker vibration. The stronger vibration actively transforms the frequencies of the weaker rhythm into the stronger Vibe, and locks them in precise rhythm.[81]

In some ways the difference between resonance and entrainment is the difference between justification and sanctification. The more adept one becomes at reaching resonance with Christ and the more one steeps one's life in the surround sound of Jesus, the more all of life becomes a Jesus Vibe, entrained by God's Spirit.

Entrainment is being tuned to the Spirit's ongoing prayer melody. As a Jesus Vibe, you cease praying the Lord's Prayer and you begin to become the Lord's Prayer. Prayer is a listening into voice. Prayer is not getting God to pay attention, but learning to pay attention ourselves to what God is doing so that we can be entrained by the Spirit. Prayer is knock-knock-knocking on heaven's door and listening to the sounds that echo back. When our prayer life, a prayer life of listening and attentiveness, becomes our listening pleasure, then entrainment happens.

This is one reason why the Spirit is up to such great things in South Korea. Get into your car at 4:30 or 5:30 in the morning, and you'll have to deal with rush-hour traffic. But people are not rushing to work. They're going to prayer meetings. Six days a week. Christians clog the early-morning highways to pray in *Tong-sung gido* (corporate loud prayer).[82] They're getting their ears restored. So that they can hear when "He speaks, and the sound of his voice / Is so sweet the birds hush their singing."[83]

5. Even Hearing Is Communal

Other people need to listen in to our listening that we might hear better.

Musicians simultaneously express themselves and listen to other performers. In the collaborate art form known as jazz, listening to each other's music makes the lights come on and the music zing. In music, you can't sing your song without listening to each other's songs.

Listening to each other is not all fun and games. I started performing in piano recitals at age six and learned to grin and bear the hearing while my colleagues banged away. The piano recital was invented by Franz Liszt in the 1830s, and the notion that they were more interesting then than now is a delusion. George Bernard Shaw, a music critic at the turn of the twentieth century, claimed that after a week of listening to pianists, he liked to go to a dentist and have his teeth drilled by a steady hand.

Even orphan fledglings, who are usually doomed to spend their lives alone because their songs cannot attract mates in the sing-off competition, are now finding partners when played CDs of the birdsong of their free cousins.[84] Even birds can't find their songs by themselves. They need other birds to sing them into their own songs.

This is so important, because what we hear must be checked by the Word and by the community, since our mishearing is so well advanced. I love the story of the English housekeeper who was invited to sit at family prayer. She would only do this once, because the prayers frightened her.

When asked which one, she said it was the invocation to "God, who hatest nothing but the housemaid." When investigated further, it happened to be the collect for Ash Wednesday, which addressed God as hating nothing "thou hast made."

My scolding mother had a scalding two-word mantra to make our listening keener: "Listen and learn." Listen to people's fears, their hopes, their concerns, their bangings, and then you learn. One of the reasons why God creates the best music in the worst places and times is because it takes the worst to get us to listen. From behind the old iron curtain, these musicians emerged with a distinctly Christian bent: Górecki, Pärt, Kancheli, Silvestrov, Schnittke, Gubaidulina, Ustvolskaya. Their music is supplying the soundtrack to my soul as I write these words.

But there is a difference between being "listened to" and "being heard." Sometimes I've been "listened to" but never "heard."[85] To be heard requires more than passive hearing, which is little more than "hearing them out" and which can go in one ear and out the other. To truly hear requires active listening, a state of total concentration where you are thinking alongside the speaker. To see, one steps back to achieve some objective distance. But to hear, one steps close and lets oneself be surrounded and saturated with the sound. You know you're tracking with someone, tracking with your ears, when phrases start to crackle, when thoughts that first seemed dense and dull start to explode in colors and clarity. Norm Wakefield challenges us to become "perceptive listeners" by practicing five kinds of listening simultaneously: (1) hearing the words; (2) watching the nonverbal; (3) discovering the meaning of the message; (4) identifying defined or undefined emotions within the message; (5) discerning the full message behind the verbal and nonverbal communication.[86]

6. Play It by Ear …

When you don't know what to do, you make it up as you go along based on your intuition, hunches, the music that guides your steps, the melodies you hear, the grace notes that come your way. You can trust these guides when you are in touch with your culture and in tune with the Spirit. Much of the church is in tune with the culture and only in touching range of the Spirit.

To ear pause, or to hear Jesus, is to be open to the possibility that God may be speaking to you in and through the very thing that you would least expect God to use. Nudgers live with the motto "You never know." That piece of junk mail that caught your eye; that thought of an old high school friend that popped into your mind; that paragraph in Philemon that keeps coming up; your extended stay in the hospital; your bankruptcy that you thought was the end of your life; or your moral failure that ended your marriage—all of these and more may very well be God's "Hear me" invitation.

To *hear* is to participate, to participate is to assign meaning, to assign meaning is to live and move and have being.[87] Participation is not consumption. Participation is relationship. Thus, the ear nudge is to connect interpersonally; it is to relate with God.

Openness to the possibility that "it just might be God" is vital to hearing God's voice. It's fairly easy to hear God in movies, music, and television as these are primarily narrative signs. Significantly more challenging is training oneself to live with open ears, ears that listen for God's grand narrative in all things. It is much more challenging to foster openness to redefining the terms and notions that gave you meaning in the past. Once a person narrows a sign's meaning, that sign becomes untouchable.

Music to My Ears

Does it fit the "music to my ears" category to recognize that as we enter this third millennium, we are nudging in one of the hinge periods of history, a historical moment for which most of us are unprepared? The call to *hear* is also the call to *here,* a call to resist fear's temptation of the rose-tinted rearview mirror, a call to sing louder than ever that "soon the night of weeping / shall be the morn of song."[88] Abraham, Jacob, Moses, and Isaiah all answered God's voice with these words: "I am here." After calming the people's fears ("Fear not"), Jesus himself said, "I am here,"[89] where "here" implies both "in the flesh" and "in the moment." "I am …" is the voice of being calling you to an "I am" life.

Will you be God's "I am" who is "here"?

When I finished writing those words, I went online to see if any contemporary poet was thinking the same thoughts. Here is what I found within five minutes:

> Now cock your ear and hear the fun
> echo away before we're lost.
> Don't you dare upset the Big Conductor;
> sing and listen; time for change.[90]
>
> —John Lavan, 28 November 2009

The music is all around us, all you have
to do is listen.[91]
—*August Rush* (2007)

 ## Discover More Online

CHECK OUT INTERACTIVES FOR YOUR PERSONAL OR SMALL-GROUP USE
AND MUCH MORE ON THE NUDGE WEB SITE:

WWW.NUDGETHEBOOK.COM

Chapter 5

PRESENCE: TASTE

Do You Have a Stomach for the Kingdom?

Tasting Jesus

The way to know were not to see but taste.[1]

—*Samson Agonistes* (1671), John Milton's companion to *Paradise Regained*

You gotta love a religion that ritualizes its most sacred moment, not with trumpets blaring or guns blazing but with food—bread broken, wine poured, and covered homemade dishes spread out on a common table. As Erma Bombeck might say, you think it's indigestion, but it's really piousness.[2]

In Christianity eating is a serious business. So serious is eating that Christianity insists you can "taste" God. That's why nudgers must be people of taste. In the eighteenth-century Enlightenment, also known as the "Century of Taste," the human species, or Homo sapiens, was primarily conceived of as a "tasting organism"[3] in keeping with the Latin *sapere*, which means "taste" or "know" (*sapienta* also meaning "wisdom"). The goal of education was to create a "person of taste," a high-minded human being who could know and pursue the "finer things" of life.

The goal of discipleship is to create people of taste. Not the kind of taste (or lack thereof) that got a rector fired by his Puritan congregation for eating custard "after a scandalous manner" (it had too much alcohol in it).[4] By "a people of taste" I mean a people who know the taste of faith and who exhibit sublime appetites for the finer things of beauty, truth, and goodness. A nudge of discipleship is by definition a nudge toward beauty, toward truth, toward love and freedom of Christ, so much so that you can taste it.

The Spanish word for "taste" is *gusto*. I once tried to break down the Christian life into a trinity of phrases, and this was the best I could do at the time: Live with Gusto, Love Well, Run Fast. What this triptych failed to convey, however, was that a faith with gusto will always have gustatory implications. The gospel is not just truth, and it's not just relationship, and it's not just truth in relationship (although that would be plenty!). The gospel is a feast that God prepares and invites us to. God wants us to sit down, eat up, and party hearty. We get this honestly: The definition of the Land of Promise was a land "flowing with milk and honey" (which is a more poetic way of saying a place with pastureland and fruit trees).

Whenever food is involved, there is opportunity for a nudge. Food nudges are some of the most powerful revelations of God's goodness and glory. And everything we do should nudge to the glory of God.

You can count on the nudge of food for a couple of simply delicious reasons.

First, the Bible says so, and the words that I read there become water and wine, wheat and meat. This is in keeping with the Hebrew tradition of Torah, which was not originally written down and visible but rather "pitched" or "showered." The Torah as water rained down from above stems from the root *yrh,* which conveys the concept of formal learning, but means literally water, or to give to drink, or to be given to drink.[5] We bow in worship to drink in the truth in the same way we stoop to drink the water.

> I know that there is nothing better for them than to be happy and
> enjoy themselves as long as they live; moreover, it is God's gift
> that all should eat and drink and take pleasure in all their toil.
>
> —Ecclesiastes 3:12–13 NRSV

The bookend commands of the Bible are "Eat freely" and "Drink freely."[6] Everything between Genesis and Revelation is one giant table on which is spread the messianic banquet—not snack, not smorgasbord, but feast on the supper of the Lamb. The Scriptures are one food fantasy after another, one giant nudge to "Come, all you who are thirsty, come to the waters" … "Come, buy and eat!" … "Listen to me, and eat what is good, and your soul will delight in the richest of fare."[7] The very being of God nudges our palates to "Come, taste me!"

Or in a more familiar phrase, "Taste and see that the LORD is good."[8] Ever since the Protestant Reformation we've been averse to this verse in any other form than as food for thought. "Intellectually comprehend and understand that the Lord is good" is how we made a cognitive nudge out of "taste and see." But the most cursory reading of the Bible reveals something else: The kingdom of God *must* have something to do with actual food and drink; because there is so much of it present. The first restaurant to be called a "café" opened in 1765 and carried this inscription over the door: *"Venite ad me omnes qui stomacho laboratoratis et ego restaurabo vos."* The Parisians who read the sign couldn't read Latin, but they could read French, printed by the proprietor Monsieur Boulanger in the window: "Come to me all whose stomachs cry out in anguish and I shall restore you."[9]

I'm not the only one to be thinking this, since some of the biggest fights in church history were food fights. Christians put other Christians to death because they didn't have the right views on this subject of food, the meaning of this one word *Eucharist* (which translates literally as "thank you" in Greek), and who can or cannot be admitted to "the Lord's table."

> This is God's table.
> Who are we to check the guest list?[10]
> —Madeleine L'Engle's favorite invitation to Communion

Paradise was lost, and Paradise is regained, by what we eat. Our dietary indiscretions got us kicked out of the garden, and our eating habits determine whether we get to live in the garden for eternity. In fact, one of the best shorthand descriptions of the gospel is this: Jesus ate good food with bad people. Or in my own personal version: Bad eating corrupts good relationships.

I know I am swimming against the stream here, but two of the twenty-first century's most popular historical figures have never resonated with me for precisely this reason. Both barefooted St. Francis of Assisi, the twenty-first-century's most popular saint, and Sufi mystic Rumi, a thirteenth-century poet who is today's best-selling poet, had food issues. If either began to enjoy his food, or something tasted especially delicious, he would mix water or ashes into it in order to ruin the flavor.[11] After all, God wouldn't want your food to taste good, right? We all know it's burned-out believers, not God, who leave everyone with the taste of ashes.

Saints are better for inspiration than imitation. When nudging Israel back to her chosen calling, Yahweh gave her "embroidered cloth, sandals, fine linen, silk, bracelets, necklaces, earrings, and a beautiful crown," and her "fame spread among the nations" because of her beauty, for it was perfect through God's splendor which he had bestowed on her.[12] I can't eat Corn Flakes for the same history of underplaying our pleasures. Invented by John Harvey Kellogg, the modest cornflake was part and parcel of his campaign against all forms of sex, and cornflakes were designed to "numb all taste buds, from tongue to toe."

When something or someone "leaves a bad taste in my mouth," it is not a good sign. When something or someone is tasteless, it is a bad sign, evidence that what is before you is bland, dull, lifeless. Jesus always brought joy to the party. Religion is not a burden, but a blessing, and when you feel underblessed and overburdened, something is wrong with your heart.

> Come Lord, stir us up and call us back, kindle and seize us,
> be our fire and our sweetness. Let us love, let us run.[13]
> —Augustine

In fact, the theme of John 6:51–58 might be known as "You Are What You Eat." What is it we're feasting on? This world is feasting on ever more thrilling forms of entertainment and escape. The gospel invites us to feast on the ultimate food: Jesus, the Bread of Life.

Jesus gives us his body and blood as food, a food that becomes part of our bodies. Food is a gift that unites with us and unites us to one another. Disciples of Jesus are what we eat. Given the "you are what you eat," it follows that our transformation is symbolized by the eating of the flesh and blood of Christ.

Or here's the nudge: "What does your mind 'feed' on?" God nudged Ezekiel to become a prophet by handing him a scroll (the Word of God) and commanding him to eat it. Ezekiel discovered that, when God's Word is internalized in his being, it tastes as "sweet as honey" in his mouth.[14] When we nudge people to open up the Bible, it is not so much to read it as to eat it and feed on it in our minds and hearts—to chew on it, marinate our minds in it, ruminate over it, and nourish our souls on it. We nudge people in biblical directions because without the Bible your brain is on a starvation diet. Give it some food, some *good* grub, some good stories, some brainstorming metaphors; and besides, the true bread for whom we hunger … is Jesus. I love how the writer of Proverbs puts it: "Come, eat of my bread and drink of the wine I have mixed. Forsake foolishness and live."[15] Faith is all that stands in the way of foolishness and fluff-brain. Or being reduced to clutching at floating signifiers …

Jesus called himself the "Bread of Heaven" and came to be our bread-fellow. Born in Bethlehem, a "place of bread," Jesus saves us by being God with us and being our companion. That word *companion* is made up of two Latin words—*com* meaning *with;* and *panis* meaning "bread."[16] Jesus is our companion, our breadfellow, our real "mother bread" to use the parlance of Panera, whose franchises start meetings with the staff breaking bread together: "We start by paying homage to mother bread," says one manager.[17]

To live we have to keep bread on the table. Jesus calls himself "living bread," not "coconut cake." That means he is of the ordinary stuff of every day, that daily bread on which we live every day.

By defining ourselves, as Paul told the Corinthians, as the "body of Christ," we are being called to become bread for the world. In the Scriptures Jesus is always saying, "Come and eat," and bread is always on the menu. The Amish have something called "friendship bread," which takes ten days to make and is based on different kitchens sharing the same starter but partaking of different finishes, as different as the kitchens and cooks who make the loaves. Jesus is the original "friendship bread."[18]

> Break Thou the Bread of Life,
> Dear Lord, to me,
> As Thou didst break the loaves
> Beside the sea;
> Beyond the sacred page
> I seek Thee, Lord;
> My spirit pants for Thee,
> O Living Word.[19]

Eating with Jesus is the epitome of all that is present
symbolically and literally in food and eating.[20]
—Loyle Shannon Jung

The predecessor to the statement "The way to a man's heart is through his sternum" was a far more generous if not politically incorrect statement: "The way to a man's heart is through his stomach." But if truth be told, how many of both sexes weren't seduced by sex so much as food? My "first love" in life was with a girl whose mother introduced me to authentic Italian food when I was thirteen, and the boundaries between my love for the daughter's auburn hair and the mother's apron were hopelessly blurred. For the first time in my life I discovered what red peppers really tasted like, and a cannoli, and a plate of pasta. That's *amore*!

> Albeit all human history attests
> That happiness for man, the hungry sinner,
> Since Eve ate apples, much depends on dinner![21]
> —Byron's joke in *Don Juan*

I shall never forget how Julia Child, the TV chef, responded to a journalist's question as to how she began her journey as the world's favorite chef. Julia told how she and her husband, Paul, lived in France for seven years.

> Early in the '50s, after one taste of French food—that unforgettable lunch—I was hooked. The wonderful attention paid to each detail of the meal was a whole new life experience for me. But you don't just spring into good cooking full-fledged. It's like looking at a painting. You need background to know what you're looking at. I was 32-years-old when I started cooking. Until then I just ate.[22]

There are three ways of taking in food: feed, eat, dine. Animals feed and eat. Only humans dine, with a menu of manners and etiquette to match the menu of "specials." We nudge people toward God because one taste of life in Christ and you will never be the same. Until you taste the riches of the cuisine of the world's most creative Chef, you're not really dining. You're only feeding, no better than sheep or goats. The crumbs from God's table[23] are bigger and better than loaves of devil's food ... with the possible exception of devil's chocolate cake, but then chocolate is always an exception.

Food was and is, by God's design, a hedge against the heresy of Gnosticism; and food grounded Jesus in humanness: Ghosts don't eat. For Jesus, the food nudge was less the "royal road to the unconscious"[24] as it was a royal road to God. Many of Jesus' sayings undoubtedly originated in a meal setting. It was in the context of his last meal with his closest followers, his disciples, that Jesus said: "I am the Way, the Truth, and the *Zoe*." The confession of Christ as "la Via, la Verita, la Vita" wasn't Jesus' apologetic to an unbelieving world; it was his point of reference to his most committed followers.

One of the chief distinctives of the Jesus movement was his table fellowship with "sinners." Jesus eats with anyone: the wicked and scurrilous often, but even the scrupulous Pharisees. Whereas in the Hebrew Scriptures food was used to maintain boundaries, Jesus used food to bridge barriers and demolish distinctions. It's not what goes into our bodies that defiles us, the New Testament teaches, but what comes out. From the whitewashed sepulchres of the outside-in, Jesus introduced inside-out heart transplants, transformance rather than conformance.

For Jesus, it's not what you put *into* your body, but what comes out. Food and the issues around food in the first-century church were hugely significant. Food was one of the primary means by which Jesus made clear the concept of transformation from the inside causing outward changes, not the other way around, making Christianity unique. Gospel faith is not about conforming to a standard; it is about being transformed into something new. Conformity can be accomplished at one level or another, but transformation is impossible without the work of Christ.

This may have been the most revolutionary aspect of the Jesus movement. Jesus pioneered a model of holiness that flipped on its head the Hebrew understanding of holiness and in so doing made it perfectly clear that saving ourselves is impossible. What was furthest from God in Judaism—a dead body, not to mention a corpse on a cross—became the very means of our salvation. Whereas a holy life meant for the Jews a life untainted by the impure, unpolluted by the dirty and unclean, for Jesus you can't have a "clean heart" without dirty hands and jam-packed tables … filled with untouchables, undesirables, the defiled and hideous and impure.[25] Instead of locking the skeletons of disease and dross into family closets, Jesus invited them to take their place at the family feast. When Jesus left the temple and its liturgies to enter the world, he was not entering contaminated ground. Rather, Jesus taught his disciples to consecrate even life's most routine, unclean routines. The kingdom coming is the act of taking what was profane and making it holy, which was the closest Jesus came to offering his disciples a political strategy.

Every good Jewish male soaked himself daily in this antibacterial prayer: "Lord, I thank thee that I was not born female, Greek, nor slave." Here is Jesus' response to that prayer, according to the apostle Paul: "There is neither Jew nor Greek, slave nor free, male nor female, for you are all one in Christ Jesus."[26] And one for all, after which they clashed swords and ran in separate directions. Oops … wrong narrative.

For Jesus holiness was less an exaltation of the ego than an integration of the other. We are salt, but salt on the rim of the container is only any good for margaritas. Salt is to be infused through water into the food to be preserved or seasoned.

For Jesus holiness was less about the moral superiority of the individual than the moral consciousness of the community. The process of holiness being the blossoming of a person from self-absorption to other-awareness and love.

For Jesus holiness was less about being good than being God's. You can be kinda good without God, for selfish motives; but you can't help *but* be good with Christ, because it is Christ who lives through us, and he defines good.

For Jesus holiness was less about clay tablets than common tables.

> *Jesus didn't just heal lepers …*
> > *he ate with them and touched them.*[27]
> *Jesus didn't just raise the dead …*
> > *he ate with them and touched them.*[28]
> *Jesus didn't just come close to hemorrhaging women …*
> > *he touched them and channeled his strength to them.*[29]
> *Jesus didn't just love prostitutes …*
> > *he ate with them and let them touch him.*[30]

And Jesus anoints us to do the same, to become the flesh of his fountain, embodiments of his love and grace so that folks who can't fathom his love can have the splint of seeing a face and feeling a hand of skin. This is often the first step to being introduced to the source.

This was no more evident than in his eating habits. Jesus ate with those deemed impure. In the kingdom of God, nothing is accursed. No place is deconsecrated. No one is unclean. No food is forbidden. The issue is not where you're sitting but whose feet you're sitting at. The issue is not what you're eating but who you're glorifying. "So whatever you eat or drink or whatever you do, do it all for the glory of God."[31] And the glory of God, in a meal with a tax collector and a prostitute, or a crack addict and a terrorist operative … the glory of God may be first experienced in the sharing of a meal as an honored guest.

In fact, the impure, unholy, unclean, pagan, corrupt—that is who the body of Christ puts at the heart of its faith and the head of its table, saying, "For this too Christ died." Rather than get stained by the impure, Jesus practiced "contagious holiness," as Craig L. Blomberg so beautifully calls it.[32] Jesus believed that holiness was more contagious than impurity. But more than that, Jesus defined holiness as the touching of impurity. Jesus not only doesn't fear contamination, he himself contaminates evil with good by the purifying power of his nudges, nudges that rubbed off on his disciples then and his disciples today.

> And here in the dust and dirt, O here,
> The lilies of his love appear![33]
> —Henry Vaughan

Distinctive and multiple table rituals congealed quickly into one called the Lord's Supper. Early followers of Jesus also brought together the sharing of meals and the singing of hymns, as modeled by Jesus, who sang a hymn with his disciples at the conclusion of the Last Supper. Pliny the Younger wrote to Emperor Trajan that Christians "were wont to assemble on a set day before dawn and to sing a hymn among themselves … to the Christ … after which it was their custom to separate and to come together again to take food."[34] The singing part of eating became so characteristically Christian that Tertullian (160–225) claimed that the marital fights of the early Christian husbands and wives consisted of "challenging each other to see who better sings to the Lord."[35]

Second, you can count on the nudge of food because food is all about trust, and it has a way of sanctifying life. Prisoners will tell you about trust. Being incarcerated means you'll be eating food prepared by folks who may not have your best interests at heart. To accept food from others is a form of trust. When you're preparing food, and handling the "staff of life," you are inextricably connected to life and death in ways that take us beyond the "stuff of life." In this plane of existence, the three basic human needs for food, security, and friendship are so linked that the three are virtually inseparable. You can't eat by yourself; at least you don't want to. It is no fat-tire accident that the oldest surviving recipe in the world is for a social beverage that fosters security and solidarity: beer.[36]

The question of which came first, beer or bread, has been a hotly debated topic ever since the botanist Jonathan Sauer proposed that the original motivation for domesticating cereal crops (moving humanity from nomadic to settled lifestyles) was to make beer rather than bread, thus making beer, some say, the foundation for the whole of Western civilization.[37] It is difficult to know what this Ur-Sumerian beer tasted like even though we have the recipe, since in ancient times it was deemed barbaric to drink beer or wine straight. Most often beer was diluted with water (three parts water to one part wine), sometimes even with seawater. To this day liturgical traditions mix water in the wine at the offertory as a descendant of this custom, as well as a descant on the Jewish requirement to water down the Passover wine so that one is symbolically reminded that the celebration is not a bacchanal but a tasteful, faithful, and refined ritual that revs us up for God's mission in the world. People who are perfectly drunk feel as though "the whole world is like water off a duck's back,"[38] whereas for Jesus the whole rubber ducky is worth dying for.

> Wine does not love man the way man loves wine.[39]
>
> —St. Thomas Aquinas

Long before we knew anything about polymeric procyanidins, the compounds in red wine that promote cardiovascular health,[40] Psalm 104 calls "wine that gladdens the heart of man" a divine blessing.[41] Church history is wet before it is dry. Wherever Christians (and later specifically Catholics) went, they made wine, which had little to do with alcohol, but everything to do with saying the Mass. Here is an anonymous tenth- or eleventh-century song called "The Heavenly Banquet," which many medieval Christians knew by heart:

> I would like to have the men of heaven In my own house:
> With vats of good cheer Laid out for them.

I would like to have the three Marys, Their fame is so great. I would like people From every corner of Heaven.

I would like them to be cheerful In their drinking, I would like to have Jesus too Here amongst them.

I would like a great lake of beer For the King of Kings, I would like to be watching Heaven's family Drinking it through all eternity.[42]

Before the Puritans set sail for America, they stuffed more wine than water onto their boats. "Sack-posset" was a medicinal brew of sack,[43] sugar, spices, milk, and beaten eggs that was traditionally served at weddings in early colonial America. (Now it's sold as a protein drink with caffeine!) France's temperance movement made the distinction between alcohol produced by fermentation and that by distillation—the latter was acceptable, with temperance "advocates" even urging increased wine production. One treatise on temperance defines a temperate diet as "twelve ounces, neither more nor less of 'bread, meat, the yolk of an egg, and soup' and 'fourteen ounces of wine' per day."[44] Beer or wine was assumed to be a part of those fourteen ounces. Temperance in times past didn't always mean teetotalism. Even temperance should be taken in temperance; all things in moderation, including moderation. More of a good thing is not always good, or holy. There is no such mathematical concept of "more equal." Perhaps if temperance had been called something like "balance," we might have recognized those critical points past which balance is unbalance.

> The Creator, though condemning man to eat to live, invites
> him to do so by appetite, and rewards him by enjoyment.[45]
> —Jean-Anthelme Brillat-Savarin

But whether bread or beer came first I care not a chicken or an egg; both are symbols of the partnership between the Creator and the created, the fruit of the earth and the work of human hands. Jesus gives us his body as food and drink. But not just any food. It's bread. And not just any drink. It's wine. Jesus didn't say, "I am the broccoli come down from heaven." Or, "I am the lentil come down from heaven." Or, "I am the pomegranate juice that came down from heaven." Jesus said, "I am the bread of life. Whoever comes to me will never be hungry, and whoever believes in me will never be thirsty."[46] Sick stomachs want bread, not enchiladas.

The way God has built participation into the creation is reflected in the bread and wine. The taste of a loaf lies in the contact of the bread with the palate, not in the grain itself; the taste of wine lies in the contact of the uncorked liquid with the palate, not in the grapes themselves. In fact, even the taste of grapes doesn't even lie in the fruit itself, but in the contact of the fruit with the palate. Truth lies not in the lines of symbols printed on the pages of a book. Truth lies in the meeting of the Word and flesh, and in that meeting we can taste the mystery of God and taste the greatness of God.

Hence the Eucharist. There is no greater example of the importance of semiotics to Christian faith than the sacraments of Baptism and Communion. Just as Baptism is not a bath, Communion is not a meal. In one of the worst upbraidings in the NT, believers are asked to "eat at home" because of the competition that was occurring inappropriately around the table. The food is there for semiotics, not for sustenance. It takes place not in ordinary time, but in sacramental time. The power of these symbols of bread and wine is in their imaging of partnership between the Creator and created. Both combine the fruit of the earth and the work of human hands. Admittedly, bread and wine are the best images to convey our participation in the divine creation, but coffee and chocolate, my two preferred primary food groups, come a close second. It doesn't hurt to dream.

It has always been my conviction that we have totally misinterpreted John the Baptist. I can get no one else to agree with me, but I am stubborn enough to try one more time to conscript you to my conviction—sort of a voice howling from the margins. Let's start with the things most people agree on:

> *JB was the forerunner and cousin of Jesus.*
> *JB was born in Judea, the son of elderly parents Zechariah and Elizabeth.*
> *JB and Jesus were born six months apart in towns that were within sight of each other.*
> *JB baptized Jesus at the Jordan River, calling him "the Lamb of God."*
> *JB appeared in the wilderness, announcing the coming of the Messiah, the arrival of the kingdom, and the repentance of sin through Baptism.*
> *Jesus apprenticed to JB and chose from John's followers the core group of his disciples.*
> *JB wore camel skin and ate locust and wild honey.*

Of course, we know a lot more about the last of the Hebrew prophets than this. (For example, John the Baptist was imprisoned and executed by Herod in about AD 30 because of a dance, making it not surprising that Baptists have been so opposed to dancing ever since.) He called Jesus out from his apprenticeship ("Are you the one?") and pointed his disciples away from himself and toward Jesus ("He must increase, but I must decrease"). But the issue becomes how do we interpret what we know; and this is where I want to start smashing the stereotypes about JB.

If asked to come up with a current image of John the Baptist, most people would conjure up a bearded, unkempt sidewalk protester holding high a handmade sign that warns, "The End Is Near. Repent." I believe that is about as far from the real John the Baptist as you can get.

The best way of thanking God is to take his goodness with all our palate ... God reads our hearts, and he knows whether we taste his kindness, or not. Enjoyment is the sincerest thanks.[47]

—C. S. Lewis's friend Austin Farrer

First of all, John the Baptist lived in the wilderness. Seldom did he make an appearance in towns and villages. The wilderness was feared for its wild animals, robbers, and other dangers. John was not an in-your-face prophet. He was somebody you really had to want to see, since you took your life in your hands when you went to hear him.

Second, we are not really sure what "animal's hair" meant. In fact, the Greek supports "animal fur" that was smooth and silky as much as "animal hair" that was rough and scratchy. The question of how a scantily clad John the Baptist could survive the extreme cold might be answered if JB draped himself in fur.

Third, the foods our ancestors prized and ate can be quite different from anything we imagine today. Our average meal is better than the special feast food in biblical times.[48] Sources of protein were always problematic in the ancient world, and one of the most nutritious and delicious protein sources was locusts. Bugs to this day are popular snacks in 113 nations, especially throughout much of Africa—even to the point where so many people were eating mopane (moh-PAH-nee) worms[49] biologists began worrying that the worms may be headed for extinction.

Of all the insects eaten, however, crickets and locusts are, gram for gram, more nutritious than pork. They boast a true food-conversion efficiency close to twenty times better than that of beef.[50] In Thailand today, farmers plant corn not for the crop, but as bait for locusts, which are then harvested and sold to local markets and urban street vendors.[51] Five-star restaurants in Mexico get their five stars partly because they serve insects, not just seasonally, but daily.[52] In case any of you are feeling a little superior at this point, remember this: What crab, lobster, and shrimp are to the sea, crickets, cockroaches, and locusts are to the soil—"the original white meat."

> No love that in a family dwells ...
> Can with this single Truth compare—
> That God was Man in Palestine
> And lives today in Bread and Wine.[53]
> —John Betjeman's Catholic "Christmas" ditty

Finally, in Jesus' day only the Mayans and Aztecs knew anything about chocolate. The equivalent experience of sweetness for the Middle East, however, was honey. And the Godiva of honey was wild honey. Eat a bar of chocolate today, and you might experience the whole of JB's diet, since the FDA allows up to 60 insect fragments per six 100-gram chocolate samples.

Here's my thesis that no one believes but that no one has disproven: What if John the Baptist weren't so much showing what it meant to live an austere, ascetic life in preparation for Jesus' coming? What if John the Baptist's diet was less about veganism or xerophagy and more about signs of kingdom food and heavenly banquets? What if locusts and wild honey were the first-century equivalents of prime rib and Godiva chocolates, in congruence with his "kingdom now" message and as a prophetic sign of the coming Messiah?

> We will look at Christians' role as "appetizers" for the world.
> We are to live in such a way that when the world bites into us,
> gets a taste of us, its appetite will be stimulated for more. We
> are to be hors d'oeuvres of the future kingdom banquet.[54]
> —Tim Dearborn

In the ancient world meals had many functions. A meal could ratify covenants, draw up treaties, anoint kings, celebrate community events. But most importantly, meals had a social function that fostered feelings of belonging and security. That's why in Jesus' day, meals were long, drawn-out rituals filled with elaborate social codes. What else do you do after a long hard day? Circle the wagons with family, friends, and guests; and exercise your skills of deipnosophy: the art of table conversation.

He who receives guests, and pays no personal care
to the repast offered them, is not worthy to have friends.[55]
—A Brillat-Savarin aphorism

The nudging of food is good for the body as well as for the soul. The spiritual nonnutritional nature of food is not just evident in the intimacy of the table. Table talk is being shown to have beneficial effects on health and heart, almost as if it were a nutritional value in and of itself. Positive experiences of community, good social relationships, especially coupled with fit food rituals, keep the heart healthy and the arteries free flowing.[56] What I hate about B&Bs—the three-hour breakfasts with strangers—are the very things that make them so heart healthy. They were also norms in Jesus' day, when you shared many if not most meals with strangers as part of life's everyday rituals of hospitality. It just may be that the more fast food on the run and road (one-fifth of all meals today are consumed in a car),[57] the greater the desire for slow-food sit-downs at the table. Evangelism today is best played out where it has always been: elbows nudging at dining tables and shoulders rubbing at kitchen sinks.

Food creates an endorphin high that is a pleasant environment for relationship. If you're going to sit around with people you're not completely comfortable with, why not make sure the lot of you have a full plate of endorphins? If you can't get along despite the postfood endorphin rush, maybe it's time for some serious heart work.

> Shared meals are often more important to creating
> community than are shared worship experiences.[58]
>
> —Daniel Sack

It would be hard to overestimate the cultural significance of meals and mealtimes.[59] The foods we eat, and how we eat them, reveal as much about ourselves as the words we speak and write. Eating is a sign language that communicates as powerfully as literary ways of expressing ourselves. Food preferences are signs of our origins, as well as signs of our discernments and directions for the future.

Disciples of Jesus are as much Homo eucharisticus as Homo sapiens. Just as Jesus was made known to them in the breaking of the bread,[60] so Jesus is made known to us in food. As people who live by the Eucharist, who live eucharistically, what kind of food nudges best convey Christ to people? How do we nudge eucharistically?

1. Nudge toward Abundance

Cardinal Basil Hume (1923–1999), archbishop of Westminster for twenty-three years and one of the best loved churchmen of the twentieth century, said that when he was a child, whenever he was tempted to steal an apple from the pantry, he thought he heard God's voice warning him against it. As he grew older, he thought he heard God say something different: "Go on. Take two apples."[61]

There is much confusion abroad as to what level of existence a disciple should expect. The upper hand currently seems to be with a minimalist mood and mentality extolling a table of sparse provisions, even poverty. The poor are seen as purer, more virtuous, less corruptible, and closer to God than all others. Conversely, the further one is from poverty, the more one is made to feel unclean, unrighteous, selfish, and guilty.

Years ago, while seeking the presidential nomination, John F. Kennedy spoke to a group in Appalachia. Most of the people in his audience were unemployed; many were mine workers. Kennedy confessed to them that he had never been in need financially. He said, "I have never been poor. I know that some of you are unemployed and you suffer. You need the basic things in life. I understand that. Although I have never been poor, I want to say to you that with compassion and empathy I think I can relate to you, and I care."

He continued in this apologetic vein for some time, until when he had finished speaking, an old-timer, a miner who had been through many a winter and many a storm, came up to him and said, "Mr. Kennedy, about that poverty you mentioned. I want to tell you, son, you ain't missed a thing!"

> Man eats too much. Thus he lives on only a quarter of what he consumes. The doctors, however, live on the remaining three-quarters.[62]
> —Ancient Egyptian papyrus

Jesus said, "I have come that they may have life, and that they may have it more abundantly."[63] But the abundance God promises us is simple things like daily bread, neighborly conversation, and the day-after-day reality of life lived in relationship with the divine. The abundance God promises us is also not to be used for our own private gain and profit, so we might build bigger and bigger barns to lord it over others and to hoard it for ourselves. Our abundance is to be shared with a needy world.

There is nothing miserly about God in the whole Bible. Jesus appeared to some to be a gluttonous alcoholic … guess everything is relative. We are introduced to a God who "pours out grace abundantly"[64] and who is lavish with love. Paul coins a term for "overflow," *huperpleonazo,* which means to be plentiful, great in quantity, with surplus amounts. God's goodness and grace are hyperfilling, superabundant, overflowing. God's favor toward us is given in abundant measure. Or as I used to sing it at holiness camp meetings: "Marvelous, infinite, matchless grace, freely bestowed on all who believe."[65]

Nudge evangelism focuses on what you have, your abundance, not on what you're lacking, your scarcity. Jesus constantly had to nudge his disciples not to focus on what they didn't have ("We only have five loves and two fish") but on what they did have ("Wow! We're not starting from scratch; we've got five and two"). Nudge people to see how God has already started something that is so far beyond the borders of our imaginings.

> Our Lord finds our desires not too strong, but too weak. We are half-hearted creatures, fooling about with drink and sex and ambition, when infinite joy is offered us, like an ignorant child who wants to go on making mud pies in a slum because he cannot imagine what is meant by the offer of a holiday at the sea. We are far too easily pleased.[66]
> —C. S. Lewis, *The Weight of Glory*

2. Nudge toward Ambrosia Nights, Balsam Days
"Why does Jesus have to taste so bad?"

This question was asked by a child after taking her first Communion.

With his first miracle of Cana wine, Jesus calls his disciples to a flavor-burst faith in the tradition of the prophets, one of whom prophesied "a feast of rich food for all peoples, a banquet of aged wine—the best of meats and finest of wines."[67] Nudgers move people toward a faith that is spicier and more flavorful than anything they've ever tasted. Fewer and fewer people want to be ladled as chicken soup for the soul anyway.

None of the aromatic roots, seeds, twigs, and nuts are essential for human health. Most are quite irrelevant to the preservation of the human species. Yet nothing has so motivated the exploration of our planet as their acquisition. The Spice Route, which spanned three millennia and girdled the globe, was paved by the search for withered berries, dead buds, gluey gums, knobbly roots, crumpled membranes, and desiccated barks.[68] The fifth-century BC Greek historian Herodotus, sometimes called "the father of history," believed that cinnamon grew in the middle of a lake, over which dangerous batlike creatures, "which screech horribly," tormented those who came to harvest it.[69] Every taste of cinnamon was a taste of darkness, daring, and escape.

The nudge toward spicy will be more important in the future than it ever was in the past for a couple of reasons. First, boomer taste buds are dulling, and the longer people live, the more seasoned their food will become. And healthy. Foodaceuticals (or what some are calling "nutraceuticals") officially began when the Food and Drug Administration proclaimed oatmeal and oat-based cereals good for the human heart. Now people are increasingly consuming foods like walnuts ("walnutritious") and pomegranate juice that have scientifically proven health benefits.

Second, Google generations boast diverse palates and prize diversity in all its forms. When my kids go out to dinner, the big debate is not whether to go to Denny's or Applebee's, but will it be sushi or Indian or Afghani. Forty percent of teenagers say that Chinese food is their favorite, followed by Mexican (21 percent) and Japanese (12 percent). USAmerican fare—good old hamburgers, hot dogs, and fries—scored only 9 percent. I know ten-year-olds who can tell you the difference between Szechuan and Hunan Chinese cuisine and why they prefer one over the other when they aren't experimenting with "fusion foods." What makes "peasant foods" like cabbage rolls taste differently when they are made in Greece, Hungary, Germany, Sweden, etc. is more the spice flavors than product content. Whether your tastes tend more toward the greasy spoon or gourmet, it's the saffron and the star anise that bring on the ambrosia nights and balsam days.[70]

Third, the soul-numbing blandness of suburbanized America with its generic franchises and placeless malls is giving rise to the celebration of particularity and the assertion of integrity. Look at Listerine, which comes now in Vanilla Mint, Cool Mint, and all sorts of colors and flavors. I don't want my antiseptic mouthwash to taste good or look good. I want it to taste awful and kill germs. To sweeten it up and make it taste like cream soda is to lack authenticity. Christianity is a strong and agitating religion. To boil down its truth to bland and unchewable mush is a *Saturday Night Live*–able offense at best and to turn it into an entirely different religion at worst.

3. Nudge toward the Hungry

What does it say that diet industries flourish right alongside fast-food industries? Obesity in the United States is associated with poverty, but poverty has little to do with hunger.

Food is all about relationships.[71] The easy pleasures of food may be a masking of our deeper hunger for connection, for truth, for life. The fact that 84 percent of USAmerican women are on a diet may say less about the outer body than the inner soul. We are seeking satisfactions for our hungers in chocolate-covered Rice Krispies and not in relationships. Above and beyond satisfying our hunger for food, eucharistic nudges nurture the right hungers and thirsts. Food is more than fuel. Food is intimacy, peace, and healing. Of her long marriage, Madeleine L'Engle wrote, "Bread we ate together became more than bread."[72]

We are all artists. And some of the artists I admire most are those who have mastered the art of living and the art of friendship. Al and Sue Deccho are my best friends on Orcas Island. I am not jealous that dozens of island-ers would make the same claim. At their home, Al and Sue have mastered the art of nurturing good hungers. Even though they don't say so, every meal is patterned after the way Jesus ate: a relaxed, unhurried, forgiving-if-you're-late, laughing, conversing, catch-up-on-the-news time of delight and healing. When Al and Sue talk about islanders, they can tell you exactly what food they served to whom and when; what the table conversation was about; and what is important to the people who dined at their table. When you leave their driveway, you have been "fed" in every way.

America is the only country that goes hunting
on a full stomach.[73]
—Comedian Chris Rock

If the Scriptures are our guide, Jesus is waiting for us where there is hunger. Jesus appears through hunger, either your own or someone else's.[74] When we fast, we are purposefully using the desire, even the pain, to keep us aware. We do not fast out of a sense of self-flagellation. We fast out of a sense of desire.

In fact, hunger is almost a precondition for recognizing the risen Lord in Luke. Eucharistic nudges are taps on the shoulder to share the banquet with the hungry. Where is Jesus to be found? In the cry of the hungry. The cry of the hungry brings Jesus to life. Hunger is sacred, not because hunger is holier than a full stomach, but because hunger is where Jesus is to be found. Christians bless bread and wine to do more than "recall" Jesus' memory. Christians bless bread and wine to recall where to find the risen Christ—in the people most welcome but least welcomed to the table.

It would be hard to count on one hand the number of cultures where people eat alone. In no other culture but ours is food a private ritual. Food is a social ritual. You prepare food not to eat it yourself but to share it with others. You share your food with those with whom you share your life.

Here is a sign that speaks volumes about how sacred the food nudges of a church are and how welcoming its table is, not just to people who are already fed and full, but to people who are hungry. On the back of each pew in St. Patrick's Cathedral in New York City are these signs: "St. Patrick's doors are open to all. Please take your handbag with you to Communion." Fair warning that eating here is not a private affair.[75]

4. Nudge toward the Worst …

When Jesus' disciples were more interested in lunch than in a "fast woman" Jesus found by a well in Samaria, he told them there were other kinds of food than what they could put in their bellies. Jesus then revealed his favorite "food": to please his Father and to fulfill the mission for which he was sent.[76]

It is in meeting the needs through us of the "worst," both the worst of the bottom and the worst of the top, that many of us ever experience the love of God, and from this experience eventually see God's love for us.

The worst affront one can inflict on the cook at home is to come home having already eaten. Working in the kitchen preparing food is a labor of love. As the food is prepared, it prepares the heart of the cook. To dis that preparation is to insult the cook. One must bring his appetite to dinner.

God has made almost every part of our lives cyclical: The desires we have, which are God ordained—food, water, sex, companionship, even a sense of his presence—all are cyclical. God has also ordained a means by which we satiate these desires. If we're hungry now, we eat. But we'll be hungry again. If for some reason we are unwilling to wait for the cycle that God has for us and take some sort of shortcut that fulfills the desire on our terms, this is called addiction. If we get angry, we may *kill* the desire, which is worse than addiction.

When we short-circuit the cyclical hunger that God has ordained, when we fill ourselves with our addictions and not our God-given appetites, we show up to the banquet with a belly full of junk food. The worst dinner guest is not the one in horrid need. The worst dinner guest is the one who ate a large meal of junk food before arriving, thereby nullifying any appreciation for the game hens.

5. Nudge toward Good-for-You Food

All impressions are nudges, and all nudges are food. It is as true that everything is "food for thought" as it is true that "you are what you eat." Paul said that when you feed on junk thoughts, you find yourself living in a junkyard, just as when you feed on junk food you look in the mirror and discover yourself living in a junk body.

Nudge away from junk-food-fattened lifestyles. Nudge toward health and holiness.

Of the three main roles Jesus performed—preacher, teacher, healer—the role of healer is most important for evangelism in the twenty-first century. It may also have been the most important for evangelism in the first century, since Marcus Borg estimates that "more healing stories are told about him [Jesus] than about anybody else in the Jewish tradition."[77]

In 1997, the World Health Organization proposed that *health* should be defined *not* as an absence of disease but as "a dynamic state of complete physical, mental, spiritual, and social well being." This definition of *health* returns us to the original definition of *salvation* in William Tyndale's first English translation of the New Testament (1524). The NT Greek words of *healing, health, wholeness,* and *salvation* are the same words, and in Tyndale's translation of the Bible they were interchangeable.[78] The good news is all about "health" and "healing" and "wholeness," and nudgers will be the first to point out how. The restoration healing of Christ is not back to where our health started to deteriorate, or even to a point just before we screwed up. It is restoration to a state we have never experienced before.

You don't think people are interested in healing? Try looking up therapists in the Yellow Pages or on Google. Just as food will increasingly be seen as medicine (foodaceuticals), so nudgers will encourage the Christian life as a healthy way of living on this planet and will challenge the unhealthy, unfit reputation it has.

Nudgers will lay bare a smorgasbord of options of what a healthy life looks like. Fats or carbs? Three square meals or continuous grazing? Raw or cooked? Organic or industrial? Veg or vegan? Meat or mock meat? The answers to these questions are so culturally based (e.g., the Cantonese of China claim that "if its back faces Heaven it's eatable"[79]) that to identify one diet with a "kingdom diet" is as wise as identifying one political party platform with the kingdom of God.

A few things are clear. First, humans are omnivores. We eat anything.

We are at opposite extremes from pandas, with their monotonous diet of bamboo. In fact, our omnivorousness is what makes our eating social—e.g., pandas do not come together to feast or dine. Humans start out univores (we consume only mother's milk), but we quickly learn both to love and to hate all different kinds of foods.

Increasing numbers of people in the future, both Christian and non-Christian, will identify themselves as herbivores. That means our food nudges need to be vegetarian-friendly. Rudolf Nureyev was a prude about alcohol and drugs, but he lived on meat. British ballerina Dame Margot Fonteyn's mother once served Nureyev chicken instead of the raw beefsteak he lived on. He looked at his plate and responded: "Chicken dinner, chicken performance."[80]

> Better is a dinner of vegetables where love is
> than a fatted ox and hatred with it.
> —Proverbs 15:17 NRSV

But before we carnivores sneer and leer at the growing hoards of herbivores and remind them that vegetables were never high on the biblical list of preferred foodstuffs,[81] we need to remember that there are good biological, ecological, and even biblical reasons for this revolution in our eating habits.

Biologically, 70 percent of antibiotics produced today are pumped into livestock, and we block this fact at our peril.[82] Food production is such a gas-guzzler of nitrogen-fertilizer "fixing" that it accounts for 20 percent of American petroleum consumption.

Ecologically, the average U.S. citizen uses about 20,000 liters of water a day (that's over 500 gallons) just for his or her consumption of beef. You don't have to be a member of PETA to have your heart broken by the sights of industrial CAFOs (Confined Animal Feeding Operations). Industrial eating cuts the food chain and obscures all relationships and connections with what we are eating. One key spiritual implication in the current revolution in eating is the restoration of the links in that chain. And we haven't even begun to address the taste issues in the difference between factory and farm. Bad food is like bad art: factory kitsch.

Biblically, Jesus ended animal sacrifice by making the Eucharist vegetarian. In spite of histories of vegetarianism, which attempt to make Jesus, Paul, and the Christian movement into a vegetarian regime up until the time of Constantine (who allegedly poured molten lead down the throats of Christian vegetarians), we don't know if Jesus ate flesh. But we do know he ate fish. Early church fathers like Tertullian, Origen, Boniface, St. Jerome, and John Chrysostom were vegetarians, but most likely they were the exceptions that proved the omnivore rule. Clement of Alexandria claimed a brother in the apostle Matthew, who ate only seeds, nuts, and vegetables. "It is far better to be happy," he wrote, "than to have your bodies act as graveyards for animals."[83]

Nudging in the future will be sensitive to the growing numbers of herbivores, and churches would be foresighted to consider not just putting in "memory gardens" for members but kitchen gardens for the whole neighborhood. Why haven't churches rediscovered French kitchen gardens or the *potager* (pronounced *potajay*), where the community can gather and grow intermingled vegetables, fruits, and flowers? What if Christians nudged their neighbors by replacing the monoculture of lawns (especially in climates where turfgrass doesn't belong) and its noisy, smoky upkeep with a unique viviculture of plants and bushes and wildflowers? Or even a vegetable garden that was planted by a group of people called "Christians" who not only weren't afraid of people stealing their produce but also invited people who needed food to make themselves at home?

It is forbidden to live in a town
in which there is no vegetable garden.[84]
—Babylonian Talmud

Second, we're all picky eaters. Foods that elicit the strongest love-hate reactions? Some that are best for you: okra, lima beans, brussels spouts, broccoli, sauerkraut, anchovies, etc. Since 20 to 30 percent of us have some kind of physical-food sensitivity and the rest of us have "food issues," it is a good nudge to ask if the person being invited to the table has food allergies, whether temperamental or medical.

> A glutton is one who raids the icebox
> for a cure for spiritual malnutrition.[85]
> —Frederick Buechner

Third, every culture and almost every family develops their own food rituals. For example, some people don't like to have their food touching on the plate. Others only like to eat one food at a meal. Others only like to eat one food at a time. These latter people have organized and call themselves "componetarians" with a Web site dedicated to this mission statement: "We believe that life is best savored one flavor at a time." It is a good nudge not to judge people's food rituals, no matter how peculiar.

The taste of faith will reflect the five tastes detected by the human tongue. Faith can be salty, sweet, sour, bitter, or *umami* (a Japanese word that describes the aftertaste shared by foods like asparagus, tomatoes, Parmesan cheese, etc.). Each taste will also have its own "mouthfeel," the quality that makes us like our potato chips crisp, our gumdrops chewy, our custards creamy, and our jelly firm. In a culture that wants to know "Why does Jesus have to taste so bad?" nudgers never leave people with a bad aftertaste, only the ferment and the foretaste.

Fourth, nudges will gently debunk spam. In a culture where inauthenticity is the norm, where the majority of our mail is fake, where fake foods adorn menus from fast food to haute cuisine, where people can live fake lives in Second Life, nudges will celebrate the real and betray the toxic. I love to serve guests pomegranate juice and then tell pomegranate and cranberry stories. Pomegranates are a beautiful and beneficial fruit that hung from the hem of the high priest's robe.[86] In fact, the "honey" part of "land of milk and honey" was not bees' honey but fruit trees, most likely pomegranates. Cranberries contain more phenols, antioxidants thought to prevent cancer, stroke, and heart disease, than any other common fruit except pomegranates. The problem is that the typical cranberry juice has few cranberries in it anymore, only flavored fructose. Hence my nudge of pomegranate juice.

6. Nudge People to "Try Something Different"

One of the images I shall never forget in the story of the Lewis and Clark expeditions was the way 10,000 pounds of the best salmon ever tasted by humans lay hanging on the racks drying out. The explorers and their crew refused to eat it and asked for dog meat.

Here are some supper ideas for you.

There are Emmaus suppers, which are surprise manifestations and revelations of what has already been going on in your life.[87]

There are Gethsemane suppers, where your soul struggles with God in the aftermath of betrayal and in anticipation of carrying crosses too heavy for you to bear, the conflict within and conflict without reflected in "Not what I will, but what You will be done."[88]

There are Bethany suppers, where you hang with your best friends and not worry about what you say or how you appear.

There are Upper Room suppers, where you gather around a new loaf of bread and a new bottle of wine to decide whether to press on or turn back.

There are Cana suppers, where in small, drab, windblown places God wants to do something miraculous and totally out of keeping with its reputation for poverty and pomegranates.

There are Mount of Olives suppers, where you picnic on high ridges and weep over those places and people you love but don't seem to know how to love back.

There are Mount Zion suppers, where you find strength in others' emotional highs even though you're at an emotional low.

There are Zarephath suppers, where an act of faith stretches beyond reason and rationality.

And there are Sermon on the Mount suppers, where a kid and some fish feed a crowd.

> The discovery of a new dish is more beneficial to humans
> than the discovery of a new star.[89]
> —Jean-Anthelme Brillat-Savarin

7. Nudge People to Taste for Themselves

You have to taste Jesus for yourself. You can describe what a fruit tastes like, but it's not until you actually touch and taste it that you find out for yourself what a fruit is about and you enjoy all its benefits.

The world eats three ways: sticks, forks, fingers. But the truth is that all of us eat with our fingers. To eat any other way is like making out and whispering sweet nothings through an interpreter. Even those who eat with forks and sticks still eat with fingers. We just mask our hand-eating with words. The success of the fast-food industry is not that it is fast, but that it is finger food.

In fact, all food is finger food. Every cook makes the food by hand. It's cleaned by hand. It's cut by hand. It's mixed by hand. It may end up on sticks and forks, but all food is at heart handmade. To be sure, there are times for forks: fettuccine Alfredo, for example. There are times for silverware/spoons: cream of mushroom soup. But even then, who could imagine either pasta or soup without bread, which is finger food?

> Eating with your hands is a sensuous indulgence, a meeting of
> soul and skin. Satisfying on a deep, animal level. It's getting

soaked in a monsoon, taking off your shoes and squishing wet
sand between your toes, making mud pies, impaling raspberries
on your fingertips and kissing them off one by one till your mouth
is juicy and full. It's squashing grapes underfoot, playing music
instead of hearing it, slapping fistfuls of your first birthday
cake into your mouth. The mutual giving and receiving between
fingers and tongue. Primal and earthy and natural.[90]

—Keridwen Cornelius

Faith in God is finger food. The Bible says, "Taste and see that the Lord is good." Encouraging people to taste the "Tree of Life" is the biggest nudge you can give. The Jesus Way is a path that leads to health (salvation), happiness (altruism), and freedom (liberty). Some people think that they've lost God's address, like Job: "If only I knew where to find him."[91] But God hasn't moved away from us ("Never will I leave you; never will I forsake you"[92]). We've allowed our lives to move away from the place of bread, and we need to be nudged to find God's address again.

Nudgers talk about Jesus the way the Food Network talks about food. Nudgers will serve what it takes to help someone get real with Jesus. The ultimate nudge makes us want to cook more than eat.

Conclusion

One of my Drew seminary students, Kerry Tilden, as part of her evangelism project, nudged her Maplewood, New Jersey, church to sponsor a Community Supported Agriculture (CSA) project where a single farm would provide locally grown, organic vegetables at a fixed price if purchased in advance. For the project to go forward, the church had to sell 50 shares (feeds 2–4/week for 25 weeks) at $500/share within a few months. They sold 100+ shares and had to turn a few families away.

Much to everyone's surprise, two-thirds of the families involved are not active in the church. Church people are meeting new people in the community and sharing information about how they use their vegetables, what new vegetables they are trying (garlic scapes and pea shoots with flowers still on them). One church member started a blog where people share online what they do with their weekly vegetables and which ones they like the best.[93] The farmer has convinced other farmers to expand the use of the delivery truck to include preordered grass-fed organic beef, organic free-range chickens and eggs, and goat cheese. Because of the demand and the up-front money, the farm agreed to partner in another CSA, requiring them to hire eleven additional employees and add forty acres to their production. Here is an evangelism project that not only brought new life to the church, but also created local jobs.

🅐 Discover More Online

CHECK OUT INTERACTIVES FOR YOUR PERSONAL OR SMALL-GROUP USE
AND MUCH MORE ON THE NUDGE WEB SITE:

WWW.NUDGETHEBOOK.COM

Chapter 6

PICTURE: USE YOUR EYES

Do You Have a Vision for the Kingdom?

Seeing Jesus

In his classic text *The Fifth Discipline* (1994), Peter Senge begins with an account of what "Hello" sounds like in South Africa. Among the tribes in northern Natal, they exchange greetings with the phrase "*Sawu bona.*" It means "I see you." The ritual reply is "*Sikhona,*" which means "I am here."

The order is important. You never say "*Sikhona*" without first having been greeted with "*Sawu bona.*" Why? Until you see me, I have no existence. Your seeing me brings me into being.[1]

> Our whole business in this life is to restore to health
> the eyes of the heart, whereby God may be seen.[2]
> —St. Augustine

The semiotics of the eyes involves seeing with the eyes of Christ and bringing Jesus into picture form. "As a man is, so he sees," wrote eighteenth-century graphic artist and watercolorist William Blake.[3] We must move beyond hearing to seeing. As the little boy said to his multitasking mother, "Mom, listen to me, but this time with your eyes." It is so easy for us to see without looking.[4]

The spiritual blindness that results in our missing the cues that Christ provides for us first to see each other and then to nudge each other is not nearly the problem of seeing full well, but *misinterpreting* what we see.

Job's friends saw, yet in their spiritually distorted sight, their eyes produced the wrong interpretation, and this resulted in serious issues between them, and therefore between them and God. Job's relationship with God changed when he went from hearing God to seeing God: "My ears had heard of you, but now my eyes have seen you."[5]

People who heard "the good news" were more impressed by what they saw than what they heard. It wasn't "hear how they talk about love" or "hear some new definitions of love" but "see how they love." Jesus' disciples had their eyesight improved with the lens of love. And their lives reflected that love. That's what made them unstoppable: Their pictures of "love come down" became the greatest stories ever made visible.

Many decades ago, some men were panning for gold in the state of Montana. (By the way, "miners" and "forty-niners" were primarily illegals … they had no legal "right" to do what they were doing on someone else's land.) The prospectors organized themselves into an informal cooperative and agreed up front that if they should strike gold they would tell no one about their find.

After weeks of hard panning and digging, one of them found an unusual stone. Breaking it open, they were excited to see that it contained gold. Soon the prospectors discovered an abundance of the precious metal. They began shouting "We've found it! We've found gold! We've struck it rich!"

They then proceeded to go to a nearby town for additional supplies. Before leaving camp, they reminded each other of the pledge of absolute secrecy. While they were in town, none of them breathed a word about their good fortune. However, when they were getting ready to return to camp, they were horrified to discover several hundred of the local townsmen preparing to follow them. And when they asked who had revealed the secret of their discovery, the answer came: "No one had to. Your faces showed it."

I, John, saw.

—Revelation 7:2

The Greek verb for "seeing" is highly irregular: from *horaō* we get the word *theory*, or to look at something from a distance; but another form of the verb *to see* comes from the noun *eidos,* which means the shape of something visible, from which we get *idea* but also *idol.*[6] The history of the last five hundred years is hidden in that one sentence.

In the Gutenberg world of modernity, the eye reigned supreme. The visual bias to knowing became part of print culture. In fact, sight became the sense of reason and the intellect. What can be known was identified with what can be seen, leading to a tyranny of the eye. This despotism of the eye has given us a new cultural currency to replace the "word"—the picture; it has given us celebrity culture; and it has given us an ophthalmic leadership fetish that collapses being a "leader" with being a "visionary," or what someone has dubbed "visionary bogosity."[7] Of all the magic keys to leadership, vision is the most magical. A series of conclusions on why smart executives fail all focus not on lack of vision, but on failure to pay attention to the visions of others.[8] A vision is too often "done" to institutions by a leader, making it a passive rather than participatory process. In some ways we need to learn how *not* to have a vision, even to make things purposively vague, which allows everyone space to shape the vision so that they are not being treated as objects but as subjects. You might call this the failure to have "hearing eyes."[9] Instead of building consensus around shared values and visions, we ought to be building trust around shared relationships and journeys.

There is tragic irony in living in a world where the richer our visual landscape, the more impoverished our capacity to perceive it. Frank Lloyd Wright felt this irony deeply and built Falling Waters, not so the cascading waterfalls could be seen all the time from the house, but so the residents would have to go out from the house to view and enjoy the falls.

Do you have eyes but fail to see,
and ears but fail to hear?[10]

—Jesus

There's more than meets the eye … to life, to love, to everything. The eyes are easily deceived and cannot be trusted, which is why God gave us eyelids but not earlids. Note how easily the eye can be fooled by the right combination of sleight of hand and word of mouth. A pencil half-immersed in water looks bent but is perfectly straight when you take it out. Every driver learns to handle mirages of water, which appear on the highway almost as often as deer. Then there are the "blind spots." We have them, or what Jesus called "logs in the eye."[11]

There is an old proverb: "Ninety percent of what you see is behind your eyes." What you see in large measure depends on what you bring to the "picture," which is one reason why we need to get the picture out there as quickly as possible so that we can determine if we're all seeing the same thing. Even then, even when we know we're all looking at the same "thing," none of us ever sees that same thing as anyone else. Every person who sees "you" sees a different you, because their eyes arrange your dots of information in ways particular to them. In summary, our eyes are portrait painters. Each of us sees others, not as they are in some pure form, but as our eyes have painted them.

Nudge evangelism restores the art of seeing. The art of seeing is first the art of seeing things as they actually are, and then after being able to see the visible as truthfully as possible, to see the invisible. Seeing in community develops the grace of common experience, and with such triangulated perceptions we are given the radar to see the invisible. Seeing in community is seeing what God is doing as our sight is percolated through all that God has invested in our lives.

To see a vision means to perceive the invisible. For disciples of Jesus, our "vision" is Christ, as the old hymn puts it: "Be Thou My Vision."[12]

> The basic command of religion is not "do this!"
> or "do not do that!" but simply "look!"[13]
>
> —Gai Eaton

Of the 50,000-plus leadership books published every year, there may be no more quoted Bible verse than Proverbs 29:18: "Where there is no vision, the people perish" (KJV).

This verse, however, is often quoted without bothering to delve deeply into what it really means.[14] The TNIV and NIV are the most lynx-eyed in seeing the correct translation: "Where there is no revelation, the people cast off restraint." A true "vision" is something received not generated, a word from God often heard in the night.[15]

The vision in days of old was "the Law." The vision today is Jesus. "I am the *light* of the world."[16] "Seeing" was one of Jesus' favorite metaphors for spiritual awareness: "The eye is the lamp of the body. If your eyes are good, your whole body will be full of light."[17] Follow Christ, and vision follows. If we can say we are called to be a people of vision, it is another way of saying we are called to be a people who follow Christ.

A denominational executive always asks his clergy, "So, what's your vision?" When he saw me one day in an elevator, we chatted and sure enough, "So, Sweet, what's your vision?" I replied, "Sir, *I* don't have a vision." He was incredulous: "What! How can you possibly say that? You must have a vision. Aren't you one of the church's visionaries? You're a leader, aren't you?"

"No, Bishop. I'm not a leader. I'm a follower. I'm following a vision, but it's not my vision. The vision is Jesus. I grew up singing a hymn I take literally: 'Be Thou My Vision, O Lord of my life.'"

Other songs that made this clear are "I Have Decided to Follow Jesus,"[18] and "Fix Your Eyes upon Jesus, Look Full in His Wonderful Face … in the light of his wonder and grace."[19] We are to set our sights on Christ, the vision that sustains and gives power. No vision, no power. No vision, division. One of the most haunting condemnations in the Hebrew Bible is that of offering God "strange fire"[20]—a divine task attempted with reliance on human skills alone. How many times do we think we can do something ourselves by greater human skill? How often do we think God got a deal when God got us?

In John 16:16, Jesus says this: "In a little while you will see me no more, and then after a little while you will see me." Jesus is saying two things here. First, you will not see me. Second, you will see me. What possibly could this mean?

Simple. Jesus promised that we really would see him again, but not like we saw him before. Jesus promised us that we would *see* him, but not as the world sees. "Before long, the world will not see me anymore, but *you will see me.* Because I live, you also will live."[21]

Before, "seeing" is a matter of eyesight.

After, "seeing" is a matter of insight.

Paul wrote to the church at Ephesus: "I pray ... that the eyes of your heart may be enlightened."[22] We have two sets of eyes: physical eyes, and a second set of eyes that are spiritual eyes, the eyes of our heart. It is these eyes that need to be trained and strengthened to see truth and follow the vision.

> "I see nobody on the road," said Alice.
> "I only wish I had such eyes," the King remarked, in a
> fretful tone. "To be able to see Nobody! And at that distance, too!"[23]
> —Lewis Carroll, *Through the Looking Glass*

On the one hand, Jesus said, "Your eye is the lamp of your body. When your eyes are good, your whole body also is full of light. But when they are bad, your body also is full of darkness. See to it, then, that the light within you is not darkness."[24]

On the other hand, Jesus said in contrast that what defiles us is not what comes into us from outside, but what comes forth from the heart: "For from within, out of your hearts, come evil thoughts."[25]

In other words: A double source determines what is dominant in you: a flow from the internal to the external, from nature to culture, and from the external to the internal, from culture to nature. The two together—the eyes combined with the heart—are what feeds the heart, and that is perception. Our framework provides interpretation of stimulus. What comes in to the heart is colored by how we interpret it. Scripture teaches that it is not what goes in that defiles; but what goes in is what is assimilated and changes the source.

Where do you look for Jesus? How do you recognize a God-vision? The first thing that needs to be said is actually the last line of *The Diary of a Country Priest*: "Grace is everywhere." But there are certain places Jesus is more likely to be than others. Or in one of my signature phrases ("That's SO God!"), where or how do we look to find God's playspaces so that we can gasp, "That's SO God!"

1. Apply RightVision

The right eye was commonly regarded as the spiritual eye, where vision gave rise to the visionary. Focus on the future. Give the future the benefit of hindsight.

> I keep the Lord always before me.
> —Psalm 16:8 NRSV

There is an old saying: "Hindsight is 20/20." History is the art of looking back to assign meaning, in order to try to explain our present. Hindsight is always 20/20 because we assign it the meaning we choose to. We fashion our history for our own sake. The truth is: What you foresee is what you get.

The challenge is to read the present in light of the past in order to have a sense of our future. Photographs can capture the past, like baby pictures. But photographs can also capture the future, like DNA.

The future is a Christian's native time zone. This is possible because the Christian finds peace in the present. Living well in the present makes the future bright. The present is not the past becoming future. The present is the future becoming past.

Granted, humans are the only species that thinks about the future. It's the time zone that, when we occupy it, we are being most human. In fact, Søren Kierkegaard claimed that to focus on the future is a chief "indication of man's nobility."[26] Only humans bury their dead with the "stuff" they'd need for the afterlife. This we know from the very earliest human bones ever discovered. Our spiritual beings, since the dawn of our creation, have known that eternity is imprinted on our souls, and our spiritual eyes have always been keeping an eye out for what is eternal. Our nudges, those from God and those we grace each other with, have to reflect both sights.

A focus on the future is also what makes us distinctively a Jesus kind of human as well. The orientation of nudge is *not* toward Google culture or any other culture, but toward the Christ who is already working in Google culture and in every culture. Jesus comes to us from beyond and pulls us from the future more than pushes us from the past. Jesus is the future—that's called Christian theology. In each "fraction" of the Eucharist is the fullness of Christ's body; in each fraction of the human species is the fullness of the Spirit; in each fraction of time is the fullness of time. The nudge acknowledges the Christ who invades culture and always has been there, like a compass reveals the magnetic lines of force that have always been there.

The Holy Spirit encourages time travel, most often to the future. Close your eyes and travel in time. Where do you go? If it's not the future, you're not living out of your inheritance. Consider yourself nudged. The default time zone of the Christian is what is ahead, not what is behind.

> Time for a hundred indecisions,
> And for a hundred visions and revisions,
> Before the taking of a toast and tea.[27]
> —T. S. Eliot, "The Love Song of J. Alfred Prufrock"

2. Use PeripheralVision

Look for the atypicals, the arrhythmias, the skipped rhythms, the "odd man out," or what one business consultant calls "positive deviance."[28] Don't expect God's presence to be most visible at the centers or the obvious. Most of the Hebrew prophets emerged not from the temple, but stormed in from the margins.

Jesus comes to us from the future, and the future is on the fringe, especially the edges of the norm. You see best the emerging patterns by your PeripheralVision, yet being peripheral is seldom encouraged. The peripheral is important not only because it widens our perspective, but because in *being* peripheral, it enters our consciousness through a means that bypasses our processing. Ever have something whiz by your head when you're busy with something else? The response is not processed like the book you're reading.

Our brains are designed to detect patterns; it's what we're designed to do. But we must notice patterns that are taking shape not just in the centers but on the periphery. Abnormalities reveal the forces by which creative patterns form, and their recognition connects the work of the age to the patterns that will adjust our lives and futures.

Signs that betray the problems of the status quo are, almost by definition, atypical when they first appear. But they quickly become the norm. For example, increasing incidences of famine in the ninth and tenth centuries were more than episodic devastations and moral conundrums. They were also signs that the days were numbered for the agrarian way of life as everyone knew it. The fringe, now the frontier, becomes the future faster than ever before.

Jesus was most at home on the fringe then, and now. Jesus was seen as an anticlerical layperson by the religious establishment. In fact, try to find a positive reference to the privileged and respected religious leaders in his stories. Most of his stories aren't even about them, but about the fringe and the common people: shepherds, farmers, servants, merchants, widows, judges, adulterers, robbers, etc.

If you've ever visited the Grand Canyon and ridden down into the canyon, you don't trust the trail to a horse. You get a mule. The safest way down and back is on the back of a mule, and that mule will hug the edge even when the path is wide. Why do mules take steps hanging on to the edge of the trail? According to one guide, "They like to know where the edge is, so they won't fall over it—so they walk right on it."[29] By the way, the best view of the Grand Canyon is from the edge.

3. CultureVision

Cultivate CultureVision,[30] the ability to see people who aren't usually on our radar screens: the pariahs, outcasts, rejects. Can we envision the hidden worlds of the less fortunate than ourselves? Can we give up TunnelVision for TogetherVision? Can we turn away from the spotlights to turn on the searchlights and find the hidden and forgotten?

Where is God to be found? Less with the victors than with the victims. We are watching for the God who is to be found (as Gandhi said) "in the next person you meet or not at all." And where is the next person you meet? Jesus nudges us to the wrong side of the tracks, there to walk the cracks, the ditches, and the back alleys.

Look to the worst, the least respectable, the invisible. That's with whom Jesus spent his three years of ministry—sinners, rejects, harlots, criminals, etc. Remember my favorite definition of the gospel? "Jesus ate good food with bad people."

Can we, whose souls are lighted
With wisdom from on high,

Can we to men benighted
The lamp of life deny?[31]
—Reginald Heber, bishop of Calcutta

You want to really look in the mirror? Look at the unseen. We discover our true identities only with the least discovered. We learn who we really are in community with the unlearned and nameless.

In Matthew's gospel, there are five women in the genealogy of Jesus, all sexually compromised in some way. Cambridge church history professor Eamon Duffy writes that "from this contaminated stream is drawn the pure abounding water of life." Duffy's writing here is so good it deserves quoting in full.

> By pointing at the beginning of his Gospel to Tamar, Matthew is letting us know what sort of God we have, what sort of a thing the Incarnation is. "God with us" means just that. The grace and truth and righteousness we recognize in Jesus, we must learn to recognize *outside* the safe world of the nice and the good, *outside* the charmed circle of religion. God's truth and power are elusive, liable to be pushed into the dark corners of our lives and our society. We need to recognize and respond to his presence in the actual, not the *ideal* world of men and women, a world which he has made and loves, and in every corner of which he dwells. But if the story of Tamar is any clue, we should not expect the righteousness of God to be blindingly apparent, nor his religion a textbook to life with the answers neatly printed at the foot of the page.... We will find the righteousness of God revealed and vindicated where we most need it, in the ambivalent and often murky encounter with those we love, but never enough; in the

society of duplicity and partial justice which is all even the best of us really aspires to.[32]

Cosmopolitan's Helen Gurley Brown, who made the magazine into the best-selling women's magazine in the world, is known for her bon mot: "Good girls go to heaven, bad girls go everywhere."[33] I suspect she borrowed it from Tallulah Bankhead's "Only good girls keep diaries. Bad girls don't have time." So if good girls go to heaven, where do redeemed girls go?

When I asked this on my Facebook wall, I got thirty-two responses, mostly from women, including "to the tattoo parlor"; "to Catholic schools"; "anywhere they want, and the Kingdom goes with them"; "to seminary"; "to the Redeemer in prayer"; "to church"; "to ORU"; "to the mission field." The closest to the answer I would have given to the question "Where do good girls go? To hell, camped out at the gates of hell, where Jesus founded his church,"[34] was this one: "Good girls go wherever there is hunger, pain, illness, or injustice—you'll find some of us there."[35] Besides, as Carrie Layton Moore put it in my favorite response, "It's not where they go, but who they go with."[36]

In some ways it is more true to say that you don't find Jesus by looking for him, but by being him, with and for those who need him most. Or in the words of the underappreciated pastoral theologian Reuel L. Howe, "If someone asked, 'How can I find God?' I would answer, 'Go find someone to love and you will find God.'"[37] Our greatest skills needed to see God are not vineyard skills but Vine living: splicing into the Vine. Nudge evangelism is greater grafting onto the Vine, deeper embeddedness in the Vine. Nudging the eye is less toward "Do you have a vision?" and more "Does a vision have you?"

> Your vision will become clear only when can you look into your own heart. Who looks outside, dreams; who looks inside, awakens.[38]
>
> —Carl Jung

That's why the ultimate in seeing is not seeing. At Matthew's last judgment, the just are vindicated on account of *not* seeing that it was Jesus whom they cared for. They were so possessed by the Jesus-vision that they fed the hungry, clothed the naked, and healed the sick as part of their everyday living. "Seeing Jesus" cannot be a theoretical visuality. The eyes do not see Jesus apart from hands that touch and tables that feed the hungry. Jesus' resurrection appearances make it clear that our witness to the grace of God in the world depends on our gracefulness.

4. Open to SurpriseVision

Look for Jesus where you least expect to find him.

This relates to places as much as to people. God lurks everywhere, but most especially where you least expect to find the divine. God makes art where no one expects to find it. God does the best of things in the worst of times. God uses our weakness and brokenness to bless and strengthen others. One of the first poems I memorized, after Henry Wadsworth Longfellow's "Hiawatha," was this one from W. H. Auden: "He is the Way. / Follow him through the Land of Unlikeliness; / You will see rare beasts and you will / have unique adventures."[39]

> Anyone can look for fashion in a boutique or history in
> a museum. The creative explorer looks for history in
> a hardware store and fashion in an airport.[40]
> —Journalist Robert Wieder

The "Luck Project" reveals that everyone makes their own "luck." Richard Wiseman, head of a psychology research department at the University of Hertfordshire in England, has found from laboratory research that people who seem to be "lucky" are actually open to new experiences and to looking down new avenues and unlikely places, whereas "unlucky" people are stuck in routines.[41]

> A wonderful harmony is created when we join
> together the seemingly unconnected.[42]
> —Philosopher Heraclitus of Ephesus

For me the greatest discovery of the "Luck Project" was that those considered lucky had the capacity to be astonished. They almost challenged life every day with these words: "Astonish me!"

Whoever funded the "Luck Project" might have saved their money for a worthier research project and simply consulted Søren Kierkegaard, who when asked if he could wish for anything, or stroke a magic lamp and have his every pleasure fulfilled, replied that his wish would not be for wealth or power or fame, but for "the passion of possibility, for the eye, eternally young, eternally ardent, that sees possibility everywhere. Pleasure disappoints, possibility does not."[43]

Can you be astonished?

5. Develop Green523Vision

Green, at 532 nanometers, is the wavelength of light to which the human eye is most sensitive.[44] How sensitive and discerning is your vision?

The human species does not have a stellar track record of getting it right at first glance. For example, the *Cambridge History of American Literature*, which first came out in 1917, omitted Herman Melville, whom some believe wrote the greatest masterpiece in USAmerican literature. Even worse, humans tend to pounce on and denounce what they see that doesn't fit into prevailing paradigms. That's why some of the greatest discoveries in science and medicine were ridiculed when they were first made: H. pylori as a contributor to ulcers; hand washing as a means to reduce puerperal fever; the sun as the center around which the earth revolves.

Discernment of what is of God and what is of the devil is relatively easy compared to what is of God and what is of the human, especially as human resources become ever more miraculous and magical. That's why the answer to the question "What does God look like?" needs to be always kept in mind. God looks like the Holy Spirit in action: where there is forgiveness, compassion, nonviolence, freedom, love, human community.

It is one thing to know where to look for God. It is quite another to have the eyes to see God once you come across Truth. How many people in Jesus' day stared him in the face, listened to him speak, yet fulfilled the prophecy of Isaiah—"ever hearing, but never understanding; ever seeing, but never perceiving."[45] What we see depends on how we look and listen. In the penetrating words of Miroslav Volf:

> Think of people who observed Jesus teach and heal and embody the life of God—and they say nothing but a "false prophet" or a "political rebel." Our eyes and ears need a heart ready to receive the truth of God's reality rather than one that longs for the comforts of false gods. Finally, even when we look in the right places with a ready heart, we still might miss the one true God. We need to be willing to let our very effort to know God slide out of our hands, opening them to God's continued and unexpected self-revelation. Otherwise, like the dog from Aesop's fable, we may end up dropping the real piece of meat in order to grab its reflection in the water.[46]

"Discernment of spirits" is a phrase that dates from the time of Jesus. It is used twice in the New Testament[47] and meant then what it means now: Distinguish between good and bad spirits. Ignatius of Loyola was the first to itemize and elaborate these in his *Spiritual Exercises* (1522–1524). Nudges given in a good spirit yield the fruits of a good spirit—"charity, joy, peace," while nudges given in a bad spirit yield the fruits of a bad spirit—"feuds, jealousy, wrangling."[48]

Some people don't know a good thing when they see it.

> Our whole business in this life is to restore to health
> the eye of the heart whereby God may be seen.[49]
> —St. Augustine

If you were to come up with some scenarios for deliriously happy life experiences, having your sight restored after being born blind would rank high on the list. But research into the rare occasions when this occurred reveals something very different: sad stories of the newly sighted living in fear, overwhelmed to the point of serious depression and even suicide. They simply had no idea what to make of the sighted world. One man who had lost his sight when he was three years old, and regained it in one eye approximately forty years later, was asked what he thought of his face. He replied: "I see it, but I don't know what to make of it." One of Jesus' miracles people easily miss is the blind man's healing. Initially it might seem Jesus had to take a second whack at it (remember "the men look like trees" comment?). But there were two separate healings here. First, Jesus healed the eye. Then Jesus healed the man's brain, which interpreted the data the eye was sending.

The sighted among us certainly take the bizarre "images" that we see every day for granted. Without Vision (i.e., Jesus), we are like the blind man in Mark 8, who when Jesus asked him if he could see, admitted that he couldn't see Jesus for the trees: "I see people; they look like trees walking around."[50] Jesus touched the man again, and the man "saw everything clearly," including Jesus. When we pray for and allow Jesus through the Spirit to touch us and open our eyes, people will stop looking like trees, and we will see Jesus in the trees and in spite of the trees. This makes Jesus' miracle of healing all the more profound. Jesus restored not only sight but physical perception and orientation to someone who had a deep spiritual perception.[51] A lot of times (read: most of the time) we are praying for things that God has already given us. "Open your eyes and look at the fields ... ripe for harvest."[52] God has already given us the fields we need for our mission. We need to be nudged to "open our eyes and look."

6. Deploy 3-DVision

It is important that we factor in delayed perceptions when it comes to re-cognizing Jesus. Like Jesus' disciples, we can count on a delay in seeing: "His disciples did not understand this at first; but when Jesus was glorified, *then they remembered*."[53] That time lag of "then they remembered" is the norm, not the exception.

> Then their eyes were opened
> and they recognized him.
> —Luke 24:31

Why did the disciples, all of them, have such trouble recognizing Jesus? Mary Magdalene saw a gardener. Two disciples saw a fellow traveler and pedestrian. Seven disciples saw a stranger on the shore. Do we need special eyes to see resurrection?

Think about what it might have been like to be a Native American and to be faced with something you had never seen before: ships that came to discover you. Nothing they saw was in their universe of perceptions. The only way they knew something was out there and coming was they observed changes in the waves and in the patterns of the water. They started with what they knew and followed those changes until gradually there began to appear something that they had never seen before: ships.

How can this be? Blue Man Group shows us how. Here is a link: www.youtube.com/watch?v=fVgB9VmWLZg (accessed 6 May 2010).

The brain fills in the picture while the eyes' rods and cones are recharging. We have "persistence of vision" because we already have an image in our brain of what we've experienced. The disciples had no prior experience of a risen Christ and were still thinking of the Messiah as a

Liberator from Roman oppression ("We had hoped he was the one to redeem Israel," said Jesus' uncle Cleopas on the Emmaus Road)[54] rather than a destroyer of the tyranny of sin and death. That's why they couldn't make the connection.

Most often we see God's hand in life's circumstances through hindsight. It takes will and skill to see what God is doing in the midst of life's circumstances. Our hope is that someday we'll trust him enough to know what he's going to do so that we can be like Jesus and just show up where God wants to perform a miracle. But in order to get there, we must spend a lot more time listening to the "unspeakable groanings of the Spirit" in us, as Paul calls them, rather than groaning for another promise.

> When true vision meets paradigm,
> paradigm always blinks first.[55]
> —Hybrid vehicle VentureOne

7. Awaken CorrectiveVision

Everyone had to see the bright star on that first Christmas Eve. The Star of Bethlehem was shining in the sky like a beacon from paradise. Why did only the magi, the intellectuals of their day, see it? What brought the magi to the manger? The magi awakened within their intellects imagination (in this case iMAGInation) and intuition.

Nudgers are able to see, not just "things," but the meaning of things, the significance of things. CorrectiveVision brings together prehension, apprehension, and comprehension. Prehension involves intuition, a word that derives from the Latin *in-tueor* or "see into." Apprehension involves imagination, the bringing together of sight and insight. Comprehension involves intellection.

Intuition, imagination, and intellection (iii) are not special gifts. Every person is iii, the intuitive "i" S. T. Coleridge designated "the living power and prime agent of all human perception."[56] When iii dies, spiritual gangrene sets in, and a nudge turns into a drudge. When iii thrives, we hear what Wallace Stevens called "the sound of words," not merely the words themselves.[57]

When you are nudging, here is how the iii of prehension, apprehension, and comprehension work to form CorrectiveVision. Paul shows how this works in his sermon to the Athenians: "Athenians, I see how extremely religious you are in every way."[58] Paul looks at their objects of worship scattered throughout the city, not as idols to condemn, but as portals for opening them up to the living God. When he finds one "to an unknown God," he pounces on the metaphor to proclaim the truth of this "unknown God" but who is now known in Jesus. In other words, intuit an image that encapsulates the encounter, the invisible power at work in that moment. Then intellectually relate this image, based on the hotchpotch of human experiences, to a biblical image, metaphor, or story. Imaginatively identify biblical figures who shared similar experiences, faced similar frustrations, experienced similar encounters with God. In this way a nudger fulfills the promise of Proverbs 20:5: "The purposes of a man's heart are deep waters, but a man of understanding draws them out."

> How many times must a man look up
> Before he can see the sky?[59]
> —Singer/songwriter Bob Dylan

8. Look for ColorVision

Want to join what God is doing? Look for beauty, and introduce people to a "beauty ever ancient, ever new" (Augustine's phrase).[60] Dostoyevsky is famous for saying that beauty can save the world. Only God can save the world, but if you want to know what God is up to, look for beauty: beauty in the ordinary as well as the more baroque beauty of the ornate and ornamental.

This sounds redundant, but isn't: So how do you recognize beauty? By noticing it. Beauty enters through the eyes. The first thing God created was light. Light is composed of color, making colors part of the divine design. In fact, if you look at creation, it appears that God is a color connoisseur: the purple of regal calmness, the red of fiery passion, the black (the uber-color that adds together all the color pigments) of dignity and purpose, the true blue of faithfulness and loyalty, the green of healing, the yellow of hope, the white of purity, the orange of joy.

> A certain minor light may still
> Leap incandescent
> Out of kitchen table or chair
> As if a celestial burning took
> Possession of the most obtuse objects now and then—
> Thus hallowing as interval
> Otherwise inconsequent
> By bestowing largesse, honour,
> One might say love.[61]
> —Sylvia Plath

The theological significance of colors[62] is most obvious in the sartorial dimensions of spirituality. In times past there were laws and kingly procla-mations regulating who could wear what colors (e.g., purple), what metals (gold, silver), and what fabric (velvet or silk). An elaborate color symbolism of heraldry was dyed and stitched on clothes. Even as Puritan preachers denounced sartorial splendor and painted faces as popish and evil straight from the "whore of Babylon," they developed their own dress as address. It is hard for us to imagine what it must have been like to simply view the attire of the Hebrews' high priest. Always dressed to the hilt, bejeweled in more wealth than entire national economies, when the jewels hit the sunlight or candlelight, color glistened everywhere.

Sometimes God's light shines like a lamp, sometimes like a laser. Sometimes God's light shines like a beacon; sometimes God's light shines like a diamond, reflecting lowly light in such a way that makes it beautiful.

9. ChristVision

You need loving eyes to see the risen Christ. If you have cynical or spiteful or hateful eyes, then your eyes will be blind to Christ … Pilate, Herod, Caiaphas the high priest all could not see the beauty of Jesus, although Pilate came close. If you cannot see the person next to you with ChristVision, you will be blind to what God is doing in his or her life.

It's so hard for people to hear "God loves you so much" when the church loves so little. "Love All. Serve All" is the corporate motto of Hard Rock Café. Does corporate culture get something church culture doesn't? Do we give people the look of love? Or the look of judgment? Do you give people the look of compassion or the look of condemnation, of condescension? Does your church give the world a live eye or the evil eye?

If holiness is seeing everyone with the eyes of Christ and seeing Christ in another's eyes, then what it means to live a "pure" life is to see Jesus in everyone. Can you see Jesus in the supreme unclean? Who is the worst person you know? Think about it for a minute…. Can you see Jesus in them?

Every age has the church it deserves or desires. Privilege desire over understanding, but be careful what you harbor as "the desires of the heart."

After you get better at "being Jesus," it's hard *not* to see resurrection. How do you live the Christian life and not see resurrection everywhere … in forsythia and daffodils, in friends and enemies?

> The task is not so much to see what no one yet has seen, but to think what nobody yet has thought about that which everybody sees.[63]
>
> —Nineteenth-century German philosopher Arthur Schopenhauer

Jesus, the Light of God, shows what is there all the time that we couldn't see in the dark: a God who created us and who loves us with an eternal passion. The light of Christ reveals the truth that we are meant for God. The "light of God's face" is Jesus Christ. Our only happiness, our true joy, is when God's light shines on us and we nudge others with "the light of [God's] countenance."[64]

10. Use Stereoscopic Vision

When it comes to nudging, it helps if you can see stereoscopically. To see Jesus more clearly and with depth, we must look out of both eyes. In other words, we must embrace paradox and develop the skill of looking at two different things at the same time, the skill that St. Augustine demonstrated when he said he defended two schools of thought: "'*Credo ut intelligam*' ('I believe in order to understand') and '*Intelligo ut credam*' ('I understand in order to believe')."[65]

> *Doch alles, was uns anrührt, dich und mich,*
> *nimmt uns zusammen wie ein Bogenstrich,*
> *der aus zwei Saiten eine Stimme zieth.*
> You and me—all that lights upon us, though,
> brings us together like a fiddle-bow
> drawing one voice from two strings it glides along.[66]
> —Rainer Maria Rilke

Nondualism is one of the hardest things for "moderns" to get. The fact that at the same time, for example, one can be both sinner and saint, lost and found, violates the most basic principles of logic: the law of non-contradiction and the law of the excluded middle. Aristotle put the law of noncontradiction like this: "The same attribute cannot at the same time belong and not belong to the same subject and in the same respect."[67] Yet Christianity violates this basic principle of logic from its very inception, creating a new chemistry between opposites: the crib and the cross, treasures and cracked pots, the local and the global, the horizontal and the vertical, the sinner and the saint, a Mary–Joseph church—a church like Mary willing to step forward into the limelight, a church like Joseph willing to disappear into the background. As Gregory Palamas, one of the wisest of Orthodox theologians, said seven centuries ago about the cruciform life, "In all statements about God there must always be paradox and silence."[68]

When you're nudging with StereoscopicVision, think of the Celtic tradition of knots. The Celts decorated everything with knotted designs, symbols of how everything is unique yet tightly woven together. The key to navigating life is to bring together the two opposite ends of the rope, the contradictory realities that we confront on a daily basis, and to tie both strands together into a knot that embraces and interconnects the opposites.[69] In the stereoscope nudge, identify the opposites of life (continuity and separation, combination and deviation) as they emerge in the everyday, and tie them together with a biblical metaphor or story knot or prayer knot (Eastern Orthodoxy uses "prayer ropes" with each knot a different prayer).

> If way to the Better there be,
> it exacts a full look at the Worst.[70]
> —Thomas Hardy

To nudge using the "knot," listen to the hurt and despair that are rumbling in a person's life. Then connect that suffering and pain to God's promises of faith, hope, and love. There is a divine message-package for every human wreckage. When you tie the knot of God wanting to do the best in the worst of times and the worst of places; when you tie the knot of being strongest in the broken places; when you tie the knot of small being large when God is in it; when you tie the knot of belief in every atheist, and atheism in every believer: then people begin to live the paradox of Christ's life-in-death at work in us: "We always carry around in our body the death

of Jesus, so that the life of Jesus may also be revealed in our body."[71] To tie
the knot of being alive means experiencing the joy, the beauty of everything,
yet the suffering of everything as well: Our music is not just out of joy, but
"a beating of gongs … to drive away devils," as Denise Levertov puts it.[72]

Part of this DoubleVision nudge is the realization that in our spiritual
life, we need both sobriety and drunkenness, we need to be heady and reflec-
tive, but at times totally intoxicated with the Spirit, or drunk with love, as
any lover will tell you. Here is how the medieval mystics tied this knot:
"Sober intoxication" they called it, especially the medieval Dominicans,
who practiced everything in moderation, including moderation.

Another part of this DoubleVision nudge is the recognition that all
of us see through a glass dimly; but second, "perhaps, the terrifying and
welcome voice may begin, annihilating everything we thought we knew,
and restoring everything we have never lost."[73] In a culture that esteems
authenticity as a number-one virtue, "To be rather than to seem" is a great
motto. But for "To be rather than to seem" to become a reality, Alexander
the Great's motto, taken from Socrates, must come into force: "Be what
you wish to seem."[74]

11. Turn on the Dark

The first step to seeing is knowing that you're in the dark. If you don't know
you're in the dark, then you need to turn on the dark. To turn on the dark
is a metaphor for keeping an open mind, for resisting easy assumptions and
automatic defaults in judgment, all of which I call light pollution. Less is
more. Sensory deprivation is a blessing to those who need less distraction.

Light can pollute dark, just as the dark can pollute the light. Stars only
come out at night. In order to see the stars, it must be dark enough to see
them. One of the greatest threats to DarkVision is light pollution. The
brightest stars in the sky no longer come from the Milky Way Galaxy, but
the night glow from our biggest cities. It's called "sky glow"—light reflected
off moisture and dust in the air.

There are a few places left where you can still see the stars. In the West Virginia mountains there is no light pollution, nor in the African dark, where I love to sit in utter silence and darkness, looking at Orion's belt, the A in Taurus, and the Southern Cross. In some Eastern cities like Seoul, South Korea, at night all the buildings "go dark." No matter how high the apartment complex or skyscraper, it is dark, enabling anyone awake to see the stars. But for most of the world, sky glow now outshines the moon for nearly half of each month.

The biological effects of night pollution are only now being appreciated. Ninety miles from Las Vegas, the neon lights are lighting up Death Valley National Park. Many of the night creatures are dying because of light pollution.[75] Certain nocturnal species and ecosystems require a nightly dose of darkness—for reproduction (snakes), for predation (bats), for food intake (zooplankton feed on algae in the dark), for growth and survival. Without dark they face extinction.[76]

There are spiritual as well as biological effects of light pollution. Most people are born at night and are born into eternity at night. Our first journey in life is from darkness to light (and even that light is filled with the three most mysterious forces in the universe: "dark energy," "dark matter," and the recently discovered "dark flow"[77]). Our last journey in life is from light to darkness. We make both of these journeys alone. This is why nudgers need NightVision, which comes only after at least two hours in the dark. We can see in the dark, but it takes time and patience. We don't have to go through life groping in the dark; we can grope the darkness.[78]

It is good to enter darkness, for darkness is the birthing place where God resides. The Hebrew word for "darkness" in Exodus 20:21 (*arafel*) is found in fifteen places in the First Testament, and eight times it refers to the presence of the Holy God.[79]

Churches are best for Prayer, that have least light:
To see God only, I goe out of sight:

And to scape stormy dayes, I chuse
An everlasting night.[80]
—Poet John Donne

The gospel of the night is a birthing gospel. Perhaps that is why in the symbol of the yin/yang the female part is dark and the male part is light. There is something matriarchal about the Night—it is mysterious, intuitive, curious, inexplicable. There is something patriarchal about the Day—it is rational, logical, analytical, clear, well outlined. Plato described two diverse ways of approaching truth: truth as mythos and truth as logos.

Logos truth is left-brained: scientific, rational, discursive, highlighting reason and science. Mythos truth—*mythos* from the Greek word meaning to close the mouth, shut the mouth, and enter the realms of darkness and speechless wonder—is right-brained: intuitive, silent, hidden, highlighting emotions and imagination. Mythos goes down; logos goes up.

The Night is mother of the Day,
The Winter of the Spring,
And ever upon old Decay,
The greenest mosses cling.[81]
—John Greenleaf Whittier

The gospel of the night is a developmental gospel, but not in the sequential way conceived by developmental theorists like Jean Piaget, Erik Erikson, Carl Jung, and Elisabeth Kübler-Ross. Like the dark room of a photographer's studio, darkness is a light-bringer, a light-birther. Dark rooms are places for creativity, community, and regeneration. Dark rooms "develop" negatives into positives.

Life needs dark rooms. Light dries and decays. It's the darkness that preserves. In the circus, they talk about having a "dark day." This means a day off. When circus performers go without dark days, they get weary, and circus life becomes almost unbearable.

Darkness is the womb in which everything exists. To trust the dark is to trust those deep, underground forces—forces of the earth, the ocean, the genes—that would bring to life the seed that is your soul. God planted deep into the ground of your being the seeds of a one-of-a-kind soul. To grow our souls into the unique creation God intends us to be, we must trust the birthing that is going on inside and around us. We must trust the "fruitive darkness."[82]

> Now understand this well: when we turn within ourselves in contemplation, the fruitive unity of God is like to a darkness, a somewhat which is unconditioned and incomprehensible.[83]
> —John of Ruysbroeck, *The Adornment of the Spiritual Marriage*

Roots lie, and live, in the dark.

Darkness is "downtime," and dreaming requires downtime, stillness, silence, rest. In "a thick and dreadful darkness,"[84] a darkness visible, a darkness risible, God gave Abram a look at the future and his descendants.

Folks living at the top of the world, where there is midnight sun, have to develop habits and ways around the light. Folks in the Pacific Northwest can develop SAD (seasonal affective disorder), where the fooling of the body with electrical lights cures the malady. God designed us for the cyclical changes of light and dark, and an upset of the balance can be catastrophic.

Play, not work, is the soil that grows dreams.

Jesus did not so much come to flood darkness with light so that darkness is destroyed as he came to show us how to enter into darkness, and mystery, so that darkness can be explored and experienced.[85] The sun illumines the night; it does not turn night into light.

We are more familiar with the Isaac Watts song about a land "where infinite day excludes the night, and pleasures banish pain"[86] than we are with the children's song by Elizabeth McEwen Shields, "Do You Know Who Made the Night." But maybe it's time we learned what Isaiah calls "the treasures of darkness."[87]

12. Reframe the Picture

The largest and most comprehensive retrospective ever presented in the United States of the career of J. M. W. Turner (1775–1851) premiered at the National Gallery of Art in Washington in 2008. Turner not only was one of the greatest landscape painters in the history of art. Toward the end of his life he moved closer and closer toward impressionist paintings and even abstract art. His paintings today are among the most sought after in the world, ranking right up there with those by Rembrandt, Picasso, and Pollock.

"I don't see clouds and water like that," a woman once said to the artist. "Don't you wish you could, ma'am?" Turner replied.[88]

Nudgers always "tell all the truth but tell it slant," as Emily Dickinson liked to put it.[89] Jesus had another way of putting it: "You have heard it said … But I say …" And the next thing he said reframed the subject, most often with a new image and a new story.

> *Was ist bekamt ist nicht erkannt.*
> What is familiar is not known.[90]
> —Hegel

The paradox of the eyes is that the closest things to you are the hardest things for you to see. We don't *know* the familiar. Something can be so familiar you can't see it. There is a one-frame cartoon that shows two little boys, one holding a book and looking at the other: "What does the word 'ubiquitous' mean? I've been seeing it everywhere lately."

The greatest example of not being able to see the familiar? Nazareth. When the people of Nazareth saw Jesus, they saw Joseph's son, whom they had known for a quarter of a century. When the lepers and the outcasts saw Jesus, they saw so much more.

Nudgers make the familiar strange. Nudgers overcome the deadening effects of the overfamiliar by reframing familiar things in unfamiliar ways. This is especially important when biblical stories are so familiar they become cozy and have a known feel. The worst thing that can be done when responses come from a well-thumbed deck is to return the slogans and repeat the fashionable phrases.

As a literary device, defamiliarization was formulated by the Russians years ago in the concept of *ostranenie*, which translates literally as "denumbing" and was designed as a distancing device to help the reader see something deadeningly familiar in a totally new light. By telling something from an oddball perspective that doesn't fit preconceived notions, by writing elliptically, epigrammatically, the writer skews the view to give a new window on the world.

> To be made uneasy is the beginning of enlightenment.[91]
> —Novelist Brian Aldiss

Nudgers must learn to use *ostranenie*, or whatever you want to call it. In making the familiar strange, nudgers make it fresh. This is one reason why I love poetic nudges so much: They distort the ordinary and, in the words of Hugo Williams, are a "slippage towards strangeness." Nudgers are also on a campaign against *cliche*: cliches of the mind, the heart, the soul. The only time nudgers use cliches is to push back against cliches. If you utilize a familiar text, always take an unfamiliar route. That's the nudge that can turn lostness into foundness, and leads out of self and into the other.

My mother's maiden name was Boggs, named after the "boggy places" of the British Isles. The American Indian name for boggy places is "Podunk," literally "the place where the foot sinks in."

I don't need to remember the "Podunk" in me because Podunk is my

middle name. And as a writer, Podunk is my mien. The Puritans said, referring to the strange manifestations that sometimes haunt the swamps and
bogs, "When the sun shines on a swamp, mist rises." I basically write about
that mist that rises from the shining of grace on sin, of hope on despair,
of promise on boggy foggy places. The mist is the making of faith. It's the
place where theory becomes practice, when thoughts become tasks. When
the mist rises, we are open to *new* sight, in that we see, but what we see is
still understood through the faith interpretation God gave us in the fog.

 Discover More Online

CHECK OUT INTERACTIVES FOR YOUR PERSONAL OR SMALL-GROUP USE
AND MUCH MORE ON THE NUDGE WEB SITE:

WWW.NUDGETHEBOOK.COM

Chapter 7

PONDER: TOUCH

Do You Have a Touch for the Kingdom?

Touching Jesus

Right now I am looking out on waters where the largest octopus on the planet lives. The giant Pacific octopus, known as *Enteroctopus dofleini,* lurks below the surface of the waters outside my study window and hunts in the two-mile stretch of Puget Sound that separates Orcas Island from Sucia Islands. These octopuses, which are some of the most beautiful, intelligent, and graceful creatures God made, can get to be bigger than a Ford Expedition, or about the size of a whale shark. They only leave their dens at night or on dark, dreary days, so it's not easy to have a "close encounter."

The octopus may be the most high-touch creature on earth. Each of its eight tentacles has 240 suckers, for a total of 1,920 suction cups. And each suction cup is a multisensory organ that at the same time it touches, smells, tastes, and hears what it grasps to tell whether it's holding some crabs and cockles or a lump of coral. The octopus can also change color in the blink of its eye, going from red to brown to communicate with other hunters or to hide in its environment. Its tongue functions as a drill, which can bore through the thickest abalone shell.

Imagine that you are that octopus, sleeping quietly in your den when a Coast Guard cutter passes overhead. Powered by diesel engines and gas turbines, the boat creates a huge ruckus in the environment. The water rocks you awake. Your sonic environment is now disrupted, and nothing seems normal. There is that "nearness to tremendousness" that Emily Dickinson talked about.[1] But do you know what is happening? Do you know what that "tremendousness" is or what it means?

That is sort of the way I feel about God. There is obviously something significant happening overhead and around me. In fact, I can experience it and tell you about my experience. But I have no clue what is happening. As multisensory as I am, and no matter how much I ponder, that Coast Guard cutter is beyond my understanding.

Elisabeth Koenig, who teaches discernment to seminary students, invites us to imagine that we're that octopus in another way.

> Imagine that your mind and heart, your values and principles, your moral faculty and your imagination, are like the octopus' suckers and tentacles, probing your inner and outer environment, "tasting" what's there to tell you what will nurture you and what will not. Imagine how your act of paying attention to all these different tastes can actually cause new discerning taste buds to grow![2]

Christianity comes with so many tactile imperatives that it is a touch culture and the church a "touching place." The highest expression of Christianity is not its doctrines, or even its art, but its manifestations of the passion people feel toward Christ and the compassion toward each other, the outsider and outlier. More than any other sense, it is the church as a touching place that makes it the paradise of pariahs. God connects to us in human touch.

> Everything humans handle has a tendency to secrete meaning.[3]
> —Marcel Duchamp

For Jesus, neither love of God nor love of neighbor/stranger took a backseat to each other. They always sat together and held hands. That's why nudges are touching times and the nudge church a touching place. This phrase "touching place" comes from John Bell and Graham Maule of the Iona Community in Scotland, who collaborated on a hymn they called "A Touching Place."

The hymn begins this way: "Christ's is the world in which we move, Christ's are the folk we're summoned to love, Christ's is the voice which calls us to care. And Christ is the one who meets us there ..."

> To the lost Christ shows his face,
> to the unloved he gives his embrace,
> to those who cry in pain or disgrace
> Christ makes, with his friends, a touching place.[4]

Google any painting of Madonna and child. You will find the same two things. First, every painting has Mary holding Jesus (only a handful in history have Joseph holding Jesus). Second, every painting has Mary looking at Jesus. The arms and the eyes—the cradling touch and the caressing look. Both need to be combined in touching-place churches. But touching places are more arms than eyes, more high-touch than high-seeing. Biblical knowing (*yada*) is not abstract or distancing but engaging and linking.

A young man was killed in a tragic, freak accident along the eastern seaboard. He had grown up in Pastor Brian Bauknight's church in Pittsburgh, and on the day of his memorial service the United Methodist sanctuary was overflowing. As part of the service, his mother asked to speak a few words to the congregation.

Although it was difficult for her to talk, she managed to say two important things. First, "I am thankful to God for every day that I was given to hug my son close." Second, "I am grateful that God has given me each of you in this church to hug me close right now."

As a little girl left the house for the bus, she said to her mother, "I'm going to be sad today." Her mother asked, "Why? Aren't you feeling well?" The little girl said, "No. But when we're sad, all the teachers take turns hugging us."

> Put your hands, Thomas, on the crawling head of a child
> imprisoned in a cot in Romania.
> Place your finger, Thomas, on the list of those
> who have disappeared in Chile.
> Stroke the cheek, Thomas, of the little girl sold in
> prostitution in Thailand.
> Touch, Thomas, the gaping wounds of my world.[5]
> —Poet Kate McIlhagga, "Thomas"

It's that way with God, too, and with God's church. The act of hugging and being hugged is the body of Christ's best nudge. Maybe the great Jonathan Edwards didn't get it exactly right. Maybe we are less "sinners in the hands of an angry God" than we are "sinners in the hands of a hugging God."[6] My favorite image of "Our Father" is a loving parent, holding on in a big bear hug, as a rebellious child flails away, struggling with all the child's might to break free, yet all the while hoping that the arms never let go.[7] The church needs to be so clear about its identity as the body of Christ that everything it does generates a gravitational pull toward the heart.

If you want to reach others, you have to reach out. D. H. Lawrence is famous for his remark that sexual intercourse is an act of holy communion. But so is the touch of tenderness, a kiss good-bye, the wiping away of tears from a child, the holding of a door open for a complete stranger: all acts of holy communion. In fact, ethics is learning the touching behaviors that turn human communion into holy communion. The touch of connection is the true currency of the church that makes things possible.

I will rule over you with a mighty hand and an outstretched arm.
—Ezekiel 20:33–40

The potential of nudging through touch is scanned in this reflection on touch by James B. Stockinger, a sociologist at the University of California at Berkeley. In his survey of our dependency on the hands of other people, the power of nudging with our hands becomes obvious. We receive ourselves as a gift from the hands of others.

> Each of us lives in and through an immense movement of the hands of other people. The hands of other people lift us from the womb. The hands of other people grow the food we eat, weave the clothes we wear and build the shelters we inhabit. The hands of other people give pleasure to our bodies in moments of passion and aid and comfort in times of affliction and distress. It is in and through the hands of other people that the commonwealth of nature is appropriated and accommodated to the needs and pleasures of our separate individual lives, and, at the end, it is the hands of other people that lower us into the earth.[8]

As a touching place, the church enables Jesus' followers to thrive because of its social environment that stimulates the senses. In fact, recent studies have shown that sensory deprivation is literally torture. Why do mammals breast-feed? The obvious answer is: food. But the deeper answer is: touch. The brain needs stimulation that comes from contact and connection if it is to develop.[9] In fact, research now reveals that the mother's touch is more important than the mother's milk. Research shows that you can live longer without the milk than without the touch. Research also reveals that more health benefits come from spending time at the watercooler than lounging by the pool in your backyard, because it's at the watercooler where you're more likely to connect and be connected. Death is a noncontact sport.

The twenty-first century is increasingly being asked to live without touch. Evidences of a touchless culture are everywhere. We live in a totally sex-obsessed culture, but a culture that refuses to explore the depth of the meaning and significance of sex. Contacts with coworkers are bathed in "don't touch" workshops. In hospitals, we can drug people; we can hook electrodes up to their brains and give them shocks against their will; we can put people in straitjackets; but we aren't allowed to hug them. Death-row inmates are not allowed "contact visits" where they can touch or hug family members except the last visit before their execution.

Even with touchless toilets, faucets, hand driers, and now holy water dispensers,[10] how many of us secretly cringe whenever we touch door handles? Who can pick up the remote in a hotel room without wondering what the last person who used it was doing? Who doesn't immediately pull down the hotel bedspread because we don't want to imagine what happened on it since it was last washed? Who can ask for a lime or lemon without worrying about the bacteria still on the skin? Who can pick up a woman's purse from the bottom for fear she has set it on the bathroom floor? Who can shake hands with a driver getting out of a car without flinching, knowing that the number-one pastime while driving alone is picking one's nose? Who licks envelopes anymore, or puts one's mouth to the top of an unwashed can?

The role that trust and touch will play in the future can only be imagined, but cannot be overstated. Since you touch not so much with hands or fingers but with skin, your skin is your major touching organism. That's how you gather information about your environment and learn what to trust. For some reason we decorate our touching organism, which already comes in a range of colors. But we desire color add-ons through cosmetics and tattoos, and the more self-conscious we become about our touching organisms, the more we lavish on decorations.[11] You might even call tattoos the new Ebenezers, altars that commemorate the touchstones of our lives.

You can also feel the vibes of the future in such phenomena as snuggies, cuddle parties, mass huggings, and even the robotic pillow called "The Hug." Shaped like a child but the size and softness of a throw pillow,[12] you can send The Hug to distant family members like your grandma. The sound of your grandma's name causes the pillow to come alive: It lights up, plays sounds, and reaches out its arms to physically hug the grandparent. Press the right paw, and the touching ends and the plush pillow says good-bye. For touching to be a third rail, as it increasingly has become in many risk-management churches, is for the church to be out of touch with the culture in which it finds itself, a culture where loneliness and isolating connectedness are some of the great diseases of our age.

I shall never forget the 2003 visit of Indian spiritual leader Mata Amritanandamayi (affectionately known as "Amma") to Columbia University, where she offered blessings in the form of "healing hugs."[13] At Columbia, people came to Arledge Auditorium hours early to line up for their hugs. I had no idea why a line was backed up the length of the block, but watched as everyone who waited was given a numbered token, an orange sticky dot, and what I later found out was a sixty-four-page guide to hugging Amma without hurting her. The key is: Don't hug her; let her hug you. One person stood in line seven hours for a hug. Everyone took off their shoes, and many chanted as they waited. Everyone also brings an "offering" to Amma.

In the category of "What Some People Won't Do for a Hug," there was the story of a man going around and faking choking episodes, apparently to get attention from women. He flails his arms, coughs, and sputters. After a woman rushes over and "saves" him with the Heimlich (a piece of apple actually hurls from his mouth), he showers her with thanks, hugs, and kisses. "'There's been no crime. Our hands are kind of tied here,' a sheriff's spokesman said."[14]

Summit, New Jersey, is a bedroom community of Wall Street. It lost more than a dozen of its residents on 9/11. In the aftermath of the collapse of the Twin Towers, the clergy of Summit felt called to do something. Some started prayer services. Others traveled to ground zero. But one pastor, Charles Rush, felt called to do something different.

Pastor Rush put on his clergy collar and went to the Summit train station. New Jersey transit was depositing at the Summit station those survivors fleeing from the carnage. The priest did not know what to do, so he simply stood there. And as the ashen, dirt-caked, cement-crusted passengers stumbled off the train, they saw him standing there, a priest silently testifying to the hope of the gospel. And they walked over to him and touched him. That's all. No words. No smile. No nods. They just touched him. Hundreds of them. Thousands of them. They just touched him.

The church has been more prone to "take a stand" on issues or "take a vote" on programs than touch. Touch is a centripetal force that includes and embraces. Taking stands is a centrifugal force that separates and divides. While the rest of the world is moving, the one taking a stand is frozen in time like kids playing freeze tag, waiting for the sign that says its okay to move again. Christ ran around touching people and tagging them. Every Jesus tag offered freedom. Every Jesus tag let the person tagged know they had been touched by God.

Jesus had a touching presence. He nudged with touch and was a master toucher. He touched people and allowed himself to be touched. He did not just heal lepers. He touched lepers. My friend Ken Ulmer, one of the greatest preachers alive today, likes to say, "We need to get the word out: The disciples were not bodyguards." The disciples didn't keep people in the crowds from touching Jesus, even the unclean and the untouchables. When they did function like bodyguards, Jesus rebuked them: "Let the children come to me ..."

Both Mary Magdalene and Thomas want to touch Jesus' body. Mary is told no. Thomas is told it's okay; but once Thomas can, he no longer needs to. Thomas is known as Thomas Didymus, Thomas the Twin, the twin of each of us. We will never know in this life whether Thomas touched Jesus or not.[15] But whether he did or didn't, Jesus invited him to.

Some things are out of our hands. Some things are in our hands. Either way, we're in good hands when our times are in God's hands.[16] In fact, sometimes we're told to keep our hands off. Just because touch is the touchstone of faith doesn't mean it's the only stone turned. This is the backstory of Uzzah, who thought it was his duty to protect the ark and to guardian the things of God. What Uzzah learned the hard way was that God can bodyguard himself. We are to carry the ark, but keep our fingerprints off the ark. We can carry the holy, but God doesn't need our smudges to ward evil from the ark. We are to just keep carrying the holy, and God will do the rest.

For Jesus, to carry the holy was to reach out and touch, not the cherubim and seraphim, but the castaways and sinners. Jesus was always reaching out to touch the untouchables, and the untouchables were always reaching out to touch him. Before healing a leper, Jesus reached out his hand and touched him.[17] Before bringing the daughter of Jarius back to life, he took her hand and said, "Little girl, get up!"[18] Before Lazarus could walk after Jesus raised him from the dead, Jesus made his disciples touch him.[19]

"If only I touch his cloak, I will be made well."[20] Everything is going against her: woman, poor, Jew, sick, bleeding (ritually unclean and thus isolated, cut off, alone). The best she could do, she thought, was touch the hem of his garment, and yet Jesus had such high-touch sensitivity that he called out, "Who touched me?" The very fact Jesus had to say, "Don't touch me," as he is entering into the mystery of resurrection, testifies to his high-touch ministry.

> Don't you sense me, ready to break
> into being at your touch?[21]
>
> —Rainer Maria Rilke

The church has often mistaken "Touch me not" as words for all time and not words for the time it takes for Jesus to become our risen Lord.

The touch nudge is the open invitation to reach out to Christ, who will grab hold of us and not let go in an enfolding, upholding embrace through all those rendering experiences of life, all of which Jesus has gone through before, even death itself. In the neogothic College Chapel of St. Patrick's College, Maynooth, there is a striking crucifixion in stained glass. The crucified Christ is depicted in an intense trinitarian ensemble, with the Father holding the arms of the cross of his crucified Son, while the Holy Spirit in the form of a dove hovers between the Father and the Crucified One, the sign of the coming "new creation"[22] out of the pain of the passion.[23]

Where's the rub?

There's the rub!

There is no rub. In an increasing number of churches, touch is the third-rail sense and the third rail of religion. In the church today, afraid of any number of lawsuits or pandemics, start "touching" and you will get into trouble, be fired, or sent to some boundary-maintenance, sexual-harassment seminars.

Even in our moments of praise and worship, we rise together but stand as one, lifting our hands up to the heavens, funneling into ourselves God's presence and turning each worshipper into a private cone of adoration. Even in our highest and holiest moments of worship, our egos resist being mere vessels for the Spirit. We want to be the focus of the attention; we want for *out story* to be heard and celebrated by God, and so we focus God's attention our way. Seldom if ever do people hold hands or touch each other in praise and worship. We are back to the holiness code of the Pharisees, for whom "Don't touch" was the prime directive.

Jesus was a healer, which meant more than curing disease. *Savior* and *salvation* are both health and healing words. Jesus' healing techniques were customized for each sick person, but there was one constant: the healing power of touch. Jesus' high-touch healing turned the religious establishment's concept of holiness on its head. Holiness is not separation from the unclean and unholy; it is touching the unclean and unholy. For Jesus, nothing and no one are accursed.[24] Whatever is unholy, impure, and corrupt, we must touch it, "for this too Christ died." Whatever is unclean, the church has to pick it up, for that is its vocation.

Holiness is not "being good." Holiness is being about the bad: touching unclean lepers; eating and drinking with criminals, tax collectors, and prostitutes; letting yourself be touched by soiled souls.

For a church that is a touching place, the question is not "Do I touch?" The church always touches. The question is, "Do I know when to touch and where not to touch?" If the life of faith is a dance, as Jesus once compared it, what kind of dance is it when you don't touch? We touch each other truthfully and healingly as dancing partners, as members of the same body. And the healing touch of love not only mends wounds, but discovers and discloses as well.

> An honest answer is like a kiss on the lips.
> —Proverbs 24:26

With every person you touch, you hold a life in your hands.

If you're on the phone, touch-nudge someone with your voice.

If someone is depressed, poke them with a joke. Sharp elbows in the ribs are our second nature.

If someone is lonely, touch them with a kiss.

If someone is sick, touch them with oil. You can sign someone's forehead, not just by the sign of ashes on the forehead on Ash Wednesday, but by the healing sign of oil any day of the year.

If someone is afraid, touch them with an anointing for mission.

If "this old house" is starting to seam and succumb to gravity, touch the cracks. The elderly should not be reduced to remembering the way it felt to be touched.

If someone has cooked you a great meal, thank them for your fullness by inviting them to rub your stomach—somebody's got to do it.

Here is the great irony: The more high-tech the culture, as John Naisbitt first pointed out in the 1970s, the less high-touch the culture. Just when a Facebook culture is jaded by the vicarious, virtual, derivative, secondary experiences of the screen and is screaming for the face-to-face, in-your-face, touch-God's-face experiences of the raw and real, the church is distancing itself from touch. The wildly successful iPhone and Apple computers have shown the appeal of touch screens, touch pads, and multitouch games. Interfaces that deploy touch are being built into software, which can already handle up to four simultaneous touch gestures: scrolling, rotating, stretching, shrinking. You can experience all four of them on the most popular iPhone app, Koi Pond. Soon screens will disappear, and the images once flat will become three-dimensional. In that holographic world, the primary way anyone will know what is true and what is telegraphic will be the resistance of the real, the pushback that comes from touch.

One of the best ways to prepare for what is coming is to develop new touching-in and touching-out rituals. When you first greet someone, touch them on the shoulder, hug them, or give them a kiss. When you say goodbye to someone, pat them on the back, squeeze their arm, or grab their hand.

One of the best touching-out rituals is what I call a TAP: Touch and Pray. "Would you mind if I prayed for you before I go?" It takes no spiritual bravado to do this. Besides, most people don't know what it's like to be at the receiving end of prayer. This touching-out ritual of prayer can be as simple as a "Bless this person I'm touching now, and may they know your peace" or the Lord's Prayer. The former head of the Vatican Bank, Archbishop Paul Marcinkus, had a fund-raising saying: "You can't run the Church on Hail Marys."[25] That may be. But if you can't run the church on Hail Marys, you *can* run your life on Our Fathers, and you *should* run the church on Our Fathers. Jesus prayed twenty-one times in the Gospels original prayers, and every one he began with "Our Father."

You can count on what we're now calling the five "God-guarantees" with every person you touch. Remember these? They're worth repeating here.

Every person you brush up against is a child of God, a Jesus-in-you
person.

Every brush is a bush.

Every best is a blest.

Every worst is a juncture for grace.

Every person needs a nudge.

Or to translate these five God-guarantees into less poetic form:

Human beings are created in the image of God.

God is already present in that person's life in the form of some burning bush.

The best things about that person are blessings from God.

The worst things about that person are arenas for redemption.

People are hungry for encouragement and love.

Not long before he died, Studs Terkel wrote a memoir. It has the best title of any memoir I have ever read. The title comes from a Dylan Thomas poem:

> And every evening at sun-down
> I ask a blessing on the town,
> For whether we last the night or no
> I'm sure is always touch and go.[26]

The title is: *Touch and Go.*[27]

Or, TAG.

Tag, you're it.

Discover More Online

CHECK OUT INTERACTIVES FOR YOUR PERSONAL OR SMALL-GROUP USE
AND MUCH MORE ON THE NUDGE WEB SITE:

WWW.NUDGETHEBOOK.COM

Chapter 8

PROMISE: USE YOUR NOSE

Do You Have L'eau de Jesus?

Breathing Jesus

In 2009, eBay ran a Christmas commercial that took head-on its main competitor, Etsy. While eBay sells manufactured goods, Etsy puts on the market homespun crafts. In the ad, a twentysomething young man tries to convince an older demographic to stop giving him handmade gifts. "No one likes them anyway," he says. As he picks up a crocheted item that his grandmother made him, he smells it, wrinkles his nose, and says, "Smells like church."

This can be seen as another example of the open scorn with which the church in North America is increasingly held by this post-Christian, pluralist culture. Or does its hint of an old and musty smellscape for the church suggest something else?

Does the church have odor issues? Do our smells de-nudge? Has the odor of the purified become the odor of the petrified and the putrid? Do Christians need aromatherapy? The common cold, usually caught through interpersonal relationships, can block one or more of the senses. Congested nose, decreased sense of taste, watery eyes, and achy joints contribute to a lessened openness to receive the sensory stimuli that are all around us. Have Christians become stuffed up?

249

Maybe Malcolm Gladwell was wrong. It's not Blink.[1] It's Sniff.

When God's glory shines, the sweetness smells. "No one has ever seen God," says John's gospel.[2] But we do get glimpses of God's glory. The divine presence marks the spot with the smell of glory. God's presence wafts sweet.

Nudge is the art of aroma persuasion. Nudge is the promise of nasal communication. Nudgers lead others by the nose to where Jesus is. Dogs teach us that the best place to be is where their master's smell is, even when they're not there in person. Nudgers trust that all people want to be where the Master's smell is.

In this chapter, we will explore briefly the glory that comes with a high smell intelligence, the possibility of your nose becoming an antenna of truth, and we will discover the undercover role of smell as a hush-hush secret agent for Jesus in an increasingly hostile, cloak-and-dagger culture.

Before I say anything, let me admit that the smell organ has inspired more than its share of nincompoopery and poppycockery, if not tomfoolery and even skulduggery. At the same time, few have appreciated smell's pivotal role in history and in religion. Nothing has so nudged the exploration of planet Earth as the demand for fragrances and tastes. Columbus, Magellan, Vasco da Gama, and Sir Francis Drake were originally lured, not by territory or gold, but significantly by the spices of the Indies. As I mentioned in the taste chapter of this book, and as historian John Keay so memorably puts it, "Atrocities would be freely committed, wars fitfully fought, states toppled, people uprooted, hundreds of ships lost, and thousands of lives squandered—all for limited quantities of various desiccated barks, shriveled berries, knobbly roots, dead buds, crumpled membranes, sticky gums, and old fruit stones, none of them exactly indispensable and most of them quite irrelevant to the generality of mankind."[3] The Jesus story begins with tightly wrapped swaddling cloths in a smelly cave and ends with strewn and stacked perfumed burial cloths in a different kind of smelly cave.

> [Perfume] decorates the day. It makes you feel as if the colors of
> the air have changed. It's a substitute for having an orchestra
> follow you about playing the theme song of your choice.[4]
>
> —Olfactory scientist Tania Sanchez

"Sniff"

"What's that you have on?"

Have you ever been asked that? Is that someone's way of telling you that you don't smell like yourself? Or that you smell better than usual? Or that you stink?

Have you ever shaken hands with somebody, and then you can't get their scent off you?

Have you ever been in a room after someone has left, but you can still smell them there?

You scent every room you spill into. You leave a smell fingerprint wherever you go. What do you smell like?

The apostle Paul once wrote that you and I are to be the fragrance that triggers memories of Christ, the essence of Jesus. "We are to God the aroma of Christ."[5]

So what does Jesus smell like?

Essence of Faith

The more science explores the nose and smell's lost language that lies buried in our brains, the more it appears that the apostle Paul has not just come up with another rich metaphor. Religion is in part the parapsychology of the nose. Nudging dwells in the nose, but mostly it just sleeps there. It's time to wake up and smell the Rose of Sharon, the Lily of the Valley.

> Noses have they, but they smell not.
>
> —Psalm 115:6 KJV

The discovery of *pheromones* or odors that transmit messages—"hormones you can smell"—will go down as one of the most significant discoveries of the twentieth century. The first text on pheromones was published in a 1974 study of insects, plants, and animals, with one chapter on "The Likelihood of Human Pheromones."[6]

Scratch that word *likelihood*. It is not just flowers that send aerosol telegrams, perceptible in minute quantities, even as low as one part per billion. From cradle to grave, we communicate with each other and with other species by chemical messages from the nose switchboard.

Here is one of the stories that turned my head in the direction of smell. In European zoos, gorilla males often killed their babies. But in one Oklahoma zoo, the males were nurturing fathers, not killers of the young. So they switched gorillas, and sure enough, once in Oklahoma, the European gorillas became nurturing. What made the difference? The Oklahoma zoo was primitive and spare. It did not have glass enclosures but open cages. The gorillas in the cheap zoo could smell the amniotic fluid when the babies were born, and the smell kicked in the paternal instinct.

How badly we can miss the importance of smell is illustrated in the "Myth of the Bad-Nose Birds."[7] Back in the early days of the nineteenth century, John James Audubon started the fiction that birds could not smell based on his turkey vultures research, which proved to him that they couldn't smell decaying meat (the real problem was that the meat Audubon tried to feed the vultures was so bad that even they turned up their noses at it).

We used to think that birds navigated their way along earth's magnetic fields. We now know that they use odor maps and sniff navigation. Birds don't so much read a map as inhale a map. In fact, European starlings released far from home get hopelessly lost if they can't smell anything.[8]

There are entire industries now built on humans sending olfactory messages and odor fingerprinting. "Fragrance marketing" is already common in the marketplace.[9] Select smells can get you to gamble more, buy more, borrow more, stay in malls longer (citrus), sell your house faster (fresh-baked bread), pay your bills more promptly, work harder, think more positively, stop panic attacks (apple-spice), calm your nerves (why do flight attendants bake cookies before you land?), and pump up your sex life (lavender-pumpkin).[10] People will pay more for Nike shoes in a store with a floral scent in the air.[11] Certain combinations of floral and spice scents cause men to see women as 4.1 pounds lighter than they actually are.[12] The scent of grapefruit causes men to see women an average of six years younger than they actually are. You don't want to know what the scents of grape and cucumber do to those perceptions of weight.

Kat Von D is a tattoo artist and star of *L.A. Ink*, a reality show that focuses on her High Voltage Tattoo business. She now has her own line of makeup that is carried at Sephora, as well as two fragrances that were recently launched: Saint and Sinner. "Every woman has two sides," says beauty addict Kat Von D, "and I've created a fragrance for both." Saint is sweet, an addictive blend of caramel, vanilla, and jasmine. Sinner plays up a dark and mysterious side with hints of vetiver, plum, and cinnamon.[13]

What happens though when you mix both scents, Saint and Sinner? Well, what do you smell like?

I'm not just talking about your body and the "armpit effect." I'm also talking about your breath. Your breath is an odor cartridge. Breath is more than 99 percent water, but roughly 3,000 other compounds have been detected in human breath. The average sample contains at least 200 compounds, including bits of DNA, proteins, and fats floating in the mist. With the right "nose," scientists can tell how healthy someone is by their breath. "The breath is a window into the blood," Joachim D. Pleil insists.[14]

Might it be that we can tell how someone is doing spiritually by their breath as well? Not just their body odor, but the smell of their breathing of life? How often have I met so-called "Spirit-filled" people where the Holy Spirit had halitosis? How many Christians profess to follow Christ, but speak with brimstone breath?

The dance of predator and prey is orchestrated by a billion chemical fiddlers. In a unit as large as a forest, a jungle, or a planet, entire symphonies of information resonate through the air, an inaudible behavioral ballet, choreographed by countless biochemical transactions.[15]

—Howard Rheingold

Part of sensing the Spirit is to use your nose. Amazingly, we now know you can taste pheromones, which link taste and smell in a bionic communication network. Smell is a sister sense to taste, setting them apart from all the other senses, both from a biologic and semiotic perspective. You can't enjoy the savory media of taste and smell without using them up. The more you look at a picture with your eyes, the smaller that picture doesn't become. The more you smell a fragrance, the more it is used up. The more you appreciate food or fragrance, the more they vanish. The more you listen to music, or look at a sculpture, the more you don't use up the objects. But with smell and taste, appreciation and preservation go in opposite directions.

The nose is a lost language in more ways than one. Humans have lost about 600 of our 1,000 scent-genes because of the use-it-or-lose-it principle. The triumph of writing, and the monopoly of the written word ("Write it down"; "Put it down!"), was especially devastating to smell, taste, gesture, and image. Undone and outdone by the eyes, the perfume industry recognizes only three major kinds of scent, because the rest of our smell repertoire is so dysfunctional and dormant. The average human being is born recognizing approximately 10,000 different odors, but we fail to lock in the connection.

Smell is the only sense where your brain connects directly with the outside world. Every other sense organ collects data by intermediaries. But your nose is directly connected to the most emotional zones of your brain—your limbic system, especially your amygdala and your hippocampus. This is why smell is an open sesame to memories: It unlocks your brain's memory board and secret storage compartments that you even forgot you had. That is also why the nose is so sensitive, that there is a delayed arrival of a smell in the second nostril that is only milliseconds long. Yet it is discernible, and it enables us to tell where an aroma is coming from.

We can recall smells with 65 percent accuracy after a year. Visual recall of photos sinks to about 50 percent after only three months. Memories are perfumes, scents that sleep in the unconscious, ready to be released at the slightest scratch of a molecule. But it's not just the brain where memory is located. Memory resides in the whole body—in nerve connections, in the cells of your immune system, in all five of your senses. Smell unlocks the memories first.

The nose nudge is what theologians call "anamnesis," the memory of what we did not know we knew. The nudge of the Jesus scent awakens the latent desire of the human heart and gets people to remember their deepest hungers and thirsts, which often get forgotten for superficial substitutes. The most basic desire of the human heart? A relationship with God. The very ubiquity of Augustine's quote ("Our hearts are restless until they find their rest in You") is proof of this hunger.

But the nose nudge also helps us remember not just our origins in God but the stories of our origins. How long can the body of Christ thrive with only twenty years of short-term memory? The nose nudge may be the cure for the church's short-term memory crisis.

Every May, in the English countryside of Derbyshire, there are a series of village festivals to offer gratitude for their wells and springs. They use only living material to decorate their wells and springs—flowers, nuts, leaves, berries, moss, and bark—which goes by the name of "Well Dressings." Best described as "stained-glass windows made of flowers," Well Dressings most often tell a story: Noah saving the animals from the flood; the plagues of Egypt; St. George slaying the dragon; or Jesus as the Good Shepherd, with Jesus' robe made of pansy petals, the sky hydrangeas.[16] Think of a Rose Bowl parade with the focus of passing on the village heritage, not the images and stories of Disney or Hollywood. These Well Dressing festivals stretch from May to September, and since every festival needs food and dance, the Well Dressings are major communal events that lock in place the biblical stories especially with smell and taste.

What if churches were to put on such memory-marking festivals to fast-track the stories of Jesus? What if the liturgical calendar of scents in which the smells change with the seasons was to frame the life of the soul? Our medieval ancestors attributed to every angel and archangel, as well as saint, a flower and scent that invested the invisible with a presence. What if our apertures to the eternal, and our prayer life, were to become more "scented"?

What you see and hear grows dim quickly, but what you smell lives on for a long time. Odor is linked with memory because, unlike the other four senses, scent bypasses the conscious brain and appeals directly to the limbic system, whereas the other senses register impressions that travel first to the rational brain centers and then arrive at emotional matrices. There is a direct connection between smells and emotions.

The fastest way to the emotions is through smells. The most powerful trigger to an emotional response is through scent. Some researchers contend that 75 percent of the emotions we generate on a daily basis are affected by smell.[17] This is one reason why just the mere talk of moving a church or altering the architecture can be so threatening. Sanctuaries smell holy, an unmistakable odor of sanctity that both reveres and makes us re-member the great cloud who have hallowed that place with their songs, prayers, and tears in unbroken worship generation after generation. When I was pastor of a church near the Abbey of the Genesee, I found myself sneaking into the monastery chapel at least once a week for a matins or vespers. It became almost an obsession. Years later, I realized why the pull was so strong: The smell of the church had become intoxicating. The chapel exhaled holy odors of incense, oiled pews, aged flooring, beeswax candles, stone walls, wine, "monk's bread," books, sweaty monks' robes, etc.

As I look back at a point where my life could have veered in one of two directions, a high-paying career in the corporate world or graduate-school debt, I chose poverty because of a smell: the Library of Congress. As many Saturdays as we could manage, some college buddies and I would get up early and drive the hundred miles from Richmond, Virginia, to Washington, D.C. There we spent the day studying in the immense reading room of the Library of Congress. The smell of dust, wood polish, leather, and ancient body odors worked their magic, and to this day I can smell that noble space (along with the apple turnovers served in a coffee shop across the street).

Just as a place like the Abbey of the Genesee or the Library of Congress can have special meaning to us and becomes invested with all sorts of charged emotions, so these sites can also be invested with negative emotions: the place where a missing child was last seen; the place where a sexual assault took place; the place (e.g., courtroom steps) where a loved one was convicted of a crime; the place where you were always dropped off for day care. A new battlefield technology delivers orders with odors. A collar is outfitted with capsules of different scents, with each smell assigned a predetermined action, which can be released by remote control. It has been proved that olfactory commands trigger emotional responses more than verbal orders.[18]

> In nature's infinite book of secresy
> a little I can read.[19]
>
> —Soothsayer in Shakespeare's *Antony and Cleopatra*

What if nudgers were to learn what memories were most cherished and prized, and then reinforce those memories with our gifts and blessings? For example, a friend loves Christmas and all the rituals of childhood associated with this season of the year. So my birthday gift to her is often Philip B all-over shampoo called Nordic Wood, which fills the shower with the aromatic freshness of green forests in Scandinavia, releasing cleansing memories of what happened around the Christmas tree.

I have another friend who is a divorced father with tender, teary memories of playing with his kids at North Carolina beaches, where they would lather each other's bodies with coconut sunscreen. There are dozens of shampoos with the dominant smell of coconut (Nexus Therapee is my favorite), and it's my way of encouraging him to begin each day singing and dancing in the shower with his kids at the beach.

God created chocolate for a reason. If love is the point of life, then what's the point of life without chocolate? Love connoisseurs are chocolate connoisseurs. No one ought to be bigger buyers of chocolate than Christians. Your nudge relationship isn't deep enough until you know which candy someone would choose: Baby Ruth, Musketeers, Butterfinger, Snickers, Hershey's, Almond Joy, Clark Bar, Good 'n' Plenty, energy bar, chocolate-covered raisins. Some church, not some movie, should have been first with the slogan "Life is like a box of chocolates."[20] Why don't churches have water fountains in the narthex and chocolate fountains in the fellowship halls? That way, the chocolate smell would nudge us to pay attention and celebrate the life that is, in this very moment, not the life we don't have or are working so hard to create, so that our hungry hearts are never satisfied.

Besides, chocolate is a vegetable.[21]

I annoy my kids with my smell nudges, I know. But every time I take them on a trip or make a family memory, I either wear a unique cologne or try to get them to douse themselves in something distinctive in hopes of locking in our time together in their souls with a memory marker. For the rest of their lives, I can count on the joys of our time together being re-membered whenever they run into that smell or spray it on them.

Smells are so strong on the emotions, they can induce physical reactions. In the past, towns were toxic. Every city was an assault on the senses and made people sick. The bigger the city, the bigger the assault. In the nineteenth century, when you visited London, New York, or Paris, a ghastly stench greeted you. The Thames River in London was called "the Great Stink," because it was less a river than a sewage pipe, and the flow of fecal sludge boasted an odor that could shut down Parliament. My grandparents' Appalachian outhouse made me throw up more than once. Pumpkin pie makes me salivate to this day because of my mother's recipe. I had a professor once with such bad breath that I get nauseated when breath reaches this state described by Kingsley Amis: "His mouth had been used as a latrine by some small creature of the night, and then as a mausoleum."[22]

If the emotions are not properly engaged, truth cannot be heard. In terms of Cocteau's paradox ("I am the lie that tells the truth"), smell is the sheath that enables the sword of truth to be picked up. Lancaster Seminary professor Frank Stalfa hammers into the heads of his students this six-word mantra: "Truth without compassion is merely aggression."[23] Truth neither has the stench of a shrinking violet nor is as perfumed as a peony. We can trust that every scent from the Father is a truth that does to us what catnip does to all cats. What comes from the pits of hell does to us what naphthalene does to moths.

I grew up going to camp meetings where the tabernacle air was fragrant with sawdust and the tent air swirled with pine. I have a theory about when the vitality of the camp-meeting tradition in evangelicalism ended: when camp meetings replaced tents with wooden cottages, and when auditoriums replaced tabernacles. Early camp meetings strewed on the floor sawdust or bundled shavings such as was used for horse bedding. Sometimes they used straw, but the danger of fire was greater with straw. The crew that put up the tents sprinkled the aisles with sawdust and shavings and piled it extra thick around the altar. They also put a noticeable mound of sawdust near the entrance to the tabernacle, so that going out and coming in, everyone knew they were invited to kneel and seek God. When the smell of holiness was cleared away and cleaned up, the camp-meeting experience lost much of its magic and power.

We all have a smell-recognition system for danger and death. There are lots of problems you can smell before you can see them (dogs and cats telegraph fires first because of this). Insects can detect oleic acid, a fatty acid that is released upon death, and will stay away from the smell. Ants have the equivalent of cemeteries for their dead, and a living ant that is drenched with a drop of oleic acid will be carried off kicking and screaming to the cemetery to be buried alive. Humans also give off the smell of death. A terminal physical crisis triggers a "death hormone" that soothes pain, slows time, and expands awareness. You can literally smell death in people. And you can smell death in churches, I am convinced. Some churches give off the smell of death. The air can be humid with Jesus just like the air can be putrid with the smell of rot and rat.

For some, perfume is a form of olfactory camouflage for one's natural body odor. For others, perfume is best used as a means of underscoring a person's existing emissions, smells that are the product of a person's metabolism and body chemistry.[24] The Jesus smell does not eradicate our unique scent, giving us all the same smell. Rather, the Jesus smell works like the art of medieval perfumers, who concocted personal scents for people by mixing and matching odors from a palette of special ingredients.

Navajo women are famous for their woven rugs and blankets. Many things make Navajo weavings so special—colorful stripes, stepped triangles and diamonds, forty to sixty weft-counts—but perhaps the least known is their closure ritual of weaving an opening in the wool for their souls to come out. In their artistry, they have already woven their souls into the fabric, which is the true "signature" of their art. Now they need to leave places for their souls to come out. When you don't leave an opening, your soul gets trapped in your goods and shrivels from the souljacking. The soul squeezing out of the hole leaves a signature scent in the same way extracting the "seminal" being of a plant (its essence, its scent) used to be an art form and a secret, an alchemical process that drew from the plant its spiritual nature, its "essence" or seminal form from which and through which the plant mysteriously grew.

The Smell Test

Some people are hired to give "organoleptic analysis," but every cook does it. It's called "the Smell Test." You smell food to make sure it's fresh, or it's done.

If you're a USAmerican, you know what America smells like. The smell that defines America? Miller Lite did a survey and found that the number-one smell in the country, the one that makes us most think of America, is smoky barbecue. Apple pie came in second, followed by the ocean, and in fourth place—garbage. (Where is the coffee?)

If you're a Christian, you know what Jesus smells like. And you can tell when something doesn't smell like Jesus. The smell of your lover is intoxicating. The smell of Jesus, the greatest Lover who ever lived, fills the soul with elation.

So what does Jesus smell like? How can we describe the smell of Jesus? A Christian can be recognized by the smell of ...

burning (burning candles, burning bush, s'mores)

fresh-baked bread

pine trees and sawdust

GOOD smells (GOOD = Get Out of Doors)

coffee

chocolate

air right after a rain

ocean spray

a new baby

sweat

ambergris, the most sought-after smell in the world (lumps of
    genuine ambergris are sperm whale vomit baked by the sun while
    bobbing about on the surface of the ocean; no two lumps are
    exactly the same, and its aroma can linger for three hundred years)

How beautiful are the feet of those who bring good news!

—Romans 10:15

Does Jesus always smell good? Then something's wrong. Jesus does not always smell like the Rose of Sharon or Lilies of the Valley. Sometimes Jesus smells bad, not because he himself smells bad, but because he likes to be around "fishy" people and welcomes bad-smelling people. Jesus isn't afraid to let others' smells rub off on him. Sometimes Jesus smells like ...

stables
gyms and locker rooms
dirty diapers
the homeless
trans e-methyl-hexenoic acid[25]
trimethylaminuria (TMAU)[26]
smelly feet

"Beautiful feet" are most often bad-smelling feet. Sometimes Jesus takes on as foul a smell as chaulmoogra oil, which was for many years the only known palliative for leprosy. If you aren't smelling awful smells sometimes, then you're not where Jesus is. Jesus' mission took him where it could be said, as was said of Lazarus: "You stink!" Sometimes Jesus has malodorous disciples and a body that gives off mixed smells. "The Russian Church has the true smell," Maurice Baring contends. "It smells of the poor, of untarred leather, onions, and human sweat."[27]

Saints are olfactory geniuses. They squirt the smell of Jesus wherever they go. It was said that when St. Hubert breathed his last, there spread throughout Brittany an odor so sweet that it seemed as if God had brought together all the flowers of spring. Some thought the odor of the Holy Spirit was more "like unto cinnamon and balsam and chosen myrrh."[28]

If nudge is on nose alert, are we more poised to smell evil or goodness? After all, Jesus is more present at a Dave Crowder than Dave Matthews concert, right? Do we first smell the evil, or the good?

Follow your nose: Gardeners can smell spring before it makes its appearance; sailors can smell land before they see it; farmers can smell rain before they hear it. Christians can smell Jesus before they hear, see, touch, or taste him. And if a person or thing doesn't pass the "smell test," then be on high alert.

> The gate of heaven is everywhere.[29]
>
> —Thomas Merton

We are surrounded by a sea of scents. When danger lurks, our sense of smell goes into overdrive.[30] Perhaps no one has better described this than Helen Keller, who was deaf and blind:

> The sense of smell has told me of a coming storm hours before there was any sign of it visible. I notice first a throb of expectancy, a slight quiver, a concentration in my nostrils. As the storm draws nearer, my nostrils dilate, the better to receive the flood of earth-odors which seem to multiply and extend, until I feel the splash of rain against my cheek. As the tempest departs, receding farther and farther, the odors fade, become fainter and fainter, and die away beyond the bar of space.[31]

The smell sharpens when something bad happens or danger is on the horizon. Smell can steer us clear of danger or scent out dry rot. "I smell a rat."

My kids can never say their father never took them camping. Of course, I don't take them camping as other fathers do. I take them "car camping." When we miss the last San Juan ferry for the evening, to save money, we camp out for the night in the car. They are not always happy about this, since I usually choose the Safeway parking lot where there is free wireless but the lights shine brightly all night long. The 5:30 ferry, however, has a standard greeter: a dog who goes to every vehicle and smells every tire and trunk in the ferry line. The number of drug dealers posing as tourists would surprise you.

It is true, the pose is exposed by the nose. A foul odor was a tell-tale presence of demons or the devil. In the past, the whiff of sulphur supposedly betrayed the presence of evil. The German writer and journalist Friedrich Percyval Reck-Malleczewen recalled his first meeting with Adolf Hitler. It was in 1920, at the Munich home of the composer and conductor Clemens von Franckenstein, where Hitler sat in a pair of spats and a floppy, wide-brimmed hat, clutching a leather riding whip. Appearing uncomfortable in the opulent setting of the villa and teetering on the edge of a chair, Hitler overrode his host's topics of conversation, "snatching hungrily at the words like a cat at pieces of raw meat." Working himself into a frenzy, Hitler rose to his feet and launched into a long, ranting monologue, all the while thwacking his boot with the riding whip. Franckenstein's servants rushed in, thinking that their employer was being attacked. After Hitler had said his peace and left, there was a long and puzzled silence. Then Franckenstein stood up and opened one of the large windows looking onto the garden.

> It was not that our grim guest had been unclean or fouled
> the room in the way that so often happens in a Bavarian
> village. But the fresh air dispelled the sense of oppression.
> It was not that an unclean body had been in the room,
> but something else, the unclean essence of a monstrosity.[32]

The question is whether or not our noses can go into high gear to smell the fragrance of Christ.

> Do not look for trials and assume extreme penances,
> but learn to accept the myrrh of suffering sent by God,

for when accepted lovingly, these bring joy.[33]
—Dominican friar/teacher/preacher Johannes Tauler

Jesus had a smell test. He called it by a different name. "Watch out for false prophets. They come to you in sheep's clothing, but inwardly they are ferocious wolves. By their fruit you will recognize them."[34] People might most reliably be known for what they are by examining their "fruits." The true and false prophets look the same. We can't tell them apart by the "truths" they utter. Even our own telling "the truth" is little evidence that we ourselves are godly. The only way to tell what's what and who's who is by their fruits. In one place Jesus says clearly, "My Father is glorified by this, that you bear much fruit, and so prove to be My disciples."[35]

Jesus' version of the smell test, which one might call the "fruit test," even led to the one time in the Bible where it says Jesus cursed. Here was a fig tree, lush with leaves, maybe even with flowers, but barren of fruit. When people are all flower and leaf but no fruit, not even a smell of fruit, it's an early-warning signal that something isn't right. The fig tree was given a brief reprieve before it would be dug up as worthless.[36]

Our mission in life? "Be fruit" and "Be fruitful and multiply." When God said, "Be fruitful and multiply," God was only calling us to reflect his nature: "Those who remain in me, and I in them, will produce much fruit."[37] A minister's life is a tree that flowers all week and bears fruit that ripens on Sunday.

We are all fruit. Take an apple. It has a pit. It is a pit-filled, pitiful core. It has hard, sometimes grizzly skin. It has soft pulp that turns brown when exposed to the light and unprotected. But that is the nature of fruit. None are perfect. In fact, unblemished, polished fruit is boring. And all fruit gives off a smell.

"Every good tree bears good fruit," Jesus said, "but a bad tree bears bad fruit."[38] Galatians 5 says to look for specific fruit, not numbers of fruit, but features of fruit that can feed a hungry world.

How do you know if your fruit is good or forbidden? If just being fruitful isn't enough, but you need certain kinds of fruit, each with its own smell, what are they? Paul gives us a hallmark and homiletic of fruit: love, joy, peace, patience, kindness, generosity, faithfulness, gentleness, and self-control.[39]

Each hallmark and homiletic of fruit gives off a certain scent. But like all fruit, you don't judge it by its skin any more than you judge a book by its cover. You can't tell what the fruit smells like when you finger it and enter into a relationship with it. The smell test on an unfingered fruit works about as well as the outer rind of a melon tells us about the fruit of the melon.

Here is the smell test of a fruit:

The smell of love over fear.

The smell of joy over woe.

The smell of peace over contentment.

The smell of patience over short-temperedness.

The smell of kindness over neglect.

The smell of generosity over selfishness.

The smell of faithfulness over deceitfulness.

The smell of gentleness over pride.

The smell of self-control over immediate gratification.

Where Jesus is living, you smell "good fruit."

Forbidden Fruit Creates Many Jams[40]
—Church sign

One of my favorite examples of nudge as "aroma persuasion," where the baking of fresh bread right out of the oven connects to the presence of the Bread of Life, comes from a friend whose life hit the wall hard in 2001. He describes it as a "747 coming out of the sky at 700 mph, nose first into the dirt from 30,000 ft. Not a piece bigger than a quarter survived."[41] In other words, one moment he was living off an executive expense account that accommodated $500 dinners. The next moment he was fending for himself in the kitchen, cooking to survive.

His kitchen survival kit sported one bulletproof bandage: He calls it "the chicken bag." Once he mastered the recipe to feed the hungers of his own family, he started using it to treat the ailments of others.

> Flowers leave a part of their fragrance
> in the hands that bestow them.
> —Ancient Chinese proverb

Here is how the chicken bag works: Buy a big bag for baking turkeys in the oven and the biggest chicken you can afford. Wash the chicken, and stick a lemon that has been cut in half inside it. Wash an entire bag of potatoes and carrots, and throw them into the bag with the chicken. Spice everything up using garlic, onion powder, salt, pepper, and paprika; then cut up a bag of onions, and throw them in for good measure. If you can afford it, buy a rack of chicken drumsticks, and place them around the chicken too. Then throw in ½ a coffee cup of water, and seal the bag with the tie. Cut a tiny slit in the top so it won't explode. Then bake the thing for 3–6 hours at 350 degrees on a flat cookie tray with a ½-inch lip (you don't want small leaks to cause problems). Unless you intensely dislike tender chicken, you can't overcook the thing. Because it's in the bag, drain the juice from the bottom into a container for a soup base.

When someone is sick or my friend is moved to bless someone with a home-cooked meal, he prepares the chicken bag at his house, but then puts it in the oven at their house. Not only do they get fed on their own terms and on their own schedule, but they arrive home to a house that smells enticing.

A house that smells like Jesus, not because it says, "I'm your Christian neighbor," but "I'm your friend," is a house where you can smell the fresh aroma of the gospel. Flowers lose their scent while they're refrigerated. The aroma of Christ doesn't fare well when frozen. It needs to be baked and taken fresh out of the oven.

Jesus, the Homeless, and Cigars

Smells are surer than sounds or sights
to make the heart strings vibrate.[42]
—Rudyard Kipling

I asked my friend Mark Hogg to tell this story for the readers of *Nudge* about one of his ministries. Mark is head of EDGE OUTREACH in Louisville, Kentucky.

EDGE OUTREACH does several health clinics every year, some overseas and some local. The local clinics are for the poor and/or homeless. This particular clinic was for the homeless in Louisville and it was the coldest day of the year ... a whopp'n 3 degrees. As with all our clinics, it is important to EDGE that every person be treated with dignity and respect—all 300 of them. We find that so many are treated as if they don't exist, and we wanted this day to be special for them ... a day when they did not feel like a charity case. So instead of just checking their eyes and giving them a prescription which they will never be able to fill, we checked their eyes and got them glasses that day. Instead of giving them a new pair of socks, we gave them a pedicure and new socks. Instead of letting them know that they have high blood pressure, we lined them up with clinics that will take personal care. And after a haircut and a fried chicken lunch, we treated them to a cigar … and not just any cigar but a tasty, fat CAO cigar.

Yup, the EDGE men met the homeless on the sidewalk, and they smoked and talked with them; and I must say, there was some lively conversation. Not only that, but men and women alike stood a little taller, smiled a little more than they had before, and commented on how long it's been since they had a treat like that. Some smoked a little, then saved the rest for another day. Some smoked it out, and some smelled the cigar. And as they did, you could see their eyes light up with memories.

I've been told that I live my life in vignettes. I catch little pictures in my mind, and I can't release them. One vignette that I will always have with me is a man that looked like Kramer from *Seinfeld*. This guy's hair was going in every direction, and he did not want a haircut. He kind of staggered, holding onto his bedroll, finishing his chicken and said, "I don't need no haircut, but I could sure do with another pedicure and cigar." Sweet memory. I think of him often. Thanks CAO—for cigars, dignity, respect, and memories.

There is an ancient story about two artists who shared the same garret. During a very long night, one of them painted on the ceiling a collage of disjointed, helter-skelter images. The next morning, the second artist eyeballed the painting intensely for a long time. Finally he said, "Try as hard as I can, that doesn't look like anything." To which the other replied, "Do you realize how hard it is to paint a picture that looks like nothing at all?"

By living our lives in helter-skelter mode, people aren't taking the easy way out. Life becomes a hard-labor camp when you live a "nothing at all" life. Nudgers leave in their wake a fragrance, a *sillage,* that reminds the weary and worn-out that there is an easier, more natural way to go through life. When you get a whiff of the Jesus Sillage, in one breath, you know that we were not designed or destined for slave-labor camps. When the smell of Jesus wafts your way, you hear echoes of mercy, whispers of grace.

The Burning Bush

> Blessed are you, Adonai our God, Ruler of the Universe,
> Creator of all the spices.[43]
> —Havdalah prayer

The Sabbath concludes in an observant Jewish home with a ceremony called Havdalah. The rituals that precede and include Havdalah involve songs, chants, drumming and clapping, stories, prayers, candles, and most importantly, breathing in beautiful scents from the often ornate Havdalah spice box. Havdalah concludes with a chalice of wine, which like the spice box, is passed to everyone present. Finally, the candle that was lit to usher in the Shabbat and separate this RIP day from the rest of the week is dipped into the wine and extinguished. Thus begins the mission and moil of a new week. At Roman banquets, the evening was over when doves' wings were dipped in perfume from glass flasks and the doves were released. At Jewish tables, the Sabbath was over when you smelled the spices and the smoke from the wine-dipped candle.

Biblical Israel was a sensory culture with a religious fluency in all five senses. God was not only heard; God was tasted, observed, touched, and smelled. We still have a language for this ("loud colors," "sour notes," "sweet smells"), but our experiences lag behind our language in Christianity's sensorially subdivided universe.

If you've allowed yourself to be nudged this far, you know that I am convinced that the eye gate and the ear gate are no longer enough to nudge Christ in people. There must now be as well a smell gate, a taste gate, and a touch gate. Truth is not meant just for the ears, eyes, or hands. Truth is for the whole body. Nudging is truth conveyed through several media to several senses simultaneously. Just as medieval supplicants felt and touched the religious image, so we must learn to reach out to the God who is already there in multisensory, synaesthetic presence.

Technically, synaesthesia is the stimulation of one sensory perception by another. Usually it takes the form of color vision: Words or numbers taking on colors. But there are cases where notes taste.[44] ES (known only by her initials) is a professional musician who tastes what she hears. A major third tastes sweet. A minor third, salty. A fourth has the flavor of mowed grass. An octave is tasteless. Less technically, synaesthesia is the ability to live life in a unity of sensory experience and expression.[45]

Nudgers must learn to be synaesthetes. Nudgers must learn sensory faith transactions.

> My soul longs for the candle and the spices.
> If only you would pour me a cup of wine for Havdalah.
> O angels high, pave a way for me,
> clear the path for the bewildered
> and open the gates that I may enter,
> My heart yearning,
> I shall lift up my eyes to the Lord,
> who provides for my needs day and night.[46]
> —Yemenite Havdalah chant

The first Havdalah, I believe, was Moses at the burning bush. The burning bush is the Rosetta Stone of recognition, of an awakening to the God who is already there that was spread across the sensory spectrum.

You can see the bush sparkle.

You can hear the bush crack and pop.

You can feel the bush's warmth.

You can taste its barbecue.

You can smell its smokiness.

All senses beckon us to the presence of God. And for the rest of the biblical story, there is an integration of sensory experience into a synaesthetic spirituality. In Exodus we read, "And all the people saw the thunderings, and the lightnings, and the [voice of the shofar], and the mountain smoking."[47] In the Hebrew Bible, God inhales the aroma of burnt sacrifices and offerings. *Perfume* means literally "the smoke that passes through," and the center of Jewish religious life was the temple, where there was a massive slaughter of animals. The temple of Jerusalem would have been smelled long before it was seen.

Jesus became God's burning bush, the new temple. The synaesthetic glory of Jesus comes today as it came then: from the sweet incense and bitter savor of his offerings—his life, death, and resurrection. In other words, we nudge others to see glory in the rejected, derided, marginalized, suffering Christ. We have learned to call glory crucified beauty, crucified truth, crucified goodness. What it means for the Son of Man to be "glorified" is very different from the world's glory. The cross is Jesus' greatest glory.

The gift of Jesus must be treated as a gift, not as a possession or a commodity. That this gift is given to be shared was made explicit in our role as "stewards of the mysteries." Our role as nudgers is to steward the mysteries, which means we neither hide the mysteries under a bushel,[48] nor cast pearls before swine.[49] But it is only through others, in and through one another, that nudgers can one day say what God said to Moses at the burning bush: "I am who I am."

When Moses stands before the burning bush and asks, "If I go to the Israelites and tell them that the God of their forefathers has sent me to them, and they ask me his name, what I shall say?" he receives an answer that more or less boils down to: "Mind your own business."[50] We nudgers need to learn to mind our own business even when sent out on a mission to be about God's business. We are not to nudge people into awareness of how God is present in our lives. As nudgers we mind God's business and help people pay attention to what God is doing in their lives.

But this one thing we must mind above all. Do you remember the first thing Moses hears at the burning bush? He is told to take off his shoes. According to the ancient interpreters of this text, this was not because he has just stepped on holy ground. No, all ground is holy where God dwells. Our problem is that we have protective habits and cushioning customs that encase and enclose us (i.e., shoes), preventing us from experiencing the divine presence … the God who is already there.

Every bush is burning. Can you see it?

Fire shows itself as light, the creative energy of God we know as HOPE.

Every bush is burning. Can you hear it?

Fire shows itself as sound, the creative energy of God we know as FAITH.

Every bush is burning. Can you touch it?

Fire shows itself as touch, the creative energy of God we know as LOVE.

Every bush is burning. Can you taste it?

Fire shows itself as taste, the creative energy of God we know as HOME.

Every bush is burning. Can you smell it?

Fire shows itself as smell, the creative energy of God we know as JESUS.

Discover More Online

CHECK OUT INTERACTIVES FOR YOUR PERSONAL OR SMALL-GROUP USE
AND MUCH MORE ON THE NUDGE WEB SITE:

WWW.NUDGETHEBOOK.COM

Postface

TRACKING GOD'S WAYS

I have never seen the notions in any other place; yet he that reads
them here, persuades himself that he has always felt them.

—Dr. Johnson (aka, Samuel Johnson, 1709–1784)

If truth is recognition, the art of attention is more important than ever
before.

The art of attention repivots the focus of the church from hermeneutics
to semiotics. Hermeneutics is the theory and practice of interpretation.
Hans-Georg Gadamer (1900–2002), one of the most representative
philosophers of the twentieth century, developed a philosophical hermeneutics. But pop culture is filled with hermeneutics as well. Part of the
enduring popularity of astrology during the modern period was its easy
hermeneutics: Memorize the twelve signs of the zodiac, learn a little Greek
cosmology, and remember the characteristics of a couple of planets (Mars
and Venus will get you far), and presto: a hermeneutic for life!

Christians were preoccupied with a different hermeneutics: the interpretation of biblical texts. Again, poet/artist William Blake prophesied the
hermeneutic battles of modern Christianity in this little ditty: "Both read
the Bible day and night / But thou readst black where I read white."[1]

Where hermeneutics is preoccupied with meaning, semiotics (or the
art and science of sign reading) is preoccupied with dancing. Semiotics
is the art and science of paying attention. A spiritual semiotics is paying
attention to what the Holy Spirit is up to in our world today.[2] The future

lies in those who can help others focus their attention and *pay attention.*

José Ortega y Gasset once attended a Martin Heidegger lecture at a philosophy conference in Germany. When the lecture had concluded, Ortega chided the philosopher, "But, Herr Heidegger, you have to treat philosophy much more freely, more lightly—one must dance with philosophy." Heidegger, knowing Ortega's reputation for electric eloquence, decided to ignore this publicly but to offer an almost inaudible aside: "I really don't know what philosophy has to do with dancing."[3]

Charles Sanders Peirce, the philosopher who taught us the most about semiotics, outlined the dance steps of a semiotic triad: "icon," "symbol," and "index." The dance of these three great orders of sign formation is the totality of semiotic relationships, he argued. But the founding statement of the field of semiotics is in Ferdinand de Saussure's *Course in General Linguistics,* published posthumously in 1915. You have to work hard to hear the music of the dance in these words, but they're there:

> Language is a system of signs that express ideas, and is therefore comparable to a system of writing, the alphabet of deaf-mutes, symbolic rites, polite formulas, military signals, etc. But it is the most important of these systems.
>
> A science that studies the life of signs within society is conceivable; it would be part of social psychology and consequently of general psychology: I shall call it *semiology* (from Greek *semeion,* "sign"). Semiology would show what constitutes signs, what laws govern them.[4]

It was not the purpose of this book to elucidate and explore semiotic theory. But rather to remind us that Christianity is a symbol system: a semiotic network of stories and images, rituals and concepts, embodiments and enactments. The key to any symbol system is the semiotic ability to read signs.

Humans have been called "the speaking species." More accurately, we should be called "the sign-reading species." A lot of species "speak." The birds and the bees signal each other. They communicate. But only humans turn that communication into a sign and symbol system. We turn almost every signal into a sign, whether that signal be an emotion, an item, an idea, a song.

For example, Adam was able to give a name to each of God's creatures. Adam even named himself, his wife, and God. Humans have the ability not just to speak and signal (left-brained functions), but to create signs about our signals (right-brained). Humans don't just use words, we create words, and we can communicate these created words, these signs, from one person to another. This is the beginning of culture.

Jesus read the signs of his times, liked to communicate in the language of signs, and challenged us to learn sign language. In his resurrected body, Jesus does not appear in forms that are immediately recognizable. That's why evangelists learn to "read" his signature, recognize his markings, decipher his signs. Those who are really gifted in semiotics are those who have discovered the sacramentality of all creation.

Semiotics is the currency of the gospel. In Augustine's *Confessions* he addresses God as the divine Beauty who reaches us through our five senses: hearing, sight, smell, taste, and touch:

> You *called* and *cried* to me and broke open my deafness.
> You *sent forth your beams* and *shone* upon me and chased
> away my blindness. You *breathed fragrance* upon me, and
> I drew in my breath and now pant for you. I *tasted* you,
> and now hunger and thirst for you. You *touched* me and I
> burned for your peace.[5]

Because of Jesus we humans can now hear, see, smell, taste, and touch the beauty of God.

It is only our capacity for sacramental thought, our ability to represent the world around us by mental symbols, and then recombine those symbols in our minds until they become sacramental, that we can reconstruct the world in our heads and dream new dreams. Other animals simply live in the world as nature presents it to them. Humans read signs to live in a sacramental world in part created by them out of symbols.

After two short years as a rural priest in the Church of England, George Herbert wrote a little book entitled *The Country Parson* (1652). It may be the most famous book on what it means to be a pastor ever written. In this classic Herbert detailed the duties of a pastor in some thirty-seven short chapters (some only a couple of paragraphs long). Herbert died at age thirty-nine from tuberculosis, so he never lived to see how famous and influential his poetry would become. Or how his organic definition of a pastor as a healer, gardener, lifelong learner, and "a diligent observer and tracker of God's ways"[6] would sleep for four centuries, only to be awakened in the twenty-first century.

It is the thesis of *Nudge* that evangelists constantly scan the environment (religious, cultural, economic) for evidences of divine activity. In fact, I am convinced that Herbert's phrase "a tracker of God's ways" is the essence of nudge evangelism.

One of my doctoral students has a close friend who is a missionary on a nearly 100 percent Muslim island in Indonesia. The people he works with are an almost completely unreached people group. Many are suspicious of his presence (he is white) and watch him constantly.

Naturally he must be very careful with everything he says and does (this same island has managed to deport almost every other missionary because of proselytizing). But his conviction is that Jesus is alive and active in that Muslim culture, and reveals himself every day through conversations, questions, gatherings, dreams, and visions. So he spends his time at attention, reading the signs God provides, pointing out these signs, and helping his new friends connect the dots. He tries never to give off a whiff of imposition, only invitation.

Time after time, when the dots are connected and Jesus pops out of the picture, a dedicated Muslim will exclaim, "So that's the Jesus I have been looking for!"

Attention is a relational term, which means that *Nudge* is a form of relational, not unilateral evangelism. In unilateral evangelism, you maximize your impact and minimize your vulnerability. In relational evangelism, you are both impacting and being impacted, which means that the nudger himself or herself can't escape being nudged.

What would a semiotician be without a sign and signifier? How about a rooster. The founding story is Jesus' warning to Peter that "before the rooster crows twice, you yourself will disown me three times."[7] Peter is living in complete denial (both of Christ, and his current state) until the rooster crows and points him back toward Jesus' prophetic words. Immediately as the cock crows, Jesus is led to the Roman government and the direct process of his crucifixion begins. While Peter was warming himself by the fire saying, "I don't know Jesus," Jesus was winding his way to the cross saying, "Yeah, but I know you, Peter." Would Peter have seen his situation if the ordained rooster had not reminded him? Followers of Christ should be like roosters, signs that remind people of Jesus' words and point people toward the words/Word/Jesus in order to help them see Jesus as he really is and themselves as they really are.

Roosters proclaim the coming of the morning, the arrival of the sun. John was a rooster; the prophets were roosters; all semioticians are roosters. They see the signs of the sun rising and they crow loudly. Maybe Moses' wish "that all the Lord's people were prophets"[8] was answered at Pentecost, when the Spirit of God was poured out "on all flesh" and all present "were filled with the Holy Spirit and began to speak."[9]

Maybe the dove and the rooster are companion birds.

NOTES

Acknowledgments

1. Deuteronomy 31:8.

2. For more see Bart Beaty, *Fredric Wertham and the Critique of Mass Culture* (Jackson: University Press of Mississippi, 2005), 156–57. See also Fredric Wertham, *Seduction of the Innocent* (New York: Rinehart, 1954), 34, 97, 192–93.

3. Judith Maizel-Long, "Theology Sung and Celebrated," in *Unmaking Methodist Theology*, ed., Clive Marsh, Brian Beck, Angela Shier-Jones, and Helen Wareing (New York: Continuum, 2004), 51.

4. Simone Weil, *Waiting for God* (New York: Putnam, 1951), 146.

Preface

1. Gerard Manley Hopkins, "God's Grandeur," in *The Poetical Works of Gerard Manley Hopkins*, ed., Norman H. Mackenzie (Oxford: Clarendon, 1992), 139.

Chapter 1

1. See, for example, "So stay awake, alert," (Matthew 24:42 MSG); and "Stay awake and be prepared," (Matthew 25:13 TLB).

2. Luke 24:47–49, author's paraphrase.

3. Rowan Williams, *Where God Happens: Discovering Christ in One Another* (Boston: New Seeds, 2005), 33.

4. Mark 4:26–27, 31–32 NKJV. The full text is as follows: "The kingdom of God is as if man should scatter seed on the ground, and should sleep by night and rise by day, and the seed should sprout and grow, he himself does not know how.... [The kingdom of God] is like a mustard seed which, when it is sown on the ground, is smaller than all the seeds on earth; but when it is sown, it grows up and becomes greater than all herbs, and shoots out large branches, so that the birds of the air may nest under its shade."

5. The phrase is that of St. Francis de Sales, picked up from Paul in 2 Corinthians 1:19 ("For the Son of God, Jesus Christ ... it has always been 'Yes'") and made into a slogan.

6. Andy Grundberg, "Beyond Itself," in *After Art: Rethinking 150 Years of Photography: Selections from the Joseph and Elaine Monsen Collection* (Seattle: Henry Art Gallery, University of Washington, 1994), 17.

7. Quoted in Charles Glass, "The Universal Instant," *TLS: Times Literary Supplement*, 03 March 1995, 7.

8. The Roman Road to Salvation had four Bible verses like the "Four Spiritual Laws" had four principles. See Romans 3:23; Romans 6:23; Romans 5:8; and Romans 10:9.

9. Dear Father, I now believe that Jesus Christ is Your only begotten Son, that He came to our earth in the flesh and died on the cross to take away all of my sins and the sins of this world. I believe that Jesus Christ then rose from the dead on the third day to give all of us eternal life.

Lord Jesus, I now confess to You all of the wrong and sinful things that I have ever done in my life. I ask that You please forgive me and wash away all of my sins by the blood that You have personally shed for me on the cross. I am now ready to accept You as my personal Lord and Savior. I now ask that You come into my life and live with me for all of eternity.

Father, Jesus—I now believe that I am truly saved and born again. Thank You, Father. Thank You, Jesus.

10. Antonio Machado, "I Love Jesus, Who Said to Me," in his *Times Alone: Selected Poems*, trans., Robert Bly (Middleton, CT: Wesleyan University Press, 1983), 109.

11. The phrase "beat my back" from preachers and altar calls describe my experience with those who knelt down with you at the altar and beat religion into your back as they prayed.

12. For instances of this, see Luis Rivera, *A Violent Evangelism: The Political and Religious Conquest of the Americas* (Louisville: Westminster John Knox, 1992).

13. British author Adrian Plass, in his *Jesus: Safe, Tender, Extreme* (Grand Rapids: Zondervan, 2006), says that too many of us are graduates "of what one might call the Mike Tyson school of evangelism" (chapter 4).

14. This is the mantra of William Wallace in the movie *Braveheart* (1995): "Every man dies; not every man really lives," www.imdb.com/title/tt0112573/quotes (accessed 19 April 2010). The full quote, attributed to A. Sachs: "Death is more universal than life; everyone dies but not everyone lives," is quoted in Herbert

V. Prochnow, *Speaker's Handbook of Epigrams and Witticisms* (New York: Harper, 1955), 69.

15. Martha Winburn England and John Sparrow, *Hymns Unbidden: Donne, Herbert, Blake, Emily Dickinson and the Hymnographers* (New York: New York Public Library, 1966), 80.

16. Nicholas Lash, *Holiness, Speech and Silence: Reflections on the Question of God* (Burlington, VT: Ashgate, 2004), 35–36.

17. Jean-Paul Sartre, *The Words* (New York: George Braziller, 1964), 102–3.

18. Richard H. Thaler and Cass R. Sunstein, *Nudge: Improving Decision About Health, Wealth, and Happiness* (New Haven: Yale University Press, 2008), 6.

19. "Nudges are not mandates. Putting the fruit at eye level counts as a nudge. Banning junk food does not." Ibid., 6.

20. The fullest elaborations of EPIC as the default interface for Google culture can be found in my *Post-Modern Pilgrims: First Century Passion for the 21st Century World* (Nashville, TN: Broadman & Holman, 2000); and *The Gospel According to Starbucks: Living with a Grande Passion* (Colorado Springs: WaterBrook, 2007); although I explore the components of this interface also in *SoulTsunami: Sink or Swim in New Millennium Culture* (Grand Rapids: Zondervan, 1999); and *Carpe Mañana: Is Your Church Ready to Seize Tomorrow?* (Grand Rapids: Zondervan, 2001).

21. See my *So Beautiful: Divine Design for Life and the Church: Missional, Relational, Incarnational* (Colorado Springs: David C. Cook, 2009).

22. Matthew 28:7.

23. Alec Clifton-Taylor, *The Pattern of English Building*, 2nd ed. (London: B. T. Batsford, 1962), 235.

24. Identified as an Old English verse with the title "With God," as printed in *The Preacher's Magazine* 4 (July 1929): 212.

25. Margaret Mead, *The World Ahead: An Anthropologist Anticipates the Future*, ed., Robert B. Textor (New York: Berghahn, 2005), 12.

26. Proverbs 25:11.

27. William Golding, *The Hot Gates: And Other Occasional Pieces* (New York: Harcourt, Brace & World, 1966), 87.

28. Johan Huizinga, *The Waning of the Middle Ages: A Study of the Forms of Life, Thought and Art in France and the Netherlands in the XIVth and XVth Centuries* (London: Edward Arnold, 1963; first published 1924), 183.

29. James 1:17–27.

30. When asked, we are to always be ready to "give the reason for the hope that you have" (1 Peter 3:15).

31. Jeremiah 20:7–9.

32. Galway Kinnell, "After Making Love We Hear Footsteps," in his *Mortal Acts, Mortal Words*, in his *Three Books* (New York: Houghton-Miffline, 2002), 77.

33. Philippians 1:21.

34. Cf. Matthew 16:2–3 MSG, TNIV. One of the oldest English weather sayings is "Red sky at night, shepherd's delight, red sky in the morning, shepherd's warning." See John Wiseman, *SAS Survival Handbook: How to Survive in the Wild, in Any Climate, on Land or Sea* (New York: Harper Research, 2004), 371.

35. Excerpted from Jackson Pollock, "My Painting," *Possibilities: An Occasional Review* 1 (Winter 1947–1948): 79; and quoted in *American Artists on Art from 1940 to 1980*, ed., Ellen H. Johnson (New York: Harper & Row, 1982), 4.

36. See Matthew 9:15.

37. Acts 17:27.

38. The actual quote is "The book of the Revelations seems to be a prophecy in the form of an opera, or dramatic poem, where divine art illustrates the object with many charming glories." Isaac Watts, "Author's Preface," in his *Horae Lyricae and Divine Songs, with a Memoir* (Boston: Little Brown, 1854), xcii.

39. John Updike, closing line of the foreword to his *The Early Stories, 1953–1975* (New York: Random, 2003), xvii.

40. This striking sentence from *Common Worship: Services and Prayers for the Church of England* (London: Church House, 2000), 198, was the inspiration for Dean Michael Perham's Lenten meditation, *Signs of Your Kingdom* (London: SPCK, 2002).

41. The dog-whistle metaphor I borrow from Ann Patchett, *Patron Saint of Liars* (Boston: Houghton Mifflin, 1992), 14.

42. Marius von Senden, *Space and Sight: The Perception of Space and Shape in the Congenitally Blind Before and After Operation* (Glencoe, IL: Free Press, 1960), 157–60.

43. Eric McLuhan, "Literacy in a New Key," *Vital Speeches of the Day* 75 (August 2009): 361.

44. Genesis 9:12–17.

45. Genesis 17:23–27.

46. Exodus 12:7, 13.

47. Exodus 13:21.

48. Judges 13:5; 16:16–20.

49. Luke 2:15–20.

50. John 19:19.

51. André Kertész, *Kertész on Kertész: A Self Portrait* (New York: Abbeville, 1985), 144.

52. Jared Diamond, *Collapse: How Societies Choose to Fail or Succeed* (New York: Viking, 2004), 11: "The society's responses to its environmental problems—always proves significant."

53. I'm quoting Michael L. Raposa in his *Boredom and the Religious Imagination* (Charlottesville: University Press of Virginia, 1999), 3–4.

54. Robert Louis Stevenson, "Happy Thought," in his *A Child's Garden of Verses*, illus., Jessie Wilcox Smith (New York: Avenel, n.d.), 27.

55. Charles Higham, "Beatlemania," in *Creme de la Phlegm: Unforgettable Australian Reviews*, ed., Angela Bennie (Melbourne: Miegunyah, 2006), 122.

56. Matthew 2:1–12.

57. Anthony J. Mayo and Nitin Nohria, *In Their Time: The Greatest Business Leaders of the 20th Century* (Boston: Harvard Business School Press, 2005). The criteria for selecting the 860 leaders were as follows:

1) had to have been a "Founder or Chief Executive Officer (CEO) of a U.S.-based company for at least five years, between 1900 and 2000."

2) had to have demonstrated "at least four consecutive years of top financial performance,"

3) and/or had to have "led a business or service that changed the way Americans lived, worked, or interacted in the twentieth century" (365–66).

58. Bill Breem, "The 3 Ways of Great Leaders," *Fast Company*, September 2005, 49.

59. 1 Chronicles 12:32.

60. Breem, "The 3 Ways of Great Leaders," 49.

61. Ian Kershaw, *Making Friends with Hitler: Lord Londonderry, the Nazis and the Road to World War II* (New York: Penguin, 2004), 141.

62. See the book of Salam Pax's postings called *The Baghdad Blog* (London: Atlantic on Behalf of Guardian Newspapers, 2003). See also his blog www.dear_raed. blogspot.com (accessed 19 April 2010.)

63. See chapter 5, "Word or Sign," of Christoph F. Potworowski, *Contemplation and Incarnation: The Theology of Marie-Dominique Chenu* (Montreal: McGill-Queen's University Press, 2001), 155–95.

64. John Ciardi, as quoted in *Worlds in Collision: Dialogues on Multicultural Art Issues*, ed., Carlos Villa (San Francisco: International Scholars Publications, 1994), 200.

65. Mary Oliver, "Low Tide," *Amicus Journal* 18 (Winter 1997): 34. Parker Palmer quotes this in his *A Hidden Wholeness: The Journey Toward an Undivided Life* (San Francisco: Jossey-Bass, 2004), 34.

66. Mary Oliver, "The Summer Day," in *New and Selected Poems* (Boston: Beacon, 1992), 94.

67. Paraphrase of Annie Dillard, as quoted in *The Meaning of Life: Reflections in Words and Pictures on Why We Are Here*, ed., David Friend and the Editors of *Life* (Boston: Little, Brown, 1991), 11. Her exact words: "We are here to witness the creation and to abet it. We are here to notice each thing so each thing gets noticed. Together we notice not only each mountain shadow and each stone on the beach but, especially, we notice the beautiful faces and complex natures of each other. We are here to bring to consciousness the beauty and power that are around us and to praise the people who are here with us. We witness our generation and our times. We watch the weather. Otherwise, creation would be playing to an empty house." Also see *Life*, December 1991, 8 p. insert after p. 65.

68. The quote in context is "Can one reach God by toil? He gives himself to the pure in heart. He asks nothing but attention." William Butler Yeats, "The Death of Synge: Extracts from a Diary Kept in 1909," in *The Autobiography of William Butler Yeats* (New York: Macmillan, 1938), 445.

69. See "Amor" in Carlos Fuentes, *This I Believe: The A to Z of a Life* (New York: Random, 2005), 9.

70. Ibid.

71. As cited by Lorraine Kisly in "Focus," *Parabola* 30 (Summer 2005): 5.

72. Iris Murdoch, *The Sovereignty of Good* (New York: Routledge, 2001), 53–54.

73. St. John of the Cross, *Ascent to Mount Carmel* (New York: Burns & Oates, 1993), 122.

74. Murdoch, *The Sovereignty of Good*, 53–54.

75. "Prayer consists of attention." The quote continues: "It is the orientation of all the attention of which the soul is capable toward God." Simone Weil, *Waiting for God*, trans., Emma Craufurd (New York: G. P. Putnam's Sons, 1951), 105.

76. Dorothy Sayers, "To the Provost of Darby [the Very Rev. P. A. Micklem], 21 March 1940," in her *1937-1943: From Novelist to Playwright*, vol. 2 of *The Letters of Dorothy Sayers*, ed., Barbara Reynolds (New York: St. Martin's Press, 1998), 158.

77. The full quote is: "I think Christianity has created a great problem in the Western world by repeatedly presenting itself, not as a way of seeing all things, but as one competing ideology among many. Instead of leading us to see God in new and surprising places, it too often has led us to confine God inside *our* place. Simeon Weil, the brilliant French resistor, said that the 'tragedy of Christianity is that it came to see itself as replacing other religions instead of adding something to all of them.'" Richard Rohr, *Everything Belongs: The Gift of Contemplative Prayer* (New York: Crossway, 2003), 93.

78. Austin Farrer, *Lord I Believe: Suggestions for Turning the Creed into Prayer* (Cambridge, MA: Cowley, 1989), 31. See also Susanne Sklar, "How Beauty Will Save the World: William Blake's Prophetic Vision," *Spiritus* 7 (Spring 2007): 20–29.

79. David Martin, "The Language of Christianity: Story, Body and Sign," in his *Christian Language in the Secular City* (Burlington, VT: Ashgate, 2002), 7, 27. See also the chapter "Recapitulating the Argument in Sign Language," in his *Does Christianity Cause War* (New York: Oxford University Press, 1997), 111.

80. Umberto Eco, *A Theory of Semiotics* (Bloomington: Indiana University Press, 1976), 7.

81. Joseph S. Nye, Jr., *The Paradox of American Power: Why the World's Only Superpower Can't Go It Alone* (New York: Oxford University Press, 2002), 67. Here is one example: Jonathan Karp resigned as editor-in-chief of Random House in June of 2005 to become publisher and editor-in-chief of a new imprint. Beginning in 2007, Warner Twelve will release just twelve books a year, with Karp devoting his entire attention to those "one of a kind" books that can "cut through the noise." Karp says, "Talented authors deserve a massive amount of attention." For more see Elizabeth Woyke, "'Massive' Attention for Authors," *Business Week*, 05 September 2005, 16.

82. Part of the phenomenal success of *The Da Vinci Code* is the culture's need for decoders: for people who know how to break codes so that they can help us read codes and break "the code" for ourselves.

83. The phrase "Attention Surplus Disorder" if that of Susan Sontag used in an explanation as to why she is not more prolific and disciplined as a writer. "Maybe I have an 'Attention Surplus Disorder.' The easiest thing in the world for me is to pay attention." As quoted by Donna Schaper in *All Is Calm: Reflections for Advent and Other Busy Seasons* (Winona, MN: St. Mary's Press, 1999), 16.

84. Simone Weil, *Notebooks* (New York: G. P. Putnam's Sons, 1956), 1, 251: "The development of the attention ought to be the sole object of education."

85. Czeslaw Milosz referred to "our tiny, tiny myness" in the poem "My-ness," first published in the *New Yorker* (1980) and reprinted in his *Unattainable Earth*, trans., Czeslaw Milosz and Robert Haas (New York: Ecco, 1986), 133.

86. Hebrews 2:1.

87. A phrase borrowed from Reg Saner's essay "The Dawn Collector" in his *The Dawn Collector: On My Way to the Natural World* (Santa Fe, NM: Center for American Places, 2005), 28–43.

88. Kenneth Paul Kramer, *Martin Buber's I and Thou: Practicing Living Dialogue* (New York: Paulist, 2003), 186–87.

89. Henry Miller, *Plexus* (New York: Grove Weidenfeld, 1987), 53.

90. See Romans 10:18 and John 1:9.

91. Psalm 19:1–4a.

92. Paul L. Mariani, *God and the Imagination: On Poets, Poetry, and the Ineffable* (Athens: University of Georgia Press, 2002), 234.

93. Walt Whitman, "Walt Whitman," *Leaves of Grass* (Philadelphia: D. McKay, 1900), 35.

94. John 11.

95. Matthew 12:39.

96. John 10:38–39. See also Matthew 12:38–40.

97. John 4:48–50; 6:26–28; 20:29.

98. Or as the author of Hebrews put it, "pioneer and perfecter of our faith, who for the sake of the joy that was set before him" (Hebrews 12:2 NRSV).

99. In John's gospel Jesus is the singular *Semeion*, not the plural *Semeia*.

100. Quoted in Philip Yancey, *Church, Why Bother? My Personal Pilgrimage* (Grand Rapids: Zondervan, 1998), 40.

101. Luke 2:34.

102. I love how Michael Jinkins puts this: "The church is the sign that endures in its fragile humanity because it does not endure in its own power but endures precisely in the power of an-Other." Michael Jinkins, *The Church Faces Death: Ecclesiology in a Post-Modern Context* (New York: Oxford University Press, 1999).

103. Bill Hull, *Straight Talk on Spiritual Power: Experiencing the Fullness of God in the Church* (Grand Rapids: Baker, 2002), 145.

104. The first of the Henry Vaughan quotes is from his poem, "Rules and Lessons," the second, from his poem, "The Morning Watch," in *The Sacred Poems and Private Ejaculations of Henry Vaughan, With a Memoir by H. F. Lyte* (Boston: Little, Brown, 1956), 93–94, 110.

105. William James, *The Varieties of Religious Experience: A Study in Human Nature: Being the Gifford Lectures on Natural Religion Delivered at Edinburgh in 1901–1902* (New York: Longmans Green, 1903), 475–76.

106. The most famous definition of a sacrament is "an outward and visible sign of an inward and spiritual grace." In scholastic formulation, *sacraments* "*significando causant*" = "they cause through signifying." In other words, the sacraments are signs that point beyond themselves to transcendent realities, and at the same time the sacraments are "causally" involved in the realization of those very same transcendent realities. In other words, the "signs" themselves effect grace.

107. Tom Brown Jr., *Grandfather: A Native American's Lifelong Search for Truth and Harmony with Nature* (New York: Berkley, 1993), 171.

108. The story may be found in Genevieve Taggard, *The Life and Mind of Emily Dickinson* (New York: A. A. Knopf, 1930), 128.

109. Quoted in *Voices of Hope: Timeless Expressions of Faith from African Americans* (Colorado Springs: Honor, 2005), 86.

110. Matthew 6:21.

111. Rainer Maria Rilke, "Da neight sich die Stunde und rührt mich an," in *Rilke's Book of Hours: Love Poems to God,* trans., Anita Barrows and Joanna Macy (New York: Riverhead, 1996), 47.

Chapter 2

1. Gerard Manley Hopkins, "The Wreck of the Deutschland," in *The Poems of Gerard Manley Hopkins,* 4th ed., ed., W. H. Gardner and N. H. Mackenzie (New York: Oxford University Press, 1967), 63.

2. Marianne Sawicki, *Seeing the Lord: Resurrection and Early Christian Practices* (Minneapolis: Augsburg Fortress, 1994), 94.

3. Gerard Manley Hopkins, "As Kingfishers Catch Fire," in *Gerard Manley Hopkins: The Major Works,* ed., Catherine Phillips (New York: Oxford University Press, 2002), 129. See Eugene Peterson's lyrical meditation on this poem, *Christ Plays in Ten Thousand Places* (Grand Rapids: Eerdmans, 2005).

4. Matthew 1:23.

5. William Stacy Johnson, "Re-thinking theology: A Postmodern, Post-Holocaust, Post-Christendom Endeavor," *Interpretation: A Journal of Bible and Theology*, 55 (January 2001), 14.

6. David Tracy, a Roman Catholic theologian at the University of Chicago, is most famous for arguing that "a church is a community that keeps alive the dangerous memories of its classics." Quoted in Eugene Kennedy, "A Dissenting Voice," *New York Times Magazine*, 9 November 1986, 28.

7. This is the thesis of Marianne Sawicki's book *Seeing the Lord*.

8. John 5:17.

9. Check out some popular contemporary "He Lives" lyrics on the Web. Here are some results: Fred Hammond, "Celebrate (He Lives)," www.metrolyrics.com/celebrate-he-lives-lyrics-fred-hammond.html; James Hall, "Jesus Lives," www.lyriczz.com/lyrics/james-hall/53030-jesus-lives (accessed 19 April 2010). Check out how well the words of "He Lives in You," by Mark Mancina, Jay Rifkin, and Lebo M (Lebohang Morake), from the *Lion King* can be applied to Jesus: www.lionking.org/lyrics/OBCR/HeLivesInYou.html (accessed 19 April 2010).

10. George Frideric Handel's Air for Soprano: "I Know that My Redeemer Liveth," from his Oratorio *The Messiah*.

11. First line of the 1933 hymn by Alfred H. Ackley, "He Lives," *The United Methodist Hymnal: Book of United Methodist Worship* (Nashville: The United Methodist Publishing House, 1989), 310. The refrain includes these words: "He lives, he lives ... You ask me how I know he lives, he lives within my heart."

12. Refrain of the 1971 song by Gloria and William J. Gaither "Because He Lives," *The United Methodist Hymnal: Book of United Methodist Worship* (Nashville: The United Methodist Publishing House, 1989), 364.

13. George W. Stroup, introduction to *Many Voices, One God: Being Faithful in a Pluralistic World*, ed., Walter Brueggemann and George W. Stroup (Louisville: Westminster John Knox, 1998), 8.

14. 2 Corinthians 6:16.

15. Matthew 18:20.

16. Alison Elliot, *The Miraculous Everyday* (Edinburgh, Scotland: Covenanters' Press, 2005), 60.

17. Colossians 3:3.

18. Sawicki, *Seeing the Lord,* 1–2.

19. For more on the both/and of Christianity, see my *SoulTsunami: Sink or Swim in New Millennium Culture* (Grand Rapids: Zondervan, 1999), 158–72; my *Carpe*

Mañana (Grand Rapids: Zondervan, 2001); my *Jesus Drives Me Crazy* (Grand Rapids: Zondervan, 2003), 73; my *AquaChurch 2.0: Piloting Your Church in Today's Fluid Culture* (Colorado Springs: David C. Cook, 2008), 172–74; and my *So Beautiful: Divine Design for Life and the Church* (Colorado Springs: David C. Cook, 2009), 44–47.

20. Zechariah 4:6.

21. Matthew 28:7.

22. Robert Wilken, *Myth of Christian Beginnings* (Garden City, NY: Doubleday, 1972), 158.

23. Gregory of Nyssa, "The Bubbling Spring," in *From Glory to Glory: Texts from Gregory of Nyssa's Mystical Writings*, sel., Jean Danielou, trans., Herbert Musurillo (New York: Scribner, 1961), 246.

24. See Matthew 14:28, 33.

25. J. Hillis Miller, *On Literature* (New York: Routledge, 2002), 36.

26. This is, of course, from verse 4 of Julia Ward Howe's "Mine Eyes Have Seen the Glory of the Coming of the Lord," also known as "Battle Hymn of the Republic."

27. Mark 1:24.

28. Luke 24:13–35.

29. John 20:11–18.

30. John 20:24–29.

31. John 21:12.

32. See Luke 24:16.

33. Alice Oswald, "Sea Poem," in her *Woods Etc.* (London: Faber and Faber, 2005), 3. See also her "Ideogram for Green," where she refers to "keeping that promise upon which sunlight takes its bearing" (Ibid., 26).

34. The first mention of McLuhan's use of this quote appears to be in Marshall McLuhan, Harley Parker, and Jacques Barzun, *Exploration of the Ways, Means, and Values of Museum Communication with the Viewing Public* (New York: Museum of the City of New York, 1969), 22.

35. Rodney Clapp, *A Peculiar People: The Church as Culture in a Post-Christian Society* (Downers Grove, IL: InterVarsity, 1996), 188.

36. Mark 12:27.

37. Sawicki, *Seeing the Lord*, 315.

38. Ibid., 252.

39. I want to thank Teri Hyrkas for this story.

40. Gerald G. May, *The Dark Night of the Soul: A Psychiatrist Explores the Connection between Darkness and Spiritual Growth* (San Francisco: HarperSanFrancisco, 2004).

41. Søren Kierkegaard, as referenced in Perry D. LeFebre, *The Prayers of Kierkegaard* (Chicago: University of Chicago Press, 1956; reprinted in 1976), 134.

42. Tom Bandy notes that "the experience of Christ, and the experience of Christ-in-mission amount to much the same thing. And in this way, semiotics connects with missiology, just as hermeneutics once connected with ecclesiology." The source of this exact quote has been lost, but Tom Bandy wrote Betty O'Brien in a 19 July 2009 email saying that most likely this is from a personal email with Len Sweet, subsequent to a Leadership Summit of church futurists on 30 November 2005 in Port Aransas, Texas.

43. Tom Bandy email to Betty O'Brien, 19 July 2009. For similar passages from Bandy, see his *Road Runner: The Body in Motion* (Nashville: Abingdon, 2002), 11–17; *Mission Mover: Beyond Education for Church Leadership* (Nashville: Abingdon, 2004), 58–59, 84–86, 126–27; and *Talisman: Global Positioning for the Soul* (St. Louis, MO: Chalice, 2006), 33–43.

44. St. Bernard, *On the Song of Songs: Sermones in Cantica Canticorum*, trans. and ed., Religious of C.S.M.V. [Sermon LXXIV] (New York: Morehouse-Gorham, 1952), 229.

45. William James, *The Principles of Psychology* (New York: Henry Holt, 1896), 443.

46. Ibid., 444.

47. Sawicki, *Seeing the Lord*, 91.

48. Herbert McCabe, "Resurrection as Epiphany," in his *God, Christ and Us*, ed. Brian Davies (New York: Continuum, 2003), 96–97.

49. The full quote is: "Pain is God's megaphore to rouse a deaf world," see "Shadowlands Script: Dialogue Transcript," www.script-o-rama.com/movie_scripts/s/shadowlands-script-transcript-winger-hopkins.html (accessed 19 April 2010). In C. S. Lewis, *The Problem of Pain* (San Francisco: HarperSanFrancisco, 2001), 93, the phrase is "pain as God's megaphone."

50. Neil Cole, *Organic Leadership: Leading Naturally Right Where You Are* (Grand Rapids: Baker, 2009), 168.

51. Matthew 25:40.

52. McCabe, "Ghosts, Burial and Resurrection," 101.

53. Jacob Petuchowski, *Our Masters Taught: Rabbinic Stories and Sauings* (New York: Crossroad, 1982), 2.

54. Matthew 11:5.

55. Romans 12:12 brings them together: "Be joyful in hope." See also 1 Peter 1:3.

56. Luke 2:10; 24:52. Alexander Schmemann points this out in *The World as Sacrament* (London: Darton, Longman, Todd, 1966), 26–27.

57. John 15:11 NASB.

58. Adam Potkay, *The Story of Joy: From the Bible to Late Romanticism* (New York: Cambridge University Press, 2007).

59. Psalm 37:4.

60. Matthew 13:11–15.

61. Matthew 13:11 NASB.

62. Matthew 11:25.

63. Simone Weil, *Intimations of Christianity Among the Ancient Greeks* (London: Routledge & Kegan Paul, 1957), 6.

64. Matthew 12:43–45.

65. Sawicki, *Seeing the Lord*, 28.

66. Luke 17:20–21 NRSV.

67. Jim Collins, *Good to Great: Why Some Companies Make the Leap ... and Others Don't* (New York: HarperBusiness, 2001), 85.

68. Thomas Mulholland, *The Shack* (Lincoln, NE: iUniverse, 2005), 22 (for example).

Chapter 2 1/2

1. As verified in Ralph Keyes, *The Quote Verifier: Who Said What, Where, When* (New York: St. Martin's Press, 2006), 161.

2. As for example in the elections in November 2007.

3. John 5:17.

4. Iris Murdoch, "Conceptions of Unity: Art," in her *Metaphysics as a Guide to Morals* (New York: Allen Lane, 1993), 23.

5. Iris Murdoch, "The Sublime and the Good," originally published in *Chicago Review* 13 (1959); reprinted in her *Existentialists and Mystics: Writings on Philosophy and Literature* (New York: Allen Lane, 1998), 219.

6. "Happy is the one who listens to me, watching daily at my gates, waiting beside my doors" (Proverbs 8:34 NRSV).

7. Mark 14:36.

8. Rabbi Jason Shulman, *The Instruction Manual for Receiving God* (Boulder, CO: Sounds True, 2006), 1.

9. Romans 2:14–15.

10. Or "sense of God." See, for example, John Calvin, *Institutes of the Christian Religion*, trans., Henry Beveridge (Grand Rapids: Eerdmans, 1965), 40–45, (vol. 1, book 2–3).

11. Quoted in Donald Nicholl, *Holiness* (New York: Seabury, 1981), 25.

12. Jack Deere, "Confessions of a Bible Deist," in his *Surprised by the Voice of God* (Grand Rapids: Zondervan, 1996), 251–69. I thank Bill Hull for pointing me to this reference in *Straight Talk on Spiritual Power* (Grand Rapids: Baker, 2002), 64–65.

13. Ibid., 251. Deere says the eighteenth-century deists believed in a Watchmaker God who wound things up and now watches as things run down—they worshipped human reason. But Bible deists worship the Bible: "The Bible and Christ merge into one entity. Christ cannot speak or be known apart from the Bible."

14. Ezekiel 3:17.

15. Habakkuk 2:1–2.

16. Jeremiah 6:17 KJV.

17. Isaiah 21:11–12.

18. This is the reasoning for the Catholic idea of intercession of saints. Clearly the saints are alive with Christ, and clearly we ask other living folks to intercede and pray for us. Thus in Roman Catholic theology, Christians have the privilege of asking the living saints to intercede in prayer.

19. The Slow Food Movement began in Italy with Carlo Petrini in the 1980s. For more, see Carlo Petrini, *Slow Food: The Case for Taste* (New York: Columbia University Press, 2003).

20. The Slow Sex Movement organized in early 2009. In 2008 Adam Tokunaga published *Slow Sex Secrets: Lessons from the Master Masseur* (New York: Vertical, 2008). One in five people surveyed admit to breaking off from making love to answer a cell phone.

21. Pete Blackshaw, "It's time for a Movement Toward 'Slow Marketing,'" *Advertising Age*, 29 June, 2009, 18.

22. For urban landscapes that encourage slowness, including closed spaces, etc., see Paul L. Knox, "Creating Ordinary Places: Slow Cities in a Fast World," *Journal of Urban Design* 10 (February 2005): 3–13, and Heike Mayer and Paul L. Knox, "Slow Cities: Sustainable Places in a Fast World," *Journal of Urban Affairs* 28 (September

2006): 321–34. For an example of what's happening in Europe, with the Città Slow movement, see Christine Sommer-Guist, "Slow City—The International Network of Cities Where Living Is Easy," trans., Hillary Crowe, Goethe Institut, www. goethe.de/kue/arc/dos/dos/sls/sdz/en1368906.htm (accessed 19 April 2010). See also "Slow Cities and the Slow Movement," www.slowmovement.com/slow_cities. php (accessed 19 April 2010).

23. Carl Honoré, *In Praise of Slowness: How a Worldwide Movement is Challenging the Cult of Speed* (San Francisco: HarperSanFrancisco, 2004), 15.

24. Nicholas Lash, *Holiness, Speech and Silence: Reflections on the Question of God* (Burlington, VT: Ashgate, 2004), 62.

25. Squire Rushnell, *When God Winks at You: How God Speaks Directly to You through the Power of Coincidence* (Nashville: Nelson, 2006), 1, 15, 29–30.

26. Nassim Nicholas Taleb, *The Black Swan: The Impact of the Highly Improbably* (New York: Random, 2007). See also the summary article "Black Swan Theory," http://en.wikipedia.org/wiki/Black_swan_theory#Coping_with_Black_Swan_ Events (accessed 19 April 2010).

27. Søren Kierkegaard, *Either/Or: A Fragment of Life*, (New York: Penguin, 1992), 233–34.

28. As quoted by Elaine Scarry in *Global Values 101: A Short Course*, ed., Kate Holbrook, Ann S. Kim, Brian Palmer, Anna Portnoy (Boston: Beacon, 2006), 26. The original quote is "We may see the reason why some men of study and thought … do make no great advances in their discoveries of it…. The reason whereof is, they converse with but one sort of men, they read but one sort of books, they will not come in the hearing but of one sort of notions." John Locke, *The Conduct of the Understanding* (New York: John B. Alden, 1891), 12.

29. Samuel Butler, *Erewhon, or, Over the Range* (London: David Bogue, 1880), 28.

30. See Philip Ball's point that "randomness has its own kind of symmetry." Philip Ball, *Critical Mass: How One Thing Leads to Another* (New York: Farrar, Straus and Giroux, 2006), 108.

31. Donald E. Knuth, *3:16 Bible Texts Illuminated* (Middletown, WI: A-R Editions, 1991). Both the book and the poster are available from www.areditions.com/books/ dk001_002.html (accessed 19 April 2010). For the inside story of how this book came to be, see Donald E. Knuth, *Things a Computer Scientist Rarely Talks About* (Stanford, CA: CSLI, 2001).

32. John 3:8.

33. Howard Nemerov, "To the Congress of the United States, Entering Its Third Century," in his *Trying Conclusions: New and Selected Poems, 1961–1991* (Chicago: University of Chicago Press, 1991), 143.

34. Jim Forest, *Praying with Icons* (Maryknoll, New York: Orbis, 1997), 37.

35. Joyce Rupp, "The Cluttered Cup," in her *The Cup of Our Life: A Guide for Spiritual Growth* (Notre Dame, IN: Ave Maria, 1997), 47–49.

36. Honoré, *In Praise of Slowness,* 15.

37. As told by Frederic and Mary Ann Brussat in a book review of *A Sideways Look at Time,* by Jane Griffiths, *Spirituality & Practice: Resources for Spiritual Journeys,* www.spiritualityandpractice.com/books/books.php?id=5211 (accessed 19 April 2010).

38. George Herbert, "Prayer," in *The Works of George Herbert in Prose and Verse, With a Memoir by Isaac Walton* (London: Bell and Daldy, 1952), 44. In my graduate school studies, one of the most off-putting, if not stupid ideas on the notion of the sacred was that of the University of Chicago's Mircea Eliade, who taught me that the sacred is "wholly other" from the mundane; that by definition the sacred is not a part of everyday existence and experience; that true manifestations of the sacred (*hierophanies*) take place in discontinuity with the ordinary.

39. Walt Whitman, "Song of Myself," in his *Leaves of Grass: First and "Death-Bed" Editions: Additional Poems* (New York: Barnes & Noble, 2004), 60.

40. As relayed by Haddon Robinson in his commentary on Joseph M. Stowell, "Who Cares?" in *Biblical Sermons: How Twelve Preachers Apply the Principles of Biblical Preaching,* ed., Haddon W. Robinson (Grand Rapids: Baker, 1989), 170.

41. Cynthia Heimel, *But Enough About You* (New York: Simon & Schuster, 1986), 69–70.

42. Denise Levertov, "Origins of a Poem," in her *Poet in the World* (New York: New Directions, 1973), 49.

43. Simone Weil, *Waiting for God,* trans., Emma Craufurd (New York: G. P. Putnam's Sons, 1951), 168.

44. D. H. Lawrence, "Hymns in a Man's Life," in "Late Essays and Articles," in *The Cambridge Edition to the Letters and Works of D. H. Lawrence* (New York: Cambridge University Press, 1979), 132.

45. Linda Stone, as quoted in Amita Tandukar, "Interruption Techniques," *Business Review Weekly,* 9 November 2006), 124. See also "Linda Stone's Thoughts on Attention and Specifically, Continuous Partial Attention," www.lindastone.net/ (accessed 20 April 2010).

46. You can find this experiment using ping pong balls in Roy H. Williams, *Does Your Ad Dog Bite?: (or Is It Just a Show Dog?) The Warm, Witty, and Revealing Thoughts of America's Most Controversial Ad Writer* (Manchaca, TX: Miracle, 1997).

47. Jesse Rice, *The Church of Facebook: How the Hyperconnected Are Redefining Community* (Colorado Springs: David C. Cook, 2009), 149.

48. "Cor Blimey," *The Economist*, 20 August 2005, 63. www.economist.com/ sciencetechnology/displaystory.cfm?story_id=4292593 (accessed 20 April 2010).

49. Kalina Christoff, Alan M. Gordon, Jonathan Smallwood, Rachelle Smith, and Jonathan W. Schooler, "Experience Sampling during fMRI Reveals Default Network and Executive System Contributions to Mind Wandering," *Proceedings of the National Academy of Sciences in the United States of America* 106, no. 21 (26 May 2009): 8719–24. The article is referenced in www.sciencedaily.com/ releases/2009/05/090511180702.htm (accessed 20 April 2010)

50. Paul Theroux, *Ghost Train to the Eastern Star: On the Tracks of the Great Railway Bazaar* (Toronto: McClelland & Stewart, 2008), 18.

51. Philippians 4:8 is what I call the "think on these things" verse.

52. Romans 5:5 NRSV.

53. John Wesley, "The Scripture Way of Salvation," in his *Sermons*, ed., Albert C. Outler, vol. 2 of the *Works of John Wesley* (Nashville: Abingdon, 1985), 2: 160, 167.

54. The actual quote in its best translation: "The language God most listens to is that of silent love." John of the Cross, "Spiritual Maxims," 285, in *The Collected Works of St. John of the Cross* (New York: Cosimo, 2007), 2:595. "Silence is God's first language, everything else is a poor translation" is from Thomas Keating, *Invitation to Love: The Way of Christian Contemplation* (New York: Continuum, 1995), 90.

55. Joseph Jaworski, *Synchronicity: The Inner Path of Leadership* (San Francisco: Berrett-Koehler, 1998), 178.

56. Wallace Stevens, "Sunday Morning," in *The Collected Poems of Wallace Stevens* (New York: Random, 1990), 67.

57. Kay Lindahl, *Practicing the Sacred Art of Listening: A Guide to Enrich Your Relationships and Kindle Your Spiritual Life—the Listening Center Workshop.* (Woodstock, VT: SkyLight Paths, 2003), 18.

58. I borrow this phrase from Andrew Nugent, *The Slow-Release Miracle* (New York: Paulist, 2006), 16.

59. Lindahl, *Practicing the Sacred Art of Listening,* 16; or Solomon ben Judah ibn Gabirol, *A Choice of Pearls: Embracing a Collection of the Most Genuine Ethical*

Sentences, Maxims and Salutary Reflections (Strassburg: Trübner, 1859), 9: "The first step to wisdom is silence; the second attention; the third memory."

60. David W. Henderson, *Culture Shift: Communicating God's Truth to Our Changing World* (Grand Rapids: Baker, 1998), 212.

61. Peter Senge, *The Fifth Discipline Fieldbook: Strategies and Tools for Building a Learning Organization* (New York: Doubleday, 1994), 377.

62. Mark Brady, "What I Have Learned from Listening," *The Wisdom of Listening* (Boston: Wisdom, 2003), 299.

63. *The Rule of St. Benedict*, trans., Abbot Parry and Esther de Waal (Leominster, England: Gracewing, 1990), 1.

64. Paul Tillich as quoted in James Simpson, *Simpson's Contemporary Quotations* (Boston: Houghton Mifflin, 1988), 183.

65. The greatest semanticist of the twentieth century, S. I. Hayakawa, argued that there are two parts to speaking: output and intake. We focus on the output but neglect the intake, the listening and receiving habits. For his classic chapter III on "How to Listen to Other People," see his famous text *Symbol, Status, and Personality* (New York: Harcourt, Brace & World, 1958), 29–35.

66. *The Rule of St. Benedict in Latin and English with Notes*, ed., Timothy Fry (Collegeville, MN: The Liturgical Press, 1981), 214–15 (chapter 19).

67. This is a variation of Marilynne Robinson phrase in *Gilead* (New York: Farrar, Straus and Giroux, 2004), 28: "Call attention to a thing existing in excess of itself."

68. *The Rule of St. Benedict*, ed., Fry, 214–15 (chapter 19).

69. Psalm 46:10.

70. George Steiner said this of William Shakespeare. See George Steiner, *After Babel: Aspects of Language and Translation* (New York: Oxford University Press, 1992), 4.

71. The poet Rainer Maria Rilke used a phrase to describe his great desire: "seekers of the inner future in that past in which was included much of the eternal." Rainer Maria Rilke, "To Lou Andreas-Salome, August 15, 1903," in his *Letters*, trans., Jane Bannard Greene and M. D. Herter Norton (New York: W. W. Norton, 1945), 1: 127.

72. See Kay Lindahl's two books, *The Sacred Art of Listening: Forty Reflections for Cultivating A Spiritual Practice* (Woodstock, VT: Skylight Paths, 2002) and *Practicing the Sacred Art of Listening: A Guide to Enrich Your Relationships and Kindle Your Spiritual Life—The Listening Center Workshop.* (Woodstock, VT: SkyLight Paths, 2003). Lindahl's major thesis is stated in the first book: "Perhaps one of the most precious and powerful gifts we can give another person is to really listen to

them, to listen with quiet, fascinated attention, with our whole being, fully present. This sounds simple, but if we are honest with ourselves, we do not often listen to each other so completely" (11).

73. Paul Hawken, "Listening Could Relieve Strife That Leads to War," *Philadelphia Inquirer*, 22 August 2002, www.converge.org.nz/pma/cra0807.htm (accessed 20 April 2010), as cited in Lindahl, *Practicing the Sacred Art of Listening*, 7.

74. Isaiah 55:3 NASB.

75. David Augsburger, *Caring Enough to Hear and Be Heard* (Ventura, CA: Regal, 1982), 12.

76. Matthew 26:41; Mark 13:33–37; 14:38; Luke 21:36. Cf. Colossians 4:2.

77. For this understanding of the shofar, see Adin Steinsaltz, "The New Year," *Parabola* 33 (Fall 2008): 89–90.

78. Esther de Waal, in an oral presentation. For more on "Vigils," see her *The Way of Simplicity: The Cistercian Tradition* (Maryknoll, NY: Orbis, 1998), 51, 163.

79. Clive Bell, "Dr. Freud on Art," *The Nation and the Athenaeum* 35 (6 September 1924): 690. Quoted in Claudia C. Morrison, *Freud and the Critic: The Early Use of Depth Psychology in Literary Criticism*, 78.

80. Meister Eckhart, "The Talks of Instruction," in *Meister Eckhart: Selected Treatises and Sermons*, trans., James M. Clark and John V. Skinner (London: Fontana Library, 1963), 68.

Here is another translation of this quote: "For indeed, people who are expectant like that are watchful, they look around them to see where he whom they expect is coming from, and they look out for him in whatever comes along, however strange it may be, just in case he should be in it. In this way we should consciously discover our Lord in all things. This requires much diligence, demanding a total effort of our senses and power of mind; then those who manage this are in a right state: taking God equally in all things, they find God in equal measure in all."

Meister Eckhart, "The Talks of Instruction [*Rede der Underscheidunge*]," in *Meister Eckhart: Sermons and Treatises*, ed., M. O'C Walshe (Shaftesbury, England: Element, 1987), 3:20.

81. Quoted in Thomas Norris, *The Trinity: Life of God, Hope for Humanity* (Hyde Park, NY: New City, 2008), 82.

82. Quoted in Mineke Schipper, *Never Marry a Woman with Big Feet* (New Haven, CT: Yale University Press, 2004) 82, 132.

83. Joseph Campbell, *Myths to Live By* (New York: Bantam, 1973) 120.

84. Michael V. Copeland, Krysten Crawford, Jeffrey Davis, et. al., "My Golden Rule: We Asked 30 Business Visionaries, Collectively Worth over $70 Billion, What Single Philosophy They Swear by More than Any Other—in Business, Life, or Both. Here Are the Secrets of Their Success," *Business 2.0*, December 2005, 109.

85. Henry David Thoreau, *Walden* (New York: T. Y. Crowell, 1910), 440.

86. An excellent comparison of the two is found in chapter 2: "The Great Commission and the Initiative of Evangelism," in D. Mark Davis, *Talking about Evangelism: A Congregational Resource* (Cleveland: Pilgrim, 2007), 28–37.

87. Acts 2:32. Jürgen Moltmann calls these words "the first words of the newborn."

88. Nicholas Lash, *Holiness, Speech and Silence: Reflections on the Question of God* (Burlington, VT: Ashgate, 2004), 75.

89. Lash, *Holiness, Speech and Silence,* 61. The Augustine quote comes from his *On Christian Teaching*, trans., R. P. H. Green (Oxford: Oxford University Press, 1999), 4.

90. Frederick Buechner, *The Sacred Journey* (San Francisco: Harper & Row, 1982), 7.

91. Lash, *Holiness, Speech and Silence,* 61.

92. S. I. Hayakawa, *Symbol, Status, and Personality* (New York: Harcourt, Brace & World, 1958), 34.

93. It is an "unreasonable demand" that "everybody else *should* mean [in these words] what I would mean if I were using them," says S. I. Hayakawa, *Symbol, Status, and Personality*, 31.

94. I first said this in my *A Cup of Coffee at the Soul Cafe* (Nashville: Broadman & Holman, 1998), 31. It has become the motto of the Auxiliary to the Virginia Fire Fighters Local 390 from Virginia, Minnesota, according to an 2 October 2009 email from Betsy Olivant.

95. Lindahl, *Practicing the Sacred Art of Listening,* 48–49.

96. Hayakawa, *Symbol, Status, and Personality,* 32.

97. Or to put this in Greek, there is not *plerosis* without *kenosis*.

98. Quoted in Lindahl, *Practicing the Sacred Art of Listening,* 51.

99. Penn Says: Gift of a Bible, Session 1, Episode 01016, www.youtube.com/watch?v=7JHS8adO3hM (accessed 17 July 2009). Or check out http://crackle.com/c/Penn_Says/A_Gift_of_a_Bible/2415037 (accessed 20 April 2010).

100. Matthew 28:7.

101. John 4:35 NASB.

102. Romans 10:14.

103. Luke 2:49 NKJV.

104. John Irving, *A Prayer for Owen Meany* (New York: Ballantine, 1989), 1. Thanks to Scott Lester for reminding me of this book, which is filled with some of my favorite quotes of all time, like "Logic is relative" (18).

Chapter 3

1. Actually, three books. Most explicitly, *11 Indispensable Relationships You Can't Be Without* (Colorado Springs: David C. Cook, 2008). But also *Out of the Question—Into the Mystery: Getting Lost in the GodLife Relationship* (Colorado Springs: WaterBrook, 2004) and *The Three Hardest Words in the World to Get Right* (Colorado Springs: WaterBrook, 2006).

2. See Matthew 4:19.

3. With thanks to my doctoral student Don Love for reminding me of this.

4. John 21:1–14.

5. Eamon Duffy, *Walking to Emmaus* (New York: Burns and Oates, 2006), 45.

6. The concluding lines of William Blake's "The Everlasting Gospel," in his *Selected Poetry*, ed., Michael Mason (New York: Oxford University Press, 1998), 264.

7. Cited in Elizabeth A. Johnson, *Consider Jesus: Waves of Renewal in Christology* (New York: Crossroad, 1990), 8.

8. Quoted in Christopher Dawson, *The Making of Europe: An Introduction to the History of European Unity* (New York: Sheed and Ward, 1945), 110.

9. William Blake, "Visions of the Daughters of Albion," in *Selected Poetry*, ed., Michael Mason (New York: Oxford University Press, 1996), 94.

10. Robert Daly, *God's Altar: The World and the Flesh in Puritan Poetry* (Berkeley: University of California Press, 1978), 22.

11. Blake, "The Marriage of Heaven and Hell," in his *Selected Poetry*, 75.

12. Joseph Ruggles Wilson, "In What Sense Are Preachers to Preach Themselves," *Southern Presbyterian Review*, 25 (1874), 360. As quoted in Bryan Chapell, *Christ-Centered Preaching* (Grand Rapids: Baker, 1994), 31.

13. Luke 15:17.

14. Gerald G. May points this out in *The Dark Night of the Soul: A Psychiatrist Explores the Connection Between Darkness and Spiritual Growth* (San Francisco: HarperSanFrancisco, 2004), 151.

15. The research of Constance Classen is summarized in Jeremy Mynott, *Birdscapes: Birds in Our Imagination and Experience* (Princeton, NJ: Princeton University Press, 2009), 149–50.

16. Latin text: Thomas Aquinas, *Opera Omnia, Sive Antehac Excusa, Sive Etiam Anecdota …: Notis Historicis, Criticis, Philosophicis, Theologicis …* (Paris: Apud Ludovicum Vives, Bibliopolam Editorem, 1875), 14: 350. English text: Thomas Aquinas, *Truth*, (2.3.19) trans., Robert W. Mulligan (Chicago: Henry Regnery, 1952), 69.

17. Tim Chester and Steve Timmis, *Total Church: A Radical Reshaping Around Gospel and Community* (Wheaton, IL: Crossway, 2008), 62.

18. W. H. Auden, "Precious Five" in his *Nones* (New York: Random, 1951), 79.

19. Closing lines of Auden, "Precious Five," 79.

20. Denise Levertov, "Dream Instruction" in *Evening Train* (New York: Mew Directions, 1992), 60–61.

21. Matthew 25:40.

22. British theologian Eric Middleton, who introduced me to this Celtic tradition, adds an occasional Sixth, Protection, which kicks in when you need it, and you need it when you confront evil. For more, see David Adam, *A Desert in the Ocean: The Spiritual Journey According to St. Brendan* (New York: Paulist, 2000), 21–23.

23. "Benedict's Secret," *The Tablet*, 1 April 2006, 24. That it was all an April Fool's joke was revealed the following week in "Moggy Folly," *The Tablet*, 8 April 2006, 18.

Chapter 4

1. Fourth stanza of Henry Van Dyke's 1907 "Hymn to Joy," aka "Joyful, Joyful, We Adore Thee."

2. Eric Clapton in his epilogue to his autobiography describes the ways he believes music and God are intertwined. In fact, he sees himself fundamentally as a spiritual healer and missionary for the blues. See Eric Clapton: *The Autobiography* (New York: Broadway, 2007), 323–28.

3. Sharon Begley, "Music on the Mind: Scientists are Finding that the Human Brain is Pre-wired for Music," *Newsweek*, 24 July 2000, 50.

4. Monika Rice, "Strange Vibrations: Doctors May Soon Listen to the Music of Your Cells," *Spirituality & Health*, March/April 2005, www.spiritualityhealth.com/NMagazine/articles.php?id=1133 (accessed 20 April 2010). The real founder of this new science may prove to be Charles Darwin, who played the piano for worms, not to entertain them, but to gauge their reactions to the sound.

5. Denise Levertov, "The Air of Life," in her *The Double Image* (London: Cresset, 1946), 41. One of my favorite quotes from Levertov, who briefly taught where I now teach at Drew University, is this one: "I believe fervently that the poet's first obligation is to his own voice—to find it and use it. And one's 'voice' does not speak only in the often slip-shod imprecise vocabulary with which one busy the groceries but with all the resources of one's life whatever they may be, no matter whether they are 'American' or of other cultures, so long as they are truly one's own and not faked." Denise Levertov, "To Bill and Floss, September 21st [1960]," in *The Letters of Denise Levertov and William Carlos Williams*, ed., Christopher J. MacGowan (New York: New Directions, 1998), 100.

6. Margaret Feinberg, *The Sacred Echo: Hearing God's Voice in Every Area of Your Life* (Grand Rapids: Zondervan, 2008). Lesslie Newbigin, in *The Gospel in a Pluralist Society* (Grand Rapids: Zondervan, 1989), focuses on hearing over speaking/talking.

7. Gwyneth Lewis, *Keeping Mum* (Highgreen, Tarset, Northunberland: Bloodaxe, 2003), 3.

8. Hillel Schwartz argues that "the last 150 years have been witness to a thorough going redefinition of the nature of sound and the ambit of noise, such that sounds which had been with people for ages were reconceived and newly calibrated.... Church bells were silenced because they belonged to a constellation of sounds whose significance was in the process of being reconfigured." Hillel Schwartz, "Noise and Silence: The Soundscape and Spirituality," in *Inter-Religious Federation for World Peace*, "Realizing the Ideal: The Responsibility of the World Religions," Section IV: "Religion and the Ideal Environment," Seoul, Korea, 20-27 August 1995, 2, www.nonoise.org/library/noisesil/noisesil.htm (accessed 20 April 2010). R. Murray Schafer defines "sacred noise" as "when you can make as much noise as you wish without being censured. It's a powerful organization within a society that can make a sacred noise. Churches in the Middle Ages could ring their bells day and night; that was the loudest sound in the city. Then, after the industrial revolution, factories could make as much noise as they wanted." Anjula Razdan, "The Father of Acoustic Ecology," *Utne* (July–August 2005), 59. www.utne.com/2005-07-01/the-father-of-acoustic-ecology.aspx?page=2 (accessed 22 April 2010).

9. From Thomas Aquinas, "Rhythm in Honour of the Blessed Sacrament," in his *On Prayer and the Contemplative Life*, with a Preface by Vincent McNabb, trans., Hugh Pope (London: R. & T. Washbourne, 1914), 103. This is said to have been written on his deathbed, and an indulgence of one hundred days was offered for the recitation of this rhythm.

10. "The Rhyme of St. Thomas Aquinas," in Edward Caswall, *Hymns and Poems, Original and Translated* (London: Burns & Oates, 1873), 161.

11. For more on "leadership" as voice activation, see my *Summoned to Lead* (Grand Rapids: Zondervan, 2004).

12. John 20:11–16.

13. See his comments in Mark 6:45, where Jesus ordered his disciples into a boat to go ahead of him to Bethsaida. Instead of following them, he detoured into the mountains to pray.

14. Joshua Leeds, *The Power of Sound: How To Manage Your Personal Soundscape for a Vital, Productive, and Healthy Life* (Rochester, VT: Healing Arts, 2001), 4.

15. Jonathan Lowe, "Heard Any Good Books Lately," *Christianity Today*, June 2006, 42, www.christianitytoday.com/ct/2006/june/18.42.html (accessed 22 April 2010). With thanks to Terry O'Casey for this reference.

16. "What we see is dictated by what we hear." So says the narrator of William Burroughs' *The Ticket That Exploded* (New York: Grove, 1967), 168.

17. Robert Frost, "To John T. Bartlett, 22 February 1914," in *Select Letters of Robert Frost*, ed., Lawrence Thompson (New York: Holt, Rinehart and Winston, 1964), 113.

18. From a biological standpoint, the ears are the first sense organ to kick in, and the last to go.

19. The eyes are very deceitful, which is why God gave us eyelids so that we can start over and start fresh, else the eyes begin to see optic illusions and mirages. "The ear has no eyelids," a phrase attributed to visionary, artist, poet Malcolm de Chazal and also to literary critic Ibn Hassan. For more on why you can trust your ears over your eyes, see my *Summoned to Lead*.

20. Numbers 12:6–8 KJV. Prophetic visions and night dreams are relatively rare in Hebrew texts compared to other sacred writings.

21. Exodus 33:11. See also Exodus 33—34.

22. David W. Henderson, *Culture Shift: Communicating God's Truth to Our Changing World* (Grand Rapids: Baker, 1998), 212.

23. Quoted in Cheryl Varian Cutler and Randall Huntsberry, *Creative Listening: Overcoming Fear in Life and Work* (Lincoln, NE: iUniverse, 2007), 86. With thanks to Barbara Turpish for this quote.

24. Dietrich Bonhoeffer, *Life Together; Prayerbook of the Bible*, trans., Daniel W. Bloesch and James Burtness (Minneapolis: Fortress, 2005), 98.

25. Ibid.

26. Marianne Sawicki, *Seeing the Lord: Resurrection and Early Christian Practices* (Minneapolis: Fortress, 1994), 122. "It is interesting that by the first century God's

name or šēm is seen, although never heard except for a rare liturgical whisper. That is, the tetragrammaton—the four-letter divine name, *yhwh*—may be read with the eyes after it has been inscribed on the scroll, but never pronounced" (123).

27. Deuteronomy 6:4–9.

28. Composer John Luther Adams, "Commentary: The Immeasurable Space of Tones," *Musicworks* 91 (Spring 2005).

29. With thanks to Bonnie Thurston, who brings all this together in "Rules of Life," *Spirituality*, 9 (March–April 2003), 73–76.

30. The first line of the prologue to *The Rule of St. Benedict in English*, ed., Timothy Fry (Collegeville, MI: Liturgical Press, 1982), 15. When I tested this linking of "listening" and "obedience" on Twitter, I lost a dozen followers, and dozens of tweets protesting my use of the word *obedience*. Are we not singing that song any longer, "Trust and Obey"?

31. Ibid., 15.

32. 2 Corinthians 12:3–9.

33. Habakkuk 2:1 NASB.

34. According to some physicists, 1 percent of the static on a TV set tuned between stations is caused by microwave radiation that last interacted with matter at the time of the Big Bang 13.7 billion years ago. Marcus Chown, *Quantum Theory Cannot Hurt You* (London: Faber and Faber, 2007), ix.

35. Quoted in James MacMillan, "Divine Accompaniment," *The Guardian*, 19 July 2003), www.guardian.co.uk/music/2003/jul/19/classicalmusicandopera.artsfeatures (accessed 12 May 2010).

36. See Masaru Emoto, *Messages from Water: The First Pictures of Frozen Water Crystals* (Netherlands: Hado Pub, 1999) and other books with similar titles by Emoto.

37. I love how the Second Vatican Council put it: "[Christ] is present in his word, since it is he himself who speaks when the holy Scriptures are read in the church." *The Documents of Vatican II*,[7], ed., Walter M. Abbott (New York: Guild, 1966), 141. Available online: "Constitution on the Sacred Liturgy, Sacrosanctum Concilium, Solemnly Promulgated by His Holiness Paul VI on December 4, 1963," [7], www.vatican.va/archive/hist_councils/ii_vatican_council/documents/vat-ii_const_19631204_sacrosanctum-concilium_en.html (accessed 22 April 2010).

38. Luke 9:35.

39. 1 John 1:1.

40. Hence the Bible translation, *The Voice* (Nashville: Thomas Nelson, upcoming) of which my contribution is the book of Genesis.

41. Quoted in Maurice Edwards, *How Music Grew in Brooklyn: A Biography of the Brooklyn Philharmonic Orchestra* (Lanham, MD: Scarecrow, 2006), 119.

42. Some philosophers have always argued this (Spinoza, Jung), but scientists are now getting into the hypothesis to prove it one way or the other. One evidence of this is the GCP (Global Consciousness Project), which asks the question: What would it mean to align minds in such a way that the impact ripples throughout the universe? For more see Jill Neimark, "For Whom the Bell Tolls: The Global Consciousness Project," *Science & Spirit* (September/October 2002): 27–29. Where might Jesus' teaching that "as a man thinks in his heart, so he is" fit into this discussion?

43. Andrew Powell, Oxford, England, "Inspiration and Persecution: Messages from the Self and Beyond," *Network* 77 (December 2001): 18. Reprinted as "Quantum Psychiatry—Where Science Meets Spirit," *Nexus* 9:3 (2002): 51–55; available online: www.rcpsych.ac.uk/pdf/powell_QP_WSMS.pdf, 3, (accessed 22 April 2010).

44. Another alternative scenario says the universe is more like the surface of a water droplet with some very unusual properties. Coauthors Shou-Cheng Zhang and Jiangping Hu of Stanford University suggest thinking of the universe as the surface of a so-called "quantum liquid," whose interior has four spatial dimensions instead of the usual three. Gravity and electromagnetism then reveal themselves in the form of tiny quivers at the edge of the liquid. See Shou-Cheng Zhang and Jiangping Hu, "A Four Dimensional Generation of the Quantum Hall Effect," *Science* 294 (26 October 2001): 823–28.

45. In 2008, an insulation project started to protect the statue from the vibration of tourists' footsteps at Florence's Galleria dell'Accademia, where it's been since 1873.

46. The best treatment of theology and super-string is Eric Middleton's *The New Flatlanders: A Seeker's Guide to the Theory of Everything* (West Conshohocken, PA: Templeton, 2007A).

47. Einstein rated his most important discovery, the greatest since Newton, he said, the concept of "the field." It is not the charges, not the particles, but the field in the space between the charges and the particles that is key to understanding physical phenomena. Albert Einstein and Leopold Infeld, *The Evolution of Physics: The Growth of Ideas from Early Concepts to Relativity and Quanta* (New York: Simon and Schuster, 1961), 244. .

48. There are feisty debates over whether *string* is the best word. Some argue for *loops*. Others argue for *threads*.

49. Ralph Waldo Emerson, "Self Reliance," in his *Essays: First and Second Series* (Boston: Houghton Mifflin, 1903), 47.

50. Psalm 32:3–5. Confessions, of both kinds, are good for us. Even the earth cries out when it is out of tune with its Creator.

51. One of the best explanations for how this works is Joshua Leeds, *The Power of Sound: How to Manage Your Personal Soundscape for a Vital, Productive, and Healthy Life* (Rochester, VT: Healing Arts, 2001), 10–14.

52. From a *Daily Telegraph* [UK] interview of R. S. Thomas, by Graham Turner, 4 December 1999: 1, 7. Available at *The Electronic Telegraph*, 4 December 1999, www. mrbauld.com/rsthomas1.html (accessed 22 April 2010).

53. R. S. Thomas, "Emerging," in his *Frequencies* (London: Macmillan, 1978), 41.

54. "The ear is the only true writer and the only true reader," Robert Frost, "To John T. Bartlett, 22 February 1914," in *Select Letters of Robert Frost*, ed., Lawrence Thompson (New York: Holt, Rinehart and Winston, 1964), 113.

"The best reader of all is one who will read, can read, no faster than he can hear the reader and sentences in his mind's ear as if aloud": Robert Frost, "Poetry and School," in *Collected Prose of Robert Frost* (Cambridge, MA: Harvard University Press, 2007), 167.

55. Joseph Caldwell, "The Rock" in Rick Moody and Darcey Steinke, *Joyful Noise: The New Testament Revisited* (Boston: Little, Brown, 1997), 135–36.

56. Wilfrid Mellers, as quoted in Ivan Hewett, "A Wryer Humor, a Deeper Calm," *TLS: Times Literary Supplement*, 31, 31 July 1998, 18.

57. Hugh MacDiarmid, "Plaited Like the Generations of Men," in his *Selected Poems*, ed., Alan Riach and Michael Grieve (New York: New Directions, 1993), 254.

58. Quoted in Caren Goldman, "Living Out Loud," *Spirituality & Health*, Summer 2000, www.spiritualityhealth.com/NMagazine/articles.php?id=970 (accessed 7 February 2009).

59. Theodore Roethke, "What Can I Tell My Bones," in his *Words for the Wind: The Collected Verse of Theodore Roethke* (Garden City, NY: Doubleday, 1958), 211.

60. 1 Kings 19:12 NKJV.

61. William Wordsworth, "Airey-Force Valley," in *The Complete Poetical Works of Wordsworth*, ed., Henry Reed (Philadelphia: Hayes 7 Zell, 1854), 192.

62. Hillel Schwartz, "Noise and Silence: The Soundscape and Spirituality," 1.

63. Mercer Schuchardt, "Default Culture," *Re:Generation Quarterly*, 5 (No. 2, 1999), 31.

64. As quoted in Ian Croften and Donald Fraser, *A Dictionary of Musical Quotations* (New York: Schirmer Books, 1985), 11.

65. Habakkuk 2:20.

66. John Jerome, *Stone Work: Reflections on Serious Play and Other Aspects of Country Life* (Hanover, NH: University Press of New England, 1996), 39.

67. Stanza 3 of Samuel J. Stone's 1866 hymn "The Church's One Foundation," *The United Methodist Hymnal: Book of United Methodist Worship* (Nashville: The United Methodist Publishing House, 1989), 545.

68. John 1:9.

69. They are now creating "optical resonators" that will soon bring us to the day when people won't have phone numbers any more, but will have their own personal wavelength instead. "The message will be: 'If you want to reach me, call cadmium red deep #83.'" See "Fiat Lux," *The Economist*, 5 February 2000, 74.

70. Revelation 1:10.

71. Sound is already being used as a weapon: "The Army is using them in Iraq. Before they go in and root out insurgents, they'll play heavy metal music for 24 hours at 150 decibels or more just to drive people crazy. Even in ancient times, armies used to make a lot of noise when they went into battle to frighten the enemy. They beat their swords against their shields and they chanted. It's been used all through history. Noise can frighten. Noise can destroy." Razdan, "The Father of Acoustic Ecology," 58, www.utne.com/2005-07-01/the-father-of-acoustic-ecology.aspx?page=2 (accessed 22 April 2010).

72. *The Republic of Plato*, trans., Benjamin Jowett (Oxford: Clarendon, 1908), 401.

73. The power of rhythm has been captured in pop culture: in movies (*Emperor's New Groove, 102 Dalmatians*), commercials (VW Beetle), songs ("Good Vibrations").

74. Psalm 40:3.

75. Louise Danielle Palmer, "The Soundtrack of Healing," *Spirituality & Health*, March/April 2005, 45ff.

76. When a young jazz musician named Fabien Maman saw how acupuncture turned the body into an instrument one could play like a harp, he explored healing with sound. In 1993, *Webster's New Encyclopedic Dictionary* credited him as the founder of sound therapy, which it defined as "treatment based on the finding that human blood cells respond to sound frequencies by changing color and shape, and the hypothesis that therefore sick or rogue cells can be healed or harmonized by sound." Janet Aschkenasy, "Fabian Maman: The Father of Sound Therapy in Concert," *Spirituality & Health*, October 2005, available at www.spiritualityhealth.com/spirit/archives/father-sound-therapy-concert (accessed 22 April 2010).

77. "I describe what I do not understand because I am lived by it. Yes, that's what it is, why I have no choice, why I am compelled," says the disembodied narrator of *Pilgerman* (1983).

78. Isaiah 30:21.

79. Margaret Feinberg, *The Sacred Echo* (Grand Rapids: Zondervan, 2008).

80. John Donne, "Hymn to God, My God, in My Sickness," in *The Poetical Works of Dr. John Donne, with a Memoir* (Boston: Little, Brown, 1855), 213.

81. Although I have not researched this, I suspect that entrainment is what is behind the voice differential in boys and girls, who have identical voice boxes until puberty releases the testosterone and estrogen. Yet by the age of five or six boys and girls sound different. In other words, the power of entrainment aligns children with cultural norms—deeper voices for men, higher voices for women.

82. Jung Young Lee, *Korean Preaching: An Interpretation* (Nashville: Abingdon, 1997), 51–52. Early Methodists called it free-prayer. In Latvia today, they call it free-style prayer.

83. C. Austin Miles, "In the Garden" (1913), *The United Methodist Hymnal: Book of United Methodist Worship* (Nashville: United Methodist Publishing House, 1989), 314.

84. Robert Dex, "Orphan Birds Given Singing Lessons," *Metro.co.uk*, 15 June 2008, www.metro.co.uk/news/176717-orphan-birds-given-singing-lessons (accessed 22 April 2010).

85. Frances M. Moran, *Listening: A Pastoral Style* (Alexandria, Australia: E. J. Dwyer, 1997).

86. Norm Wakefield, *Between the Words: The Art of Perceptive Listening* (Grand Rapids: F. H. Revell, 2002).

87. For a detailed theory of assigning meaning to signs, see Umberto Eco, A *Theory of Semiotics, Advances in Semiotics*, ed., Thomas A. Sebeok (Bloomington: Indiana University Press, 1979), esp. sections 1 and 2.

88. Stanza 3 of "The Church's One Foundation."

89. See for example Mark 6:50. "I am here" is often translated as "It is I."

90. "Change," posted on http://poemsfromreality.blogspot.com/ (accessed 22 April 2010).

91. Opening lines from the movie *August Rush* (2007), available on DVD, (Burbank, CA: Warner Home Video, 2008).

Chapter 5

1. John Milton, "Samson Agonistes: A Dramatic Poem," in *The Poetical Works of John Milton Complete in One Volume* (London: Jones, 1824), 104, (line 1091).

2. This is my paraphrase of a favorite 4th of July quote from a 1982 Erma Bombeck column (rerun in 1985) about loving a country that "celebrates its independence every July 4 … with family picnics where … the potato salad gets iffy, and the flies die from happiness. You may think you have overeaten, but it is patriotism."

3. Denise Gigante, *Taste: A Literary History* (New Haven: Yale University Press, 2005), 11.

4. This story of Lionel Playters of Uggleshall is referenced in Keith Thomas, *The Ends of Life: Roads to Fulfilment in Early Modern England* (New York: Oxford University Press, 2009), 135. See also John Cordy Jeaffreson, *A Book about Clergy* (London: Hurst and Blackett, 1870), 2:195–96.

5. Marianne Sawicki, *Seeing the Lord: Resurrection and Early Christian Practices* (Minneapolis: Fortress, 1994), 123.

6. See Genesis 2:16 and Revelation 21:6.

7. Isaiah 55:1–2.

8. Psalm 34:8.

9. See Matthew 11:28.

10. As referenced by poet Luci Shaw in private conversation. Another version is "It's God's table. What gives us the right to check the guest list?" A similar phrase can be found in William C. Placher, *Jesus the Savior: The Meaning of Jesus Christ for Christian Faith* (Louisville, KY: Westminster/John Knox, 2001), 126: "The table of the Lord's Supper is his, not ours; it is not our place to institute selectivity that he never imposed."

11. The psalmist once talks of eating ash like bread and mingling tears with drink (Psalm 102:9). But more often the psalmist and other biblical writers compare the life of faith to a sumptuous banquet. The best short reflection written on Francis is in the chapter on "Ashes and Dirt" in novelist David James Duncan's theological ramblings called *God Laughs & Plays: Churchless Sermons in Response to the Preachments of the Fundamentalist Right* (Great Barrington, MA: Triad Institute, 2006), 77–87.

12. Ezekiel 16:10ff.

13. St. Augustine, *Confessions*, trans., Henry Chadwick (New York: Oxford University Press, 1991), 138.

14. Ezekiel 3:3.

15. Proverbs 9:5–6 NKJV.

16. See the definition of *companion* as cited in Webster's Third New International Dictionary of the English Language (Springfield, MA: Merriam Webster, 1993), 461. For more on this see William C. Placher, *Jesus the Savior: The Meaning of Jesus Christ for Christian Faith* (Louisville, KY: Westminster John Knox, 2001).

17. Quoted by Kate Rockwood, "Rising Dough: Why Panera Bread Is on a Roll," *Fast Company*, October 2009, 70. www.fastcompany.com/magazine/139/rising-dough.html (accessed 22 April 2010).

18. For my development of the metaphor of "sour-dough starter," see my "A Sourdough Spirituality," PreachingPlus.com, 28 July 2002.

19. Mary A. Lathbury, "Break Thou the Bread of Life," (1877), in Cynthia Pearl Maus, *Christ and the Fine Arts: An Anthology of Pictures, Poetry, Music and Stories Centering in the Life of Christ* (New York: Harper, 1938), 196.

20. Loyle Shannon Jung, *Food for Life: The Spirituality and Ethics of Eating* (Minneapolis: Fortress, 2004), 27.

21. Byron's *Don Juan: A Variorum Edition*, ed., Truman Guy Steffan and Willis W. Pratt (Austin: University of Texas Press, 1957), 3:404.

22. Quoted in *Reader's Digest* 120 (1982): 137.

23. "We do not presume to come to this your table, merciful God, trusting in our own righteousness, but in your wide-spread and great love of compassion and hospitality. Apart from you, we are not worthy so much as to gather up the crumbs under your table. But you are the same God whose way is always to have mercy. Grant us, therefore, gracious God, so to eat the bread of your blessed Christ and to drink the cup, that we may evermore dwell in your Kingdom and your Kingdom in us" (traditional "Prayer of Humble Access"). For denominational variations, see for example, *The United Methodist Hymnal: Book of United Methodist Worship* (Nashville: The United Methodist Publishing House, 1989), 30, or *The Book of Common Prayer and Administration of the Sacraments and Other Rites and Ceremonies of the Church According to the Use of the Protestant Episcopal Church in the United States of America* (New York: Oxford University Press, 1952), 82.

24. Introduction to *Eat, Memory: Great Writers at the Table: A Collection of Essays from the New York Times,* ed., Amanda Hesser (New York: W. W. Norton, 2009), 11.

25. For this reason, it is incomprehensible to me that in some parts of the Russian Orthodox tradition, only celibate women can bake sacramental bread, lest the unclean sully the sacred provisions.

26. Galatians 3:28.

27. Mark 1:40–45; Luke 17.

28. See the story of the dead daughter of Jairus in Mark 5:21–43.

29. Matthew 9:20–22.

30. Luke 7:39.

31. 1 Corinthians 10:31.

32. Craig L. Blomberg, *Contagious Holiness: Jesus' Meals with Sinners* (Downers Grove, IL: InterVarsity, 2005).

33. Henry Vaughan, "The Revival," *The Complete Poems* (New Haven: Yale University Press, 1981), 370.

34. As referenced in James W. McKinnon, *Music in Early Christian Literature: Cambridge readings in the literature of music* (New York: Cambridge University Press, 1987), 27.

35. Ibid., 44.

36. It can be found on a 3,800-year-old clay tablet as part of a hymn to Ninkasi, the Sumerian goddess of brewing. Victor Harold Matthews and Don C. Benjamin, *Old Testament Parallels: Laws and Stories from the Ancient Near East* (New York: Paulist, 1997), 238–39.

37. Sauer posed the question to Robert J. Braidwood. See "Symposium: Did Man Once Live by Bread Alone," *American Anthropologist*, 55:4 (1953): 515–26. See also Braidwood's earlier article, "From Cave to Village," *Scientific American*, October 1952:62–66. For a discussion of this with another viewpoint, see also Thomas W. Kavanaugh, "Archaeological Parameters for the Beginnings of Beer," *Brewing Techniques*, September/October 1994), http://brewingtechniques.com/library/backissues/issue2.5/kavanagh.html (accessed 22 April 2010). Richard Conniff, *The Natural History of the Rich: A Field Guide* (New York: W. W. Norton, 2002), 67: "Many archaeologists regard the proliferation of feasts around the start of the agricultural epoch as a result of improvements in food production. [Brian] Hayden argues that they were also a cause. Giving a lavish feast and prevailing in 'competitive battles' with rival feast-givers was important enough to drive the search for new and more impressive kinds of foods—not staples but status foods, not porridge in every pot or bread on every table but party foods. Hayden points out that the first domesticated crops in many cultures around the world were actually intoxicants and delicacies. Some were even party utensils: In Japan, Mexico, and the eastern US, one of the earliest domesticated crops was the bottle gourd, used chiefly as a serving vessel at feasts. Elsewhere it was the chili pepper—not a staple food but, as in some Maya cultures even today, a status symbol. Wheat may have been domesticated for bread, but some researchers say beer came first."

38. This is Hugo Williams' perfect description of inebriation in his *No Particular Place to Go: Down and Out in America* (London: Gibson Square, 2002), 42.

39. Quoted by Paul Murray, *The New Wine of Dominican Spirituality* (New York: Burns & Coates, 2006), 154.

40. Moderate wine drinking has been shown to reduce the risk of heart attack by as much as 40 percent. See "Uncorking the Past," *The Economist*, 22 December 2001, 29–32.

41. "He makes grass grow for the cattle, / and plants for man to cultivate— / bringing forth food from the earth: / wine that gladdens the heart of man, / oil to make his face shine, / and bread that sustains his heart" (Psalm 104:14–15).

42. Marcia Colish, *Medieval Foundations of the Western Intellectual Tradition* (New Haven: Yale University Press, 1999), 80.

43. Sack was the first wine introduced into the new world. Columbus brought it over. The word *sack* comes from the Spanish word *sacar*, which means to export or take out. A 1491 law said that said wine for export should have no taxes, so all wines exported were called "sack." Shakespeare, who may have been addicted to sack, in his "Henry IV Part II" has Falstaff sing sack's praises in a long speech that concludes: "If I had a thousand sons, the first human principle I would teach them should be, to forswear thin potations and to addict themselves to sack." (William Shakespeare, "King Henry IV, Part II," in his *The Complete Works*, ed., Charles Jasper Sisson [New York: Harper & Row, 1953], 538: Act 4, Scene 3.)

44. Luigi Cornaro, *Discourse on a Sober and Temperate Life*, trans. from the Italian Original (London: Printed for Benjamin White, 1768), 30. But Cornaro testified that when he increased each by just two ounces, his health failed drastically.

45. Jean-Anthelme Brillat-Savarin, *The Physiology of Taste: Meditations on Transcendental Gastronomy*, trans. from the French (New York: Liveright, 1948), xxxiii.

46. John 6:35 NRSV.

47. See Austin Farrer, *The Brink of Mystery*, ed., Charles C. Conti (London: SPCK, 1976), 67

48. There are exceptions, of course. The Assyrian Ashurnisapal II boasted that he had given a ten-day feast, including thousands of cattle, calves, sheep, lambs, ducks, geese, doves, stags, and gazelles, as well as fruit, vegetables, cheese, and nuts, for 47,074 people. See Najmieh Batmanglij, *A Taste of Persia: An Introduction to Persian Cooking* (London: I. B. Tauris, 2007), 7–8.

49. Caterpillars of Gonimbrasia belina, a moth that feeds on mopane trees. Dave Harcourt, "Mopane Worm Problems Effect the Poorest—Southern African

Traditional Foods," *Eco Worldly*, http://ecoworldly.com/2009/03/11/mopane-worm-problems-effect-the-poorest-southern-african-traditional-foods/ (accessed 22 April 2009).

50. Janet Raloff, "Insects: The Original White Meat," *Science News*, 07 June 2008, 20.

51. Ibid., 21.

52. If you'd like to try some grasshopper gumbo here in the States, check out New Orleans' cooking show demonstration bar called Bug Appetit. Part of Audubon Nature Institute's Insectarium, a 23,000 square-foot museum which opened in 2008, also offers bugged dining, www.auduboninstitute.org/insectarium.html (accessed 22 April 2010). For more academic environments for your entomophagy (en-toh-MOFF-uh-jee), try Cornell University's fall Insectapalooza, the North Carolina Museum of Natural Sciences' autumn Bugfest, or Purdue University's spring Bug Bowl.

53. Closing lines of John Betjeman, "Christmas," in his *Faith and Doubt of John Betjeman: An Anthology of Betjeman's Religious Verse*, ed., Kevin J. Gardner (London: Continuum, 2005), 83.

54. Tim Dearborn, *Taste & See: Awakening Our Spiritual Senses* (Downers Grove, IL: InterVarsity, 1996), 81.

55. Jean-Anthelme Brillat-Savarin, *The Physiology of Taste: Meditations on Transcendental Gastronomy*, trans. from the French (New York: Liveright, 1948), xxxv.

56. Carolyn Shaffer and Kristin Anundsen, *Creating Community Anywhere: Finding Support and Connection in a Fragmented World* (New York: Putnam, 1993), and Robert E. Ornstein and David S. Sobel, *The Healing Brain: Breakthrough Discoveries About How the Brain Keeps Us Healthy* (Cambridge, MA: Malor, 1999).

57. Four years later it was reported that "the number of dinners made at home from scratch continues to freefall. It dropped another 7 percent over the last two years, and now accounts for 32 percent of all evening meals in the U.S., according to the National Restaurant Association." See Christ Martell, "Carryout Dinners Increase: Home Cooking Decreases," *Wisconsin State Journal*, 25 February 2006, available at www.redorbit.com/news/science/406151/carryout_dinners_increase_home_cooking_decreases/index.html (accessed 22 April 2010).

58. Daniel Sack, *Whitebread Protestants: Food and Religion in American Culture* (New York: St. Martin's Press, 2000), 62.

59. The anthropologist Mary Douglas made this point forcefully in "Deciphering a Meal," *Daedalus 101* (Winter, 1972): 61–81.

60. Luke 24:35.

61. As quoted by Timothy Radcliffe, *Why Go to Church? The Drama of the Eucharist* (New York: Continuum, 2008), 77.

62. Tim Dearborn, *Taste & See: Awakening Our Spiritual Senses* (Downers Grove: IL: InterVarsity, 1996), 76, quoting from Arthur Wallis's *God's Chosen Fast* (Ft. Washington, PA: Christian Literature Crusade, 1971), 81.

63. John 10:10 NKJV.

64. 1 Timothy 1:14–17 NKJV.

65. Romans 5:20–21 is the inspiration for this song "Grace Greater Than Our Sin," by Julia H. Johnston, first published in D. B. Toner, *Hymns Tried and True* (Chicago: Bible Institute Colportage Association, 1911), 2.

66. C. S. Lewis, *The Weight of Glory, and Other Addresses* (San Francisco: HarperSanFrancisco, 2001), 26.

67. Isaiah 25:6.

68. See John Keay, *The Spice Route: A History, California Studies in Food and Culture* (Berkeley: University of California Press, 2006), 7.

69. Herodotus, *The Histories*, trans., George Rawlinson (New York: Quality Paperback Book Club, 1997), 273.

70. Ambrosia means "sweet smelling or delicious." In Greek mythology it was the food of the gods who lived on Mount Olympus, the food that kept them immortal. Without this food, they became weak. A food that when humans ate it, they became strong. The gods mixed Ambrosia with Nectar as a drink.

71. Relationships without surely, but also relationships within, balancing calories, fats, carbs, proteins, etc.

72. Cited by Luci Shaw at Mountain Advance, Canaan Valley, 2005. From the closing lines of Madeleine L'Engle, *Two-Part Invention: The Story of Marriage* (New York: Farrar, Straus & Giroux, 1988), 232. See also these lines from Madeleine L'Engle's poem "Lover's Apart": "We two are one and bread is broken / and laughter shared both near and far / Deepens the promises once spoken." Madeleine L'Engle, *Madeleine and Luci Shaw. Friends for the Journey: Two Extraordinary Women Celebrate Friendships Made and Sustained Through the Seasons of Life* (Vancouver: Regent College Pub, 2003), 106.

73. It's not just a comic's line as Alastair Graeme Darrach chides us in his *There Is Something Wrong With the World* (Bloomington, IN: AuthorHouse, 2007) 48: "We are … the only generation that goes hunting on a full stomach."

74. Luke 8:49–56; 14:1–14; 15:11–32; 16:19–31.

75. With thanks to Facebook friend Teri Hyrkas for this sign.

76. John 4:32, 34.

77. Marcus Borg, *Meeting Jesus Again for the First Time: The Historical Jesus & the Heart of Contemporary Faith* (San Francisco: HarperSanFrancisco, 1994), 31.

78. For more on this, see my *Health and Medicine in the Evangelical Tradition:* "Not by Might nor Power" (Valley Forge, PA: Trinity Press International, 1994).

79. Hugh D. R. Baker, *Hong Kong Images: People and Animals* (Hong Kong: Hong Kong University Press, 1990), 149.

80. Julie Kavanagh, *Nureyev: The Life* (New York: Pantheon, 2007), 226.

81. For a later source, see the Babylonian Talmud: "If a man goes to stay at a person's house, on the first day he will receive chickens, on the second day fish, on the third day meat, on the fourth day lentils, and so on down until he is fed vegetables." As cited in Miriam Feinberg Vamosh, *Food at the Time of the Bible: From Adam's Apple to the Last Supper* (Nashville, TN: Abingdon, 2004), 52.

82. As reported by Union of Concerned Scientists, "70 Percent of All Antibiotics Given to Healthy Livestock," 8 January 2001, online at www.mindfully.org/Health/Antibiotics-Healthy-Livestock.htm (accessed 22 April 2010).

83. Steven Rosen, *Food for the Spirit: Vegetarianism and the World Religions* (New York: Bala, 1987), 18.

84. Jacob Neusner, *Our Sages, God, and Israel: An Anthology of The Talmud of the Land of Israel* (Chappaqua, NY: Rossel, 1984), 111.

85. Frederick Buechner, *Beyond Words: Daily Readings in the ABC's of Faith* (San Francisco: HarperSanFrancisco, 2004), 130.

86. Exodus 28:33–34.

87. Luke 24:30–31.

88. See Mark 14:36 NASB.

89. Jean-Anthelme Brillat-Savarin, *The Physiology of Taste: Meditations on Transcendental Gastronomy*, trans. from the French (New York: Liveright, 1948), xxxiv.

90. Keridwen Cornelius, "Eating with Your Hands," *Gastronomica: The Journal of Food and Culture*, 9 (Summer 2009), 14.

91. Job 23:3.

92. Hebrews 13:5.

93. http://maplewoodcsa.blogspot.com/ (accessed 19 August 2009).

Chapter 6

1. Peter M. Senge, *The Fifth Discipline Fieldbook: Strategies and Tools for Building a Learning Organization* (New York: Currency, Doubleday, 1994), 3.

2. St. Augustine, "Sermon 37," in his *Sermons on Selected Lessons of the New Testament*, in A Select Library of the Nicene and Post-Nicene Fathers of the Christian Church, ed., Philip Schaff (New York: Christian Literature Co., 1888), 6:5.

3. "Blake to Dr. Trusler, 23 August 1799," in *The Letters of William Blake, with Related Documents*, ed., Geoffrey Keynes, 3rd ed. (New York: Oxford University Press, 1980), 9.

4. It was a favorite expression of St. Francis de Sales to warn about how easy it was to *Voir sans regarder*, or "see without looking."

5. Job 42:5.

6. Marianne Sawicki, *Seeing the Lord: Resurrection and Early Christian Practices* (Philadelphia: Fortress, 1993): "The verb for *seeing* in Greek is *horaō*, and it is extremely interesting. It encodes the Greek cultural experience of what it means to know. *Horaō* is quite an irregular verb, and its principal parts have different stems. From this verb comes the word that means a gaze from afar: *theōria*. From another form of the verb to see comes the noun *eidos*, which means the shape of something that is visible. The Greek philosophers used *eidos* to designate that aspect of a thing which can be known by the human mind, its essence. It gives us our word 'idea.' An *eidōlon* is a vision, a fancy, a ghost, or a portrait; the Septuagint uses this term for false gods, and it gives us the English word 'idol.' The form for the perfect tense of the verb 'to see,' *oida*, literally 'I have seen,' is used as a virtual present-tense construction, 'I know.' The Greeks understood that there were cognitive components to other activities besides seeing; nevertheless they accorded to theoretical knowledge the most important status at the expense of other kinds" (122).

7. Thomas de Zengotita, *Mediated: How the Media Shapes Your World and the Way You Live in It* (New York: Bloomsbury, 2005), 255.

8. Sydney Finkelstein, *Why Smart Executives Fail: And What You Can Learn from Their Mistakes* (New York: Portfolio, 2004).

9. I first encountered the phrase "hearing eyes" in the writings of the Russian poet Mayakovsky.

10. Mark 8:14–21.

11. See Matthew 7:3.

12. Ancient Irish hymn, "Be Thou My Vision," trans. Mary E. Byrne (1905); versed by Eleanor H. Hull (1912), *The United Methodist Hymnal: Book of United Methodist Worship* (Nashville: The United Methodist Publishing House, 1989), 451.

13. Gai Eaton, *King of the Castle: Choice and Responsibility in the Modern World* (London: Bodley Head [for] The Imperial Iranian Academy of Philosophy, 1977), 18. Philip Toynbee quotes this in his *Part of a Journey: An Autobiographical Journal, 1977–1979* (London: Collins, 1981), 125. With thanks to Bruce Eldevik, Luther Theological Seminary, St. Paul, MN, for the bibliographic information.

14. G. K. Chesterton puts a spin on this proverb that mocks our tendency to substitute sacramental phrases for real analysis: "Where there is no people the visions perish" in his *The Collected Works of C. K. Chesterton: The Illustrated London News, 1908-1910*, The Collected Works of C. K. Chesterton, 28 (San Francisco: Ignatius, 1987), 572.

15. OED gives this as the first definition of *vision*: "an appearance of a prophetic or mystical character, or having the nature of a revelation, supernaturally presented to the mind in sleep or in an abnormal state."

16. John 8:12.

17. Matthew 6:22.

18. "I Have Decided to Follow Jesus," *The Faith We Sing* (Nashville: Abingdon, 2000), 2129. While often listed as anonymous, it has also been attributed to the Hindustani prince, S. Sundar Singh, with additional verses, http://library.timelesstruths.org/music/I_Have_Decided_to_Follow_Jesus/ (accessed 22 April 2010).

19. Helen H. Lemmel's 1922 chorus, "Turn Your Eyes Upon Jesus," *The United Methodist Hymnal: Book of United Methodist Worship* (Nashville: The United Methodist Publishing House, 1989), 349.

20. Leviticus 10:1 NASB.

21. John 14:19.

22. Ephesians 1:17–21.

23. Lewis Carroll, "The Lion and the Unicorn," in *Alice's Adventures in Wonderland and Through the Looking-Glass* (Philadelphia: John C. Winston, 1923), 257.

24. Luke 11:34–35.

25. Mark 7:15, 20–21 TNIV.

26. Søren Kierkegaard, *Edifying Discourses: A Selection* (New York: Harper, 1958), 32.

27. T. S. Eliot, "The Love Song of J. Alfred Prufrock," in his *Complete Poems and Plays* (New York: Harcourt, Brace & World, 1952), 4.

28. Rosabeth Moss Kanter, *Super Corp* (New York: Crown Business, 2009), 247. For more on the origin and development of positive deviance by Monique and

Jerry Sternin (Tufts University), see Richard T. Pascale, Mark Millemann, and Linda Gioja, *Surfing the Edge of Chaos: The Laws of Nature and the New Laws of Business* (New York: Three Rivers, 2000), 176–79.

29. Stephen C. Compton, *Rekindling the Mainline: New Life through New Churches* (Bethesda, MD: Alban Institute, 2003), 154.

30. I get the phrase "culture vision" from Mary Catherine Bateson, *Peripheral Visions: Learning Along the Way* (New York: Harper Collins, 1994), 53: "What would it be like to have not only color vision but culture vision, the ability to see multiple worlds of others?"

31. Reginald Heber, "From Greenland's Icy Mountains: Before a Collection Made for the Society for the Propagation of the Gospel," in *The Poetical Works of Reginald Heber* (London: J. Murray, 1841), 122.

32. Eamon Duffy, *Walking to Emmaus* (New York: Burns & Oates, 2006), 162.

33. Jennifer Scanlon, *Bad Girls Go Everywhere: The Life of Helen Gurley Brown* (New York: Oxford University Press, 2009), 9.

34. I talked about this in a sermon I wrote several years ago that I titled "Hellbusters."

35. From Facebook friend Pam Harris.

36. For a whole book on this theme, see my *11 Indispensable Relationships You Can't Be Without* (Colorado Springs: David C. Cook, 2008).

37. Reuel L. Howe, *Herein Is Love: A Study of the Biblical Doctrine of Love in Its Bearing on Personality, Parenthood, Teaching, and All Other Human Relationships* (Chicago: Judson, 1961), 45–46.

38. Carl Jung, as quoted in John B. McGuire and Gary B. Rhodes, *Transforming Your Leadership Culture* (San Francisco, CA: Jossey-Bass, 2009), 103.

39. W. H. Auden, "The Flight into Egypt," from "For the Time Being: A Christmas Oragorio," in his *Collected Longer Poems* (New York: Random, 1969), 196.

40. Quoted in Rob Bevan and Tim Wright, *Unleash Your Creativity: Secrets of Creative Genius* (Oxford, Eng.: Infinite Ideas, 2005), 58.

41. See Richard Wiseman, *The Luck Factor: Changing Your Luck, Changing Your Life: The Four Essential Principles* (New York: Miramax, 2003). In an interview in *Fast Company*, Daniel Pink asked Wiseman, "How did you uncover that in your lab?" Answer: "We did an experiment. We asked subjects to flip through a newspaper that had photographs in it. All they had to do was count the number of photographs. That's it. Luck wasn't on their minds, just some silly task. They'd go through, and after about three pages, there'd be a massive half-page advert saying, 'STOP COUNTING. THERE ARE 43 PHOTOGRAPHS IN THIS NEWSPAPER.'

It was next to a photo, so we knew they were looking at it. A few pages later, there was another massive advert—I mean, we're talking big—that said, 'STOP COUNTING. TELL THE EXPERIMENTER YOU"VE SEEN THIS AND WIN 150 POUNDS ($235).' For the most part, the unlucky would just flip past these things. Lucky people would flip through and laugh and say, 'There are 43 photos. That's what it says. Do you want me to bother counting?' We'd say, 'Yeah, carry on.' They'd flip some more and say, 'Do I get my 150 pounds?' Most of the unlucky people didn't notice." Daniel H. Pink, "How to Make Your Own Luck," interview with Richard Wiseman, *Fast Company*, July 2003, 78ff., www.fastcompany.com/magazine/72/realitycheck.html (accessed 22 April 2010).

42. As quoted in Roger von Oech, *Expect the Unexpected (Or You Won't Find It): A Creativity Tool Based on the Ancient Wisdom of Heraclitus* (New York: Free Press, 2001), 59.

43. Søren Kierkegaard, "Diapsalmata," in his *Either/Or,* ed., Howard V. Hong and Edna H. Hong (Princeton, NJ: Princeton University Press, 1987), 1:41.

44. *Green 532* is the title of a book of poems by Randolph Healy: *Green 532: Selected Poems 1983–2000* (Applecross, Western Australia: SALT, 2002).

45. Isaiah 6:9.

46. Miroslav Volf, *Free of Charge: Giving and Forgiving in a Culture Stripped of Grace* (Grand Rapids: Zondervan, 2005), 23.

47. See 1 Corinthians 12:10; 1 John 4:1.

48. Galatians 5:19–22.

49. St. Augustine, "Sermon 37," in his *Sermons on Selected Lessons of the New Testament,* in A Select Library of the Nicene and Post-Nicene Fathers of the Christian Church, ed., Philip Schaff (New York: Christian Literature Co., 1888), 6:5.

50. Mark 8:24.

51. Compare this with the Jewish thought of Abraham: Joshua Heschel, *God in Search of Man: A Philosophy of Judaism* (New York: Farrar, Straus, and Giroux, 1976), 85, 188.

52. John 4:35.

53. John 12:16 NRSV.

54. Luke 24:21.

55. See http://pro-zev.com/product/catalog/181/index.html (accessed 22 April 2010).

56. S. T. Coleridge, *Biographia Literaria*, ed., J. Shawcross (Oxford: Oxford University Press, 1907), 1:202. The quote continues: "and as a repetition in the finite mind of the eternal act of creation in the infinite I AM."

57. Wallace Stevens, "The Noble Rider and the Sound of Words," in his *The Necessary Angel: Essays on Reality and the Imagination* (New York: Alfred A. Knopf, 1951), 3–36.

58. Acts: 17:22–23 NRSV.

59. Bob Dylan, "Blowing in the Wind." Listen to it at www.morkol.com/index.php/artistas/song/289/Bob_Dylan/Blowing_in_the_wind (accessed 22 April 2010).

60. Or in a more modern translation, "beauty so old and so new." Augustine, *Confessions* [xxvii (38)], trans., Henry Chadwick (New York: Oxford University Press, 1991), 201.

61. Sylvia Plath, "Black Rook in Rainy Weather," in her *The Collected Poems*, ed., Ted Hughes (New York: HarperPerennial, 1992), 57.

62. Herman Pleij, *Colors Demonic & Divine: Shades of Meaning in the Middle Ages and After* (New York: Columbia University Press, 2002).

63. Identified as being from Arthur Schopenhauer, *The World as Will and Representation*, as quoted in Athena McLean and Annette Leibing, *The Shadow Side of Fieldwork: Exploring the Blurred Borders between Ethnography and Life* (Malden, MA: Blackwell, 2007), 20.

64. Psalm 4:6 KJV.

65. Augustine, "On What is Written in Isaiah: Unless You Believe, You Shall not Understand," [Sermon 43], in his *Sermons II (20-50) on the Old Testament*, trans., Edmond Hill (Brooklyn: New City, 1990), 240–41.

66. Rainer Maria Rilke, "Liebes-Lied," or "Love-Song," in his *New Poems*, trans., J. B. Leishman (New York: New Directions, 1964), 48–49.

67. Aristotle, *Metaphysics*, trans., W. D. Ross (Lawrence, KS: Digireads.com, 2006), 35.

68. As quoted in Diarmaid MacCulloch, "The Axis of Goodness," *The Guardian*, 18 March 2006, www.guardian.co.uk/books/2006/mar/18/highereducation.news (accessed 22 April 2010).

69. The best unfoldment of Paul Ricoeur's "knot of faith" theory is Alan Jamieson, *Journeying in Faith: In and Beyond the Tough Places* (London: SPCK, 2004), 31–32.

70. Thomas Hardy, "In Tenebris, II" in *Collected Poems of Thomas Hardy* (New York: Macmillan, 1925), 154.

71. 2 Corinthians 4:10.

72. Denise Levertov, "Three Meditations," in her *Selected Poems*, ed., Paul A. Lacey (New York: New Directions, 2002), 24. The poet who has understood this DoubleVision better than most is Denise Levertov. See her *The Double Image* (London: Cresset, 1946), where she shows off her understanding of opposites.

73. The closing words of Northrop Frye, *Words with Power: Being a Second Study of "The Bible and Literature"* (San Diego: Harcourt Brace Jovanovich, 1990), 313.

74. Mary Renault, *The Nature of Alexander* (New York: Pantheon, 1975), 45. See also Plato and Xenophon, *Socratic Discourses* (New York: Dutton, 1954), 33.

75. Ben Harder, "Light All Night: New Images Quantify a Nocturnal Pollutant," *Science News*, 169 (18 March 2006): 171, http://findarticles.com/p/articles/mi_m1200/is_11_169/ai_n26695544/ (accessed 22 April 2010).

76. Ibid. Light pollution is killing the California glossy snake (at one time the most abundant reptile in Southern California). Light pollution is killing the Western long-nosed snake.

77. "Dark flow" is an unexplained force drawing galaxy clusters toward a stretch of sky. Some posit dark flow as the gravitational pull of other universes.

78. "Then the LORD said to Moses, 'Stretch out your hand toward the sky so that darkness will spread over Egypt—darkness that can be felt'" (Exodus 10:21).

79. Exodus 20:21; Deuteronomy 4:11; 5:22; 2 Samuel 22:10: 1 Kings 8:12; 2 Chronicles 6:1; Psalms 18:9; 97:2

80. John Donne, "A Hymne to Christ at the Author's Last Going into Germany," in *The Poems of John Donne*, ed., Herbert J. C. Grierson (New York: Oxford University Press, 1968) 1:353.

81. John Greenleaf Whittier, "A Dream of Summer," in *The Complete Poetical Works of John Greenleaf Whittier, With Illustrations* (Boston: J. R. Osgood, 1876), 85.

82. John of Ruysbroeck, "The Book of the Sparkling Stone" in *Medieval Netherlands Religious Literature*, trans., Edmund College (London: Heinemann, 1965), 95.

83. John of Ruysbroeck, *The Adornment of the Spiritual Marriage*, in his *The Adornment of the Spiritual Marriage, The Sparkling Stone, The Book of Supreme Truth*, trans., C. A. Wynschenk, ed., Evelyn Underhill (London: John M. Watkins, 1951), 146.

84. Genesis 15:12ff.

85. See Denise Levertov's comment that a poet's work "is not to flood darkness with light so that darkness is destroyed, but to enter into darkness, mystery, so that it is experienced." Denise Levertov, "H.D.: An Appreciation," in her *The Poet in the World* (New York: New Directions, 1973), 246.

86. Isaac Watts, "There Is a Land of Pure Delight," *The Methodist Hymnal: Official Hymnal of the Methodist Church* (Baltimore: Methodist Publishing House, 1939), 528.

87. Isaiah 45:3.

88. Quoted in John Stewart Collis, *Living with a Stranger* (New York: Braziller, 1979), 94.

89. Emily Dickinson, "Tell All the Truth," in *Complete Poems of Emily Dickinson*, ed., Thomas H. Johnson (Boston: Little Brown, 1960), 506.

90. Georg Wilhelm Friedrich Hegel, *Hegel: Texts and Commentary; Hegel's Preface to His System in a New Translation*, ed. and trans., Walter Arnold Kaufmann (Garden City, NY: Anchor, 1966), 48.

91. Brian Wilson Aldiss, *Harm* (London: Duckworth, 2007), 215.

Chapter 7

1. Emily Dickinson, *Poems* (New York: Alfred A. Kinopf, 1993), 62.

2. Dr. Elisabeth Koenig, "Discernment," *Spirituality & Health*, 6 (May/June 2003), 45. Koenig teaches discernment at New York's General Theological Seminary.

3. Quoted in Octavio Paz, *Marcel Duchamp, Appearance Stripped Bare* (New York: Arcade, 1989), 24, as "Everything that man has handled has a fatal tendency to secrete meaning."

4. John L. Bell and Graham Maule, *Love from Below, Wild Goose Songs*, 3 (Chicago: GIA, 1990), 67.

5. Kate McIlhagga, "Thomas," in her *The Green Heart of the Snowdrop* (Glasgow: Wild Goose, 2004), 133.

6. The Dean of George Fox Evangelical Seminary, Dr. Charles J. Conniry Jr., is fond of saying: "If I may be so bold as to emend the great Jonathan Edwards, we are not 'sinners in the hands of an angry God,' we are sinners in the hands of a forgiving God and a giving God."

7. Peter Balaban first gave me this image on 31 October 2002. It had such an impact in my life that I noted and dated the conversation.

8. These words are from Stockinger's University of California PhD dissertation, "Locke and Rousseau: Human Nature, Human Citizenship, and Human Work," as printed in Robert Neelly Bellah, et al., *The Good Society* (New York: Alfred A. Knopf, 1991) 104. With thanks to Jason Clark for pointing me to this statement.

9. Bruce E. Wexley, *Brain and Culture: Neurobiology, Ideology and Social Change* (Cambridge, MA: MIT Press, 2006).

10. In an H1N1 world, you now can put your hand under a faucet, and out comes holy water, thanks to an electronic sensor. See "Italian Invents Anti-Swine Flu Holy Water Dispenser," 14 November 2009, www.talktalk.co.uk/news/odd/reuters/2009/11/14/italian-invents-anti-swine-flu-holy-water-dispenser. html (accessed 22 April 2010); or Tiffany O'Callaghan, "Holy Water Dispenser in the Era of Swine Flu: An Electronic Dispenser," posted 13 November 2009, http://wellness.blogs.time.com/2009/11/13/holy-water-in-the-era-of-swine-flu-an-electronic-dispenser/?xid=rss-topstories&utm_source=feedburner&utm_medium=feed&utm_campaign=Feed%3A+time%2Ftopstories+%28TIME%3A+Top+Stories%29 (accessed 22 April 2010).

11. As of 2007, one in four U.S. adults between eighteen and fifty has at least one tattoo (as compared to 6 percent for all ages in 1936). In the future, semipermanent tattoos will be the norm, and then almost everyone will have a tattoo. For statistical sources on tattoos see for example, http://tattoos-101.tattoofinder.com/tattoo-statistics>, (accessed 22 April 2010).

12. Robotics researchers at Carnegie Mellon in Pittsburgh, financed by a grant from the National Science Foundation, came up with this electronic hug to provide physical touch for distant family members. Jeffrey Selingo, "Does Grandma Need a Hug? A Robotic Pillow Can Help," *New York Times*, 11 November 2004, G5, www.nytimes.com/2004/11/11/technology/circuits/11hugs.html (accessed 22 April 2010).

13. In 1993, Amma was president of the Centenary Parliament of World Religions in Chicago. She also keynoted the UN's 50th Anniversary Commemoration in 1995. For a biographical sketch of Amma, see www.thefamouspeople.com/profiles/mata-amritanandamayi-80.php (accessed 22 April 2010).

14. AP News Service, March 7 2003, "Man Fakes Choking to Get Women's Attention," www.redorbit.com/news/oddities/3179/man_fakes_choking_to_get_womens_attention/index.html (accessed 22 April 2010).

15. No text mentions the touching, according to Glenn W. Most, *Doubting Thomas* (Cambridge, MA: Harvard University Press, 2005), 141: "In over a thousand years of detailed, intense, devout exegesis of John 20, only two interpreters seemed to have recognized … that Thomas might not have actually touched Jesus: one Latin scholar, Augustine … and one Greek one, Zigabenus."

16. Psalm 31:15.

17. Matthew 8:3; Mark 1:41.

18. Mark 5:41 NRSV.

19. "Unwrap him" (John 11:44 NLT).

20. Matthew 9:21 NRSV; see also Mark 5:27–30.

21. Rainer Maria Rilke, *Rilke's Book of Hours: Love Poems to God*, trans., Anita Barrows and Joanna Macy (New York: Riverhead, 1997), 66.

22. 2 Corinthians 5:17; Galatians 6:15.

23. See Helen M. Roe, "Illustrations of the Holy Trinity in Ireland, 13th to 17th Centuries," in *Journal of the Royal Society of Antiquaries of Ireland* 109 (1979): 101–50.

24. See the New Jerusalem of Revelations 22:2–3.

25. Quoted in Gilian Ania, *Fortunes of the Firefly: Sciascia's Art of Detection* (Market Harborough: University Texts, 1996), 70. Marcinkus retired to Arizona following a banking scandal in Italy; he died there in 2006 and was buried in his hometown, Chicago. See also Margalit Fox, "Archbishop Marcinkus, 84, Banker at the Vatican, Dies," *New York Times*, 22 February 2006, www.nytimes.com/2006/02/22/business/22marcinkus.html (accessed 22 April 2010).

26. From the poem recited by Rev. Eli Jenkins in Dylan Thomas, *Under Milk Wood: A Play for Voices* (New York: New Directions, 1954), 87.

27. Studs Terkel, *Touch and Go: A Memoir* (New York: Free Press, 2007).

Chapter 8

1. Malcolm Gladwell, *Blink: The Power of Thinking Without Thinking* (New York: Little, Brown, 2005).

2. John 1:18.

3. John Keay, *The Spice Route: A History, California Studies in Food and Culture*, 17 (Berkeley: University of California Press), 2006, 6–7.

4. Tania Sanchez, "How to Connect Your Nose to Your Brain," in Luca Turin and Tania Sanchez, *Perfumes: The Guide* (New York: Viking, 2008), 5.

5. 2 Corinthians 2:15–17.

6. The book, Martin C. Birch, *Pheromones* (New York: American Elsevier, 1974), contained the chapter, "The Likelihood of Human Pheromones," by Alex Comfort, which had originally appeared in *Nature*, 16 April 1971, 432–79.

7. Susan Milius, "Myth of the Bad-Nose Birds," *Science News*, 20 August 2005, 120–23.

8. Bird olfaction and scent communication are now widely researched topics. See, for example, Francesco Bonadonna and Gabrielle A. Nevitt, "Partner-Specific Odor Recognition in an Antarctic Seabird," *Science*, 29 October 2004, 835, which reports that prions can repeatedly distinguish the odor of their mates from that of other birds. Ornithologists have reported natural odors for 177 avian species. For example, the feathers of the crested auklet smell like tangerines, a scent which intensifies during breeding season. See Milius, "Myth of the Bad-Nose Birds," 120–23.

9. A couple of examples: Jazz Diet Pepsi was announced to the public by its smell. The soft-drink company placed an ad laced with scents of black cherry and French vanilla in the October 2006 edition of *People* magazine. Four months later, British travel agency Thomson Holidays sprayed its store windows with a scratch-and-sniff scent of coconut suntan lotion, in order to remind those passing by that they, via Thomson Holidays, could leave February's icy chill for beaches in sunnier climes. See Rick Docksai, "The Scent of the Future," *The Futurist*, November–December 2008, 9.

10. A combination of lavender and pumpkin, which you might call Viagra by the nose, increases arousal by 40 percent in men, maximizing blood flow to the penis.

11. As far back as the late 1990s, Scientists at Smell and Taste Treatment and Research Foundation of Chicago were asked to do this, as reported by Leslie Alan Horvits, "Aromachologists Nose Out the Secret Powers of Smell," *Insight on the News*, 10 November 1997, http://findarticles.com/p/articles/mi_m1571/is_n41_v13/ai_20000519/ (accessed 13 April 2010).

12. If you liked the scent, you saw the woman as twelve pounds lighter. See "Special Odor Reduces Perceived Weight up to 12 Pounds," on the Smell and Taste Treatment and Foundation Web site, www.smellandtaste.org/index.cfm?action=research.perceived (accessed 13 April 2010).

13. I got this story from my friend Stacy Spencer, who preached a marvelous sermon on Luke 7:37–38 (NKJV): "And behold, a woman in the city who was a sinner, when she knew that Jesus sat at the table in the Pharisee's house, brought an alabaster flask of fragrant oil, and stood at His feet behind Him weeping; and she began to wash His feet with her tears, and wiped them with the hair of her head; and she kissed His feet and anointed them with the fragrant oil," www.facebook.com/note.php?note_id=138656349598 (accessed 13 April 2010). See also "Kat Von D Wants to Know: Saint, Or Sinner?" on Sephora's Beauty & the Blog, http://blog.sephora.com/2009/08/kat-von-d-wants-to-know-saint-or-sinner.html (accessed 13 April 2010).

14. Joachim D. Pleil is research physical scientist at the U.S. Environmental Protection Agency.

15. Howard Rheingold, "The Smell of Things to Come," in *Excursions to the Far Side of the Mind: A Book of Memes* (New York: William Morrow, 1988), 59.

16. See "Discover Derbyshire and the Peak District," www.derbyshire-peakdistrict. co.uk (accessed 22 April 2010). Click "Well Dressings."

17. So says Martin Lindstrom in *Brand Sense: Build Powerful Brands through Touch, Taste, Smell, Sight and Sound* (New York: Free Press, 2005).

18. As reported in "Obey My Orders," *Utne*, March–April 2006, 21.

19. William Shakespeare, *Antony and Cleopatra*, Act 1, scene 2.

20. My favorite section of Michael Frost and Alan Hirsch, *The Shaping of Things to Come: Innovational Mission for the 21st Century* (Peabody, MA: Hendrickson, 2003) is entitled "The Chocolate Shop Church" (60–63).

21. This is how it was explained to me: Chocolate is derived from cocoa beans. Bean=vegetable. Sugar is derived from either sugar cane or sugar beets. Both of them are plants, in the vegetable category. Thus, chocolate is a vegetable. To go one step further: Chocolate candy bars also contain milk, which is dairy. So candy bars are a health food. Chocolate-covered raisins, cherries, orange slices, and strawberries all count as fruit: So eat as many as you want.

22. Kingsley Amis, *Lucky Jim* (Harmondsworth, Middlesex, England: Penguin, 1992), 61.

23. Thanks to Facebook friend Barbara Turpish for this quote.

24. The latter is being argued by Manfred Milinski of the Max Planck Institute in Ploen, Germany, and Claus Wedekind of the University of Edinburgh, "Evidence for MHC-Correlated Perfume Preference in Humans," *Behavioral Ecology* 12 (March 2001): 140–49. "Previous work has shown that a cluster of genes called the major histocompatibility complex, or MHC, helps to determine body odour. The MHC is part of the immune system, and varies from individual to individual, although relatives have more similar MHCs than do the unrelated." The quote is from "Cor, You Don't Half Smell," *The Economist*, 27 January 2001, 80.

25. A chemical that lends a distinctive odor to the sweat of schizophrenics.

26. Some people smell worse than others naturally. This chemical produces a disorder called fish-odor syndrome.

27. Maurice Baring, as quoted by Donald Nicholl, *Triumphs of the Spirit in Russia* (London: Darton, Longman and Todd, 1997), 211.

28. *Aurora Consurgens: A Document Attributed to Thomas Aquinas on the Problem of Opposites in Alchemy* (Toronto: Inner City Books, 2000), 139, 379.

29. Thomas Merton, *Conjectures of a Guilty Bystander* (London: Sheldon, 1977), 155.

30. Wen Li, James D. Howard, Todd B. Parrish, Jay A. Gottfried, "Averse Learning Enhances Perceptual and Cortical Discrimination of Indiscriminable Odor Cues," *Science*, 28 March 2008: 1842–45.

31. Helen Keller, *The World I Live In* (New York: Century, 1908), 67–68.

32. This story is told in Azriel Louis Eisenberg, *Witness to the Holocaust* (New York: Pilgrim, 1981), 39. Also quoted in Christopher Clark, *Vases, Tea Sets, Cigars, His Own Watercoulours, London Review of Books*, 09 April 2009, 31.

33. Tauler was born about 1300 in Strasbourg, best friend of another Dominican Henry Suso.

34. Matthew 7:15–16.

35. John 15:8 NASB.

36. Luke 13:6–9.

37. John 15:5 NLT.

38. Matthew 7:17.

39. Galatians 5:22 NRSV.

40. Mary Katherine Compton and David Compton, *Forbidden Fruit Creates Many Jams: Roadside Church Signs Across America* (New York: New American Library, 2001).

41. Vern Hyndman has given me permission to tell his story.

42. As quoted by Dr. Joe Schwarcz, *The Genie in the Bottle: The Fascinating Chemistry of Everyday Life* (New York: Barnes and Noble, 2001), 82. The correct second line, however, is "to make the heart strings crack," Rudyard Kipling, "Lichtenberg," in his *The Five Nations* (London: Methuen, 1908), 191.

43. Stephen M. Wylen, "Havdalah," in his *The Book of the Jewish Year* (New York: UAHC Press, 1996), 17.

44. As described in Gian Beeli, Esslen, and Lutz Jäncke, "Synaethesia: When Coloured Sounds Taste Sweet," *Nature*, 3 March 2005, 38.

45. Blue Man Group has made a fortune off their mastery of synasthetics, as sounds become colors, and colors become textures.

46. Sixteenth-century Yemenite poet, Sa'adiah, "For the Candle and the Spices," in "Perfume and Spice," *Jewish Heritage* online magazine, http://jhom.com/topics/spices/poem.html (accessed 14 April 2010).

47. Exodus 20:18 KJV. Bracketed part reads: "the noise of the trumpets."

48. Matthew 5:15 KJV.

49. Matthew 7:6 KJV.

50. Nicholas Lash, *Holiness, Speech and Silence: Reflections on the Question of God* (Burlington, VT: Ashgate, 2004), 14.

Postface

1. William Blake, "The Everlasting Gospel," in *The Complete Poetry and Prose of William Blake*, newly rev. ed., ed., David V. Erdman (Berkeley: University of California, 1982), 524.

2. This also implies a reshifting of focus toward pneumatology (the doctrine of the Holy Spirit) from ecclesiology (the doctrine of the church); and from kerygmatics to charismatics.

3. The source of this remarkable anecdote is Hans-Georg Gadamer, who was present for this exchange. See his *A Century of Philosophy: A Conversation with Riccardo Dottori* (New York: Continuum, 2006), 126–27.

4. Ferdinand de Saussure, *Course in General Linguistics*, ed., Charles Bally and Albert Sechehaye (New York: Philosophical Library, 1959; originally published in 1915), 16.

5. St. Augustine, *Confessions*, 10:38.

6. It was first published as "A Priest to the Temple or, The Country Parson, His Character and Rule of Holy Life" in George Herbert, *Herbert's Remains, or, Sundry Pieces of That Sweet Singer of the Temple, Mr. George Herbert, Sometime Orator of the University of Cambridge: Now Exposed to Publick Light* (London: Printed [by T. Maxey] for Timothy Garthwait, at the little North Door of Saint Paul's, 1652. George Herbert, *The Temple, Sacred Poems and Private Ejaculations, with A Priest to the Temple, or The Country Parson, With a Life of the Author*, by Rev. J. Lupton (London: William Tegg, 1864), 257. The most recent reprint is *A Priest to the Temple, or The Country Parson: with Selected Poems* (Ithaca, NY: Cornell University Press, 2009).

7. Mark 14:30.

8. Numbers 11:29.

9. Acts 2:4.

BIBLE RESOURCES